Tahir [illegible] the noble Afghan [illegible] man. After completing a BA in International Relations, he worked with the Institute for Cultural Research in the United Kingdom, and with the Institute for the Study of Human Knowledge in the USA. He has written widely on the customs and lore of the Middle East, Central Asia and Africa, contributing to many well known international journals and magazines.

BY THE SAME AUTHOR

The Middle East Bedside Book
Cultural Research
Journey Through Namibia
Guide to Jordan

Beyond the Devil's Teeth

Journeys in Gondwanaland

TAHIR SHAH

PHŒNIX

Dedicated to the great traveller Sir Wilfred Thesiger,
in gratitude for his hospitality and encouragement

A PHOENIX PAPERBACK

First published in Great Britain
by The Octagon Press Ltd in 1995
This paperback edition published in 1997 by Phoenix,
a division of Orion Books Ltd,
Orion House, 5 Upper St Martin's Lane,
London WC2H 9EA

A CIP catalogue record for this book
is available from the British Library.

ISBN: 1 85799 980 0

Printed and bound in Great Britain by
The Guernsey Press Co. Ltd, Guernsey,
Channel Islands.

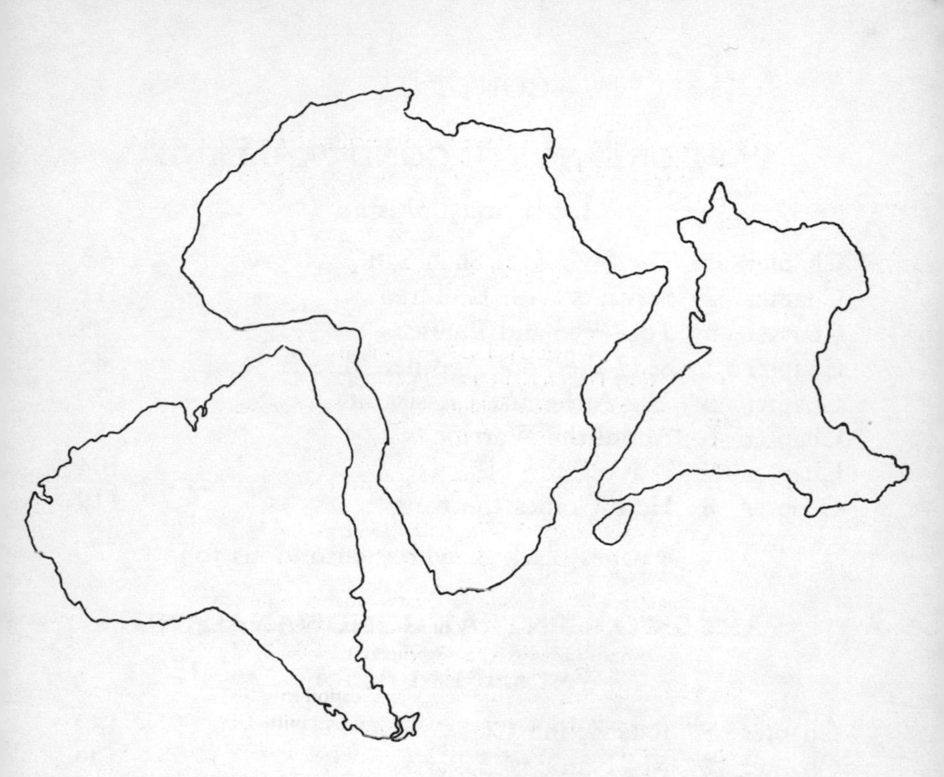

The Gondwanaland Puzzle

Two hundred million years ago, the Earth's continents were joined to form one giant landmass. When this divided in two, the southern section - now known as 'Gondwanaland' - continued to move. Then, forty-five million years ago, it split apart - to become what are now recognised as the Indian subcontinent, Africa and South America.

CONTENTS

PART ONE: NORTH GONDWANALAND

India and Pakistan

PART TWO: CENTRAL GONDWANALAND

West and East Africa

PART THREE: WEST GONDWANALAND

South America

PART ONE: NORTH GONDWANALAND

India and Pakistan

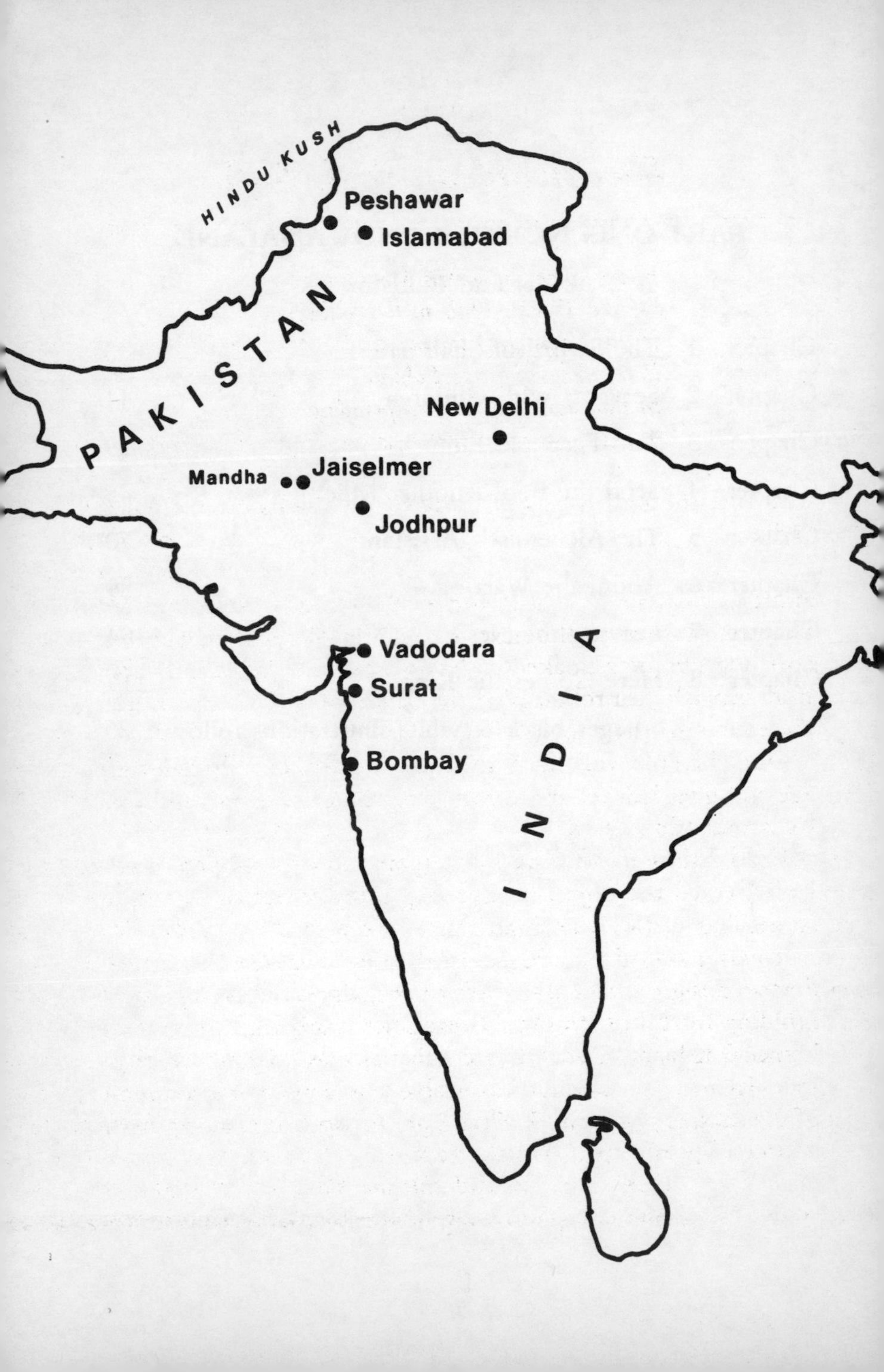
HINDU KUSH
Peshawar
Islamabad
PAKISTAN
New Delhi
Mandha
Jaiselmer
Jodhpur
Vadodara
Surat
Bombay
INDIA

CHAPTER 1
The Sword of Shah Safi

In the Glens of Seven Mountains,
Of the Twelve Hills in the Valleys,
Is the mountain Lingawangad,
Is the flowering tree Pahindi;
In that desert so far out-spreading
Twelve coss round arose no dwelling.

The Tale of Lingo, *retold by J. Forsyth,* The Highlands of Central India.

A maze of passageways stretched in all directions. As I wandered from one cavern to the next, I could smell shish kebabs and coriander. Figures cloaked in desert dress murmured in Arabic from beneath their robes. Were they uneasy that I had discovered the source of their fortune?

One chamber was filled with ancient artifacts, dulled with age and guarded by an old man. He observed me carefully as I examined his hoard.

Hidden deep under a stack of papers and a torn shawl of silk I discovered the object. Only on picking it out did I realise something of the true significance of the find.

It was a sword of what seemed to be seventeenth century Persian design. Certainly worth twenty times the asking price. Holding the hilt, I slowly slid back the scabbard, to reveal an immaculate blade of watered steel, damascened in gold. Mughal, Indo-Islamic . . . Engraved in Arabic letters was the inscription of the master swordsmith *Shah Safi*: his signature, along with a kind of poetic spell, which read:

Chastise all evil with this fair blade
And through its magic your glory shall never fade.

The guardian mumbled the price and, trembling slightly, I handed him a new note. Then, as I stood dazed before him, trying to come to terms with what I had bought, he said in a loud Cockney voice,

' 'Ere d'you want a bag for that, mate?'

I had quite forgotten that this was London's Bermondsey Market early on a Friday morning, and the treasure's purveyor was a stallholder like any other.

He thrust my fifty-pound note under layers of woolly clothing and handed me a crumpled piece of wrapping paper.

As I was leaving, I looked back and nodded to my benefactor. He sat huddled against the cold under a sign, on which was scrawled in almost illegible lettering:

Thieves will be HURT.

* * *

Some weeks later I lounged at the back of a large London auction room. Against the low hum of conversation were the sounds of lot numbers being called, and a hammer clicking down at the end of each sale. My sword, labelled lot 732, waited to be sold.

As I sat there, thoroughly bored, I noticed a dagger, also numbered for the sale. The blade had been hammered from a coarse piece of iron: and its hilt reminded me of a weapon I had seen some time before. The design was typical of a people in Central India, a tribe for which I had an unusual fascination: the Gonds.

I thought back to a trip I had made to India some years before, and of a curious place in which I had found myself. One particular conversation had seemed important:

The waiter poured me a glass of straw-coloured tea. He turned and went to lie in the shade, removing his artificial right leg, and using it as a pillow. Every few minutes the makeshift café under the railway bridge was swamped with steam and smoke from passing trains. I was in Gondia, Central India.

As the waiter snored loudly, a mysterious old man — wrapped in a navy blue blanket — came and sat next to me. His skin was dark, his face was square, and a clump of shiny black hair poked out from each ear. As I scratched away at a notepad, the man watched me in silence.

Observing my interest for his town as I looked around inquisitively, he said:

'It was once very different, you know.'

'But it looks as though nothing's changed here for centuries,' I replied.

The old man chuckled, and the blanket rippled with his laughter.

'Look around! Where we sit now was jungle not long ago: there were dense forests, monkeys swinging from tree to tree, and panthers stalking through the undergrowth. Now, instead of big cats, there are camels: it's not a jungle, but a desert!'

Putting away my notes, I looked in all directions. It seemed hard to believe that panthers ever roamed these parts.

The man had more to say:

'For thirty years I've lived here. I am making a study for Calcutta University . . . my work you see, is concerned with the Gonds, and how their society vanished.'

'Who are the *Gonds*?' I asked.

The man pulled his wrapping closer, as if a freezing chill had run down his spine.

'*Who* are the Gonds?' he echoed. 'Well, this great tract of land used to be known as *Gondwana*: it was named after its people, the Gonds.'

The café filled with a fog of black coal smoke as a steam-engine roared by. The one-legged waiter snorted in his sleep and, when the smoke had cleared, the old man continued:

'The Gonds were a stocky, dark people, quite unlike the other tribes of Central India. They told of a time when their ancestors ran wild. In an epic rhyme they sang the adventures of their prophet — whose name was Lingo. With the poetic metre like that of Hiawatha, the epic story is, in some ways, similar to the tales of the Norsemen.'

The old man paused and, twisting the clumps of hair which sprouted from his ears, the tale began . . .

'One day the Goddess Parvati gave birth to twelve clans of Gonds: they lived in the jungles and were very wild. They ate anything that moved. Goddess Parvati loved them, but her husband — the Great God — did not. He sent a squirrel amongst the Gonds, which they chased. When the rodent scurried into a cave, the Gonds followed. Then the Great God sealed the cave with a boulder: trapping all but four Gond men inside.'

'Did the Gonds perish in the cave?' I asked.

The academic ignored my interruption. And, when I was silent, he continued with the story.

'Parvati was very sad because her Gonds had vanished. In her misery she went to the God of Gods. When he listened to her tale, he presented her with the bud of a flower. The bud opened and gave birth to Lingo, the prophet of the Gonds.'

As the old academic wriggled deeper into his chair, I wondered how long his fable might be. India is famous for its epic poems. Some are said to be so long that they take almost a lifetime to tell.

Noticing that my attention was straying, the story-teller coughed and caught my eye.

'When Lingo was nine years old,' he said raising his voice, 'he yearned to meet other people. So he climbed a tree and spied the four Gond men, who were barbarians. Lingo felled some trees, made a field, and grew some rice. From a giant he stole a firebrand as well as the giant's seven daughters. The flames and the women he gave to the Gonds.'

'What were the giant's daughters like?' I asked.

Instead of answering my question, the man abruptly removed his dentures, rubbed them on his blanket, and stuffed them back in his mouth. Then he frowned.

'What happened then?' I inquired weakly, hoping to break the uneasy silence.

'Well, one day,' began the voice again, 'when the Gond men went hunting in the forest, the women tried to seduce Lingo. So he pounded each one with a pestle. The Gonds were angry when they found their wives battered black and blue. So they killed Lingo and played marbles with his eyeballs.

'But the Gods breathed life back into the prophet Lingo and sent him to find the other Gond people. Which he did. When he had saved them from the cave, he became their leader.'

The ancient paused for a moment, as if his strength were failing. Yet I sensed that there was more to tell. Looking deep into my eyes, he whispered:

'The Gond kingdoms have fallen, their people live dispersed in poverty: the teak trees and the jungles have been cleared . . . but the importance of the Gonds must not be forgotten!'

'What importance is that?'

'Gondwanaland!' shrieked the weary academic, his fingers grasped around each other.

The waiter sat up, woken by the cry. He reached for the prosthesis and strapped it onto his stump.

'What is Gondwanaland?'

'Long ago India, Africa and South America formed one supercontinent,' continued the scholar. 'This colossal landmass, known as Gondwanaland, was named after the Gonds and Gondwana.'

'How on earth did a theory like that get named after such a remote and unknown tribe?'

The man explained:

'Gondwana,' he said, 'was found to have many species of flora and fauna which existed in other parts of the Gondwanaland.'

'Are there other features common to the different areas of Gondwanaland?' I asked.

The old man sipped his tea, narrowed his eyes, and observing me straight on, screeched:

'That is something for you to find out!'

* * *

As I sat at the back of the draughty auction hall, wondering about Gonds and super-continents, a hammer banged down and lot 732 — my sword — was sold for six thousand pounds.

I went about London gripped by a strange and unhealthy greed. As my mind set to work, I began to consider what eastern treasures one might find at the source. If one could buy a Mughal sword in England for fifty pounds, how much would it cost in India?

Gonds, India and riches became fused in my mind.

In the early morning activity of London's antique markets, I would often hear tales of wondrous things to be found in Bombay's Chor Bazaar, the Thieves' Market. British antiques were said to lie there in abundance, unwanted, underpriced, or discarded along with rare artifacts from Mughal India, the splendid empire which the British had displaced.

With the profit from my Bermondsey buy, I arranged an expedition. I bought maps and guides and finally a ticket to Bombay — the Chor Bazaar and its treasures were waiting.

One morning, a few days before I was about to leave, I received a letter from an old travelling companion of my grandfather. He invited me to his house for tea.

On arriving at the house in the countryside, some miles from London, I was led into the *durbar*, reception room. The walls were hung with ancient Bokharan tapestries; the floors concealed by Afghan rugs bearing the *filpai* — elephants' foot — design.

Furniture carved with Arabic calligraphy, and brass trays were dotted about.

I explained to my host my plans to go to India and see what I might find: as I, too, had an interest in eastern antiques.

He showed me the most prized pieces in his collection: Turkish *yataghan* swords, their hilts carved from walrus ivory and silver; daggers with damascened blades and rock-crystal pommels; and a number of ancient amulets and talismans with hidden spells.

After we had drunk some tea, and I had listened to my host, he stopped for a moment and sat in silent concentration. Then, from a large elaborate display, he took down a pair of camel saddle-bags which had hung on a hook. The bags were embroidered with geometric designs and symbols.

'I want to present you with these,' he said. 'Your grandfather and I were presented with them by a dervish on our travels in the Middle East some fifty years ago. The mystic promised that they would always bring their bearer good fortune.'

Thanking the old gentleman warmly, I left.

When I was ready to start packing, I opened the saddle-bags to check their full capacity. They were lined with a fine grey felt, in which lingered the musky smell of camel. Grains of some, doubtless desert, sand were rubbed deep into the seams.

The two main pockets were quite sufficient to hold all that I intended to take. As I filled the pouches with my clothes and maps, I discovered something odd: at the bottom of one pouch there was a secret pocket. It had been craftily concealed beneath an extra felt flap. At first it seemed empty, but then I noticed that something was hidden there. Inside was a scrap of parchment. As I unfolded the sheet, the edges cracked; it was old and delicate.

Inscribed on it was a verse from the Quatrains of Omar Khayyam, the eleventh-century Persian mystic. Reading the words aloud I prepared for a most amazing journey:

The sages who have compassed sea and land,
Their secret to search out and understand,
My mind misgives me if they ever solve
The scheme on which the universe is planned.

CHAPTER 2

Servants with Children

Eating raw and eating rotten;
Eating squirrels, eating jackals . . .
Eating lizards, frogs, and beetles,
Eating rats, and mice, and bandicoots;
So the Gonds made no distinction.

The India Guest House was hot at night, and was always so: except when it rained. A fan above my squalid box of a room rotated, blowing the hot air downwards across the four graffiti-covered walls. There were no windows. This was the third night.

A servant with a fixed smirk ground mashed cockroaches deeper into a plug hole with the end of a spoon, and grinned wider as I stared and gagged.

I was in Colaba — the 'A-1 part of town' — as the taxi driver had assured me, en route from Bombay's Sahar International Airport.

The steps and walls of the street were plastered red, as if a gangland gunfight had taken place, and the corpses had just been removed. Blood-red splashes of half-masticated *paan* — the concoction of betel leaf, lime and tobacco which Indians love to chew — decayed amongst bits of straw and coconut husks, as I walked out into the sunshine.

It was hard to get to grips with a city where all the elements of human existence mingled: from the most affluent businessmen and visiting landed gentry, to the poorest wafer of human servility. Bombay is a mixture of all that is human.

I wandered about the streets looking, smelling, and listening to a new kind of chaos: almost melodious and well-practised. It seemed as if such disorder had been going on since the beginning of time and would continue until time came to an end. It had experienced all, seen everything, and been exposed to the most bizarre and peculiar qualities of man. I was to find it impossible to surprise.

Colaba is an island edged with reclaimed land. It is lit with street lamps, drained by sewers, and has shops in which chocolate can be bought. Yet children with elephantiasis played in rags, their noses streaming like those of any other children. I heard the shouts of beggars: '*Doh Rupia, Doh Rupia!* (Two Rupees, Two Rupees!).'

I saw coffee brewing on tiny stoves, stalls selling surgical gloves in rows, imported Lux soap, cans of Coca-Cola, underpants and paperbacks, as I walked into the waves of dark heads, gripped by a strange excitement.

Treasure and the Gonds. Bombay was where they intersected: for here, by current repute, the relics of the Mughals and the British Raj alike were concentrated. More than that, I had discovered that Bombay — in the vernacular *Mumbai* — was a form of Parvati, deity of the Gonds, derived from *Maha Amma*, Great Mother. Coincidence or omen?

Back at the guest house I tried to acclimatise. A travel-worn adventurer had once told me that leaning with one's head dangling over the end of a bed was the best way to achieve this. It was while I was in this position, the blood rushing to my temples, that the door swung open.

The western woman who entered seemed to be tattooed from head to toe. She rubbed a stick of sandalwood incense between her fingers as she gushed excitedly in a Texan drawl:

'I just had to show someone,' she said.

Having adjusted myself to a more usual position I asked what she had to show.

'It's very special and so symbolic,' she gasped.

'What is?' I asked.

Unravelling a long white crepe bandage from her left arm she revealed a newly-tattooed epic scene.

What I made out to be a dragon was being ingested by what looked like a scorpion: which in turn was in the process of being swallowed by a field-mouse.

'It's very nice,' I said politely; 'What exactly does it mean?'

The woman's eyes burned with evident horror that I should not understand such an elementary scene as this. At that moment her husband arrived. A towering hulk of a man with long blond hair and six days' growth of beard, he wore no shirt. He, too, was heavily tattooed with outlandish symbols and motifs. As his wife danced about in the confinement of my box, with what she confided were secret movements, whose meaning she was forbidden to divulge, the man addressed me:

'We just came from a monastery in Kathmandu, where we stayed with the head priest as his guests. Of course not anyone could just go and stay with a priest like that.' He looked at me accusingly as if that was my very intention. 'A very, very wonderful thing happened while we were there.'

'What was that?' I inquired with interest.

'The priest wanted our electric tattooing needles, and in exchange he presented us with the chisel they had used for the very same purpose — that is to say, tattooing — for hundreds of years.'

I was appalled that such an ancient tradition had ended so suddenly. But the tattooed figure had more to say:

'You know what was even more wonderful than that?'

'What was?'

'Well, as we were leaving the monastery, we heard our very own, one hundred per cent American, tattooing needles being put to work. And I said to Jan, "You know Jan, the monastery's gone electric!" '

In desperation I wandered the streets of Bombay to find a new place to live. The tattooist-mystics had come to my room late at night, brandishing the Nepalese chisel: seeking virgin skin. Jan's delirium had been uncontrollable. She had rubbed her hands across my bare chest, calling for a ceremony of demonic proportions and guaranteeing its wholly genuine Tantric provenance.

The Texans hummed in unison outside my door, in an attempt to recreate the natural monastic surroundings for the blunt knife. It was then I had realised that it was time to leave.

As I turned onto Veer Nariman road for the first time, I found what were to be my new hangouts, my new homes. On the right was the Chateau Windsor Hotel, and opposite, on the left, Gaylord's restaurant. Both were imbued with tradition and hospitality, lubricated with endless supplies of servants, who laughed and listened, and became my friends.

I moved up into a rooftop room aired by breezes rolling off the Arabian Sea. The bathroom had no bath or shower, so the television — which did not work — was thrown in free of charge. By now I had been in Bombay long enough for the arrangement to seem perfectly natural.

The hotel ran on peculiar lines. I would go down to use the shower on the floor below, and return to find a troop of six or more miniature, khaki-shorted servants pilfering from my possessions. Some had dusters, others mops, or even only decorative smiles.

A managerial lady, standing five foot five, towered above them as she called out constant instructions in Hindi. Pulling the towel tighter to my waist, I would point to the door. The army of khaki uniforms and servile giggles then ambled out. I would go back into the bathless bathroom, to find four more lurking with the last-stand resistance of knobbly-kneed schoolboys, caught hiding behind the bicycle sheds during lessons. They looked sheepish and bowed themselves out.

* * *

As the primitive lift wound down from the fifth floor, I was saluted by the gentleman with a silver moustache and green beret who never left the lift. Gradually, with cables grinding up above us, we were lowered down the shaft. In a brief and jolty examination of the walls which enclosed us, I noticed a small sign, which read:

Servants are not allowed to make use of
the lift unless accompanied by children.

The monsoon had come. In the depths of the umbrella bazaar I spent much of the afternoon negotiating to buy an umbrella. The bazaar was knee-deep in mud. A man, squatting on the gutter's edge, juggled a set of cobweb spokes. He was a master craftsman who could reconstruct a delicate framework, like the skeleton of some primeval creature, to shield one from the hardest monsoon waters. Rebuilt and modified contraptions, beautifully restored, were sold as new. Some must have been upwards of a hundred years old. An antique umbrella was placed in my palms and I inspected it like a new revolver, looking down the barrel in respect for such workmanship. We haggled for what seemed like hours and, having marched off in pretended indignation more than once, I threw down some notes and left protected.

The Chateau Windsor, by almost alarming contrast with where I had been living, filled me with a deep sense of pride. I could now ring my parents' friends without being ashamed of my lodgings. An operator with four days' growth of beard grinned conspiratorially at me and pointed to an antique Bakelite telephone. I called an old friend of my mother's who lived nearby. The line was triple-crossed and punctuated by a loud buzzing. My words echoed as if off a satellite. 'Hallooo!' came a distant voice. I yelled into the mouthpiece with some difficulty, as it was fixed at stomach level to the wall. My mother's friend answered and I managed to shout my address before we were cut off. An hour passed and a telegram was handed to me: an invitation to dine by the lady to whom I had spoken.

In the depths of Colaba Market, far from the tourist cameras and souvenir shops, vegetables and videos were sold in heaps. All night, Xerox stalls guarded by blinking assistants clattered and flashed, in the mysterious practice of copying stacks of books.

It was in this darkness that I found V.V. Gupta: the master tailor. He was to become a contact and friend in my hardest hours. His shop was sandwiched precariously between another — which sold explosives mainly to small boys with evil, glinting eyes, and a stall vending fighting-kites of all shapes and colours to their sisters. I commissioned a shirt to be crafted in an indestructible beige sackcloth. Somehow the tailor had convinced me that this crude fabric was ideally suited, in colour and quality, to my sunburnt skin. The shirt would be ready the next afternoon.

One day seemed to melt into the next, a symptom that perhaps I, too, was falling victim to Bombay's general lethargy. Time passed, and I was aware of neglecting my treasure-seeking goals. Instead, I felt compelled to people-watch for hours on end — and was particularly enthralled by foreigners on their travels. The hours I invested lurking at the Leopold Café set me on a course to study fellow travellers on my own adventures.

As I sat there, on the hard-backed chairs, I peered out onto Colaba's bustle. Leopold's was like an island cocooned in what seemed to be the last bastion of internationalism. Yet its clientele were there for their own enjoyment. They had come to India with highly selective vision to solve their own insecurities.

The summer rain fell continuously, washing away the past year's filth until the streets sparkled. A herd of sacred cows had found their way to the Strand, bringing traffic to a standstill. Weaving through the centre of the drove, I made my way to the tailor's shop. There I found V.V. Gupta sewing a scarlet polyester petticoat.

He held out a sackcloth shirt with double cuffs and a large label announcing 'Fancy Tailors', stitched prominently to the outside. I was so impressed that I placed an order for numerous pairs of boxer shorts which he assured me he would complete immediately. He and his wife then burst into laughter and said the 'panties' would take a week. What I had not realised was that this order would expand into an ongoing obligation to keep this man supplied with work. I had become, in proper Indian fashion, his patron.

In order to make the relevant grassroot-level contacts, I realised the necessity of hiring an assistant, secretary and legman. I consulted V. V. Gupta who told me to return at midnight, for he knew just the man.

That night, shortly before the stroke of twelve, I waded down the waterlogged Strand. Its photocopiers flashed with robotic precision, like lighthouse beacons to guide the lost. Continuing into the darkness towards my nocturnal meeting — I fantasized about the paragon of a secretary who, like a bloodhound in pursuit, would lead me straight to treasure.

V. V. Gupta ushered me into his shop, on tiptoes, as if to a Masonic ritual of the thirty-third degree. He poked his head around the street making sure that the explosives man and the kite vendor had retired. They had, and I entered the cluttered shop.

It was amongst piles of uncut sackcloth that I first saw Prideep. He sat, thin and swarthy, in a bundle in one corner, shadows from a hurricane-lamp playing about his imp-like face. This, then, was the man who was to take me to great riches. We were formally introduced. Prideep held out a wrinkled hand with inch-long fingernails painted red. Then he smirked and giggled for no reason, and looked deeply into the pupils of my eyes.

An eager, gap-filled mouth, with broken teeth, opened. I examined the remarkable dentistry of bridges, braces and crowns, which reflected the lamplight.

I hired Prideep on the spot, agreeing to pay the enormous wage of 100 rupees, about £2, a day for his expertise — which Gupta guaranteed was worth every *paisa*. Suddenly I had a co-worker. To cement the alliance I presented my new assistant with a small notepad and a yellow and green Bic ballpen. He clawed them to his chest and grinned. I never saw the pad again.

It was perhaps put away, perhaps sold. But the pen was always present in his top shirt pocket: a symbol of his elevated state.

It was explained in subdued whispers that Prideep could not write, but had every intention of learning. So he would like to keep the writing equipment for the time being, if that was all right. I said that it was. Then I was politely advised that, although Prideep spoke no English, he had the capacity to learn, and would, of course, acquire this language during his service. I looked at V. V. Gupta in some alarm, while a pair of twinkling eyes shone, and Prideep waved and laughed, and cackled some more. I wondered whether his enthusiasm was from the knowledge that he was to be financially successful from now on, or through true eagerness for the job.

V. V. Gupta explained to Prideep exactly what he would need to do. Prideep nodded eagerly. We would begin the next morning.

The eggs benedict was runny at Gaylord's. And incessant cups of coffee were poured with scientific precision from a conical flask into a china cup. After breakfast I strolled south to the promontory of Colaba to begin great things with Prideep.

Every early morning walk through the crowded streets revealed more of the hidden realities behind the clichés of Indian life. As I scattered coins at the lines of strategically-placed beggars, a white Indian-made Ambassador car pulled up. Three living torsos were unloaded: not an arm or a leg between them. They were dropped off each morning, and collected in the evening, by a pimp whose sideline they were; he fed them and took their earnings. They would roll back and forth under the sun and monsoon rain, singing in perfect harmony.

I would pass Churchgate Station, the main commuter artery to the city. It discharges millions of people whose broken shoes grind down the paan-splattered rubbish into dust. Newspapers and pineapples are sold, and old men sit on the gutters performing their morning ablutions. Some people spit and clear their throats, others choke in the dust, combing back greasy black hair with long, waxed nails. Rows of *dabba* boxes are weaved through the chaos. Within their round tin walls were packed heavy lunches of curry and rice, mutton and chapaties. For, in India, a midday meal is more than a couple of crusty sandwiches wrapped in brown paper. Performing one of Bombay's miracles, the dabba-wallahs deliver hundreds of thousands of cooked lunches every day. Transported on bicycles, barrows, carts and on heads, the boxed lunches are collected from each office-worker's own home every weekday. Like a secret society, with cryptic signals, words and secret routes, the dabba-wallahs manage, for a small fee, to convey each meal to its rightful owner without error in time for lunch.

I was becoming addicted to Bombay. There was squalor and poverty, but I had begun to realise my good fortune and would never again forget it. To be healthy and well-clothed and to have even a few tattered rupee notes in one's pocket, was a source of enormous satisfaction.

I passed tree-lined streets, a cricket ground and the curly, determinedly artistic façades which run down to the Arabian Sea. Wavy lettering announced names such as 'Belvedere Court' and 'Oval View'. All this had been once so very British.

Prideep was chewing on a stick when we met at the pre-arranged rendezvous. He politely offered the unchewed end to me. In such ways he was always courteous, though rather quiet, which was sometimes disconcerting. We began to communicate through signs. Soon, though, I was to find out that Indian sign language was different from that to which I was accustomed. I pretended to pull a dagger from my belt: thus suggesting that I wanted to see old Mughal daggers. V.V. Gupta had explained that this was one of my interests. Prideep nodded.

Things seemed to be going well. We set off at a brisk enough pace. Then a second problem manifested itself. Prideep insisted on walking behind me as a sign of his humility. This made matters very complicated, especially when he was supposed to be leading me somewhere. I tried to suggest that he might walk alongside me and not even in front. He would have none of it.

Twice I stepped on people's toes and once tripped over a sleeping sacred cow, whilst turning to see which corner my assistant had taken. Prideep firmly refused to allow me to take taxis and, when I finally leapt into the back of one, he jumped on a bus and I had to follow it in the cab. All the time he assured me in sign language that we were getting closer to the treasure.

When the afternoon heat was at its worst and lines of *dabba* boxes were being pushed through the traffic on huge barrows, Prideep pointed to the ground. We had, it seemed, arrived. My heart began to pound at the idea of jewel-encrusted sword-hilts. I was ushered into a large white shop.

My loyal and wise assistant motioned for me to wait. Like a bloodhound he tracked down the manager who handed him a small parcel wrapped copiously in newspapers. Adrenalin coursed through my veins. I watched the papers being pulled apart. That was as far as the excitement went. Inside was a very large and very fat silvery trout. The scales were coming off. My lower jaw dropped at the complete misunderstanding. Prideep screwed up his eyes and smiled widely, expecting enormous praise. Turning on my heel, I decided that a translator was necessary.

V. V. Gupta was a worried man. As I sat in his shop with Prideep, long-faced characters with devilish looks would enter, go through a back door, and return, stuffing bundles — wrapped in coarse jute cloth — down their shirt-fronts. I pretended not to notice. V. V. Gupta rubbed his calloused palms across his face and moaned:

'How will I ever do it?'

'What are you so worried about?' I asked.

'I promised my two children that I would send them to Harvard to study; it's very expensive you know.'

I did a double-take and looked around the shop. Did I hear

right? The tailor brought out some prospectuses. I suspected that some devious deals were taking place on the premises. Surely a small-time Bombay tailor was not earning the hundreds of thousands of dollars necessary for one Harvard education, let alone two?

However, we were here on different business. I had confided to him the difficulty of communicating with Prideep, and had been summoned to Gupta's emporium.

V.V. Gupta lifted his face and whispered,

'Are you ready to meet *him*?'

Osman was a Muslim and was six foot three. His features were unmistakably those of a Pashtun: deep penetrating eyes, a hawk-like nose and a solid square chin. A man of severe proportions, he was acutely refined — his manners were impeccable, his clothing neat and orderly and his fingernails carefully manicured. And he spoke fine English.

V.V. Gupta apologised profusely that Osman had been the best translator he could come up with at short notice. It was explained over tea that Osman had once worked at the United States Embassy in New Delhi. His position had been assistant janitor. Osman, whose voice was deep and warm, was to get equal wages to those of my illiterate secretary. My team was now a fully-fledged band.

I decided to take him and Prideep on a tour of the Prince of Wales Museum to see fine Mughal exhibits.

Built by the British in 1911 in an Indo-Saracenic style, with domes and galleries in white mosaic, the museum was, curiously, the only place in Bombay I ever saw gardeners who were happy.

I stood entranced in front of cases containing Mughal armour, and ruby-encrusted swords with jade hilts. Osman reported that Prideep understood now what I was looking for. But this comprehension seemed to cause him to slouch and fall into a decline. He was very quiet. I pointed to the hand-written calligraphic Korans and miniature paintings of the emperors Shah

Jahan and Akbar, Babur and Arungzeb. A lump came to my throat from seeing such beauty after the barbarisms of Bombay.

When we emerged from the museum, Prideep looked nervous. I told him and Osman to go and find hungry people who could secure such treasures discreetly from private vendors. Great discretion, I had been told, was necessary. This was because, while masses of valuables were still in the hands of now-impoverished aristocratic families, everyone knew everything in India, and to sell things openly meant irredeemable loss of face. It was the hungry people, motivated by need, who would be our key, acting as go-betweens. My assistants cackled in unison. Prideep mouthed the word *hungree* and they ran off into the evening sunlight.

At the Chateau Windsor, the liftman saluted and I was moved into a smaller, cheaper, room which overlooked the kitchen on one side and the main lavatory on the other. Having become the sponsor of so many citizens of Bombay, and hence burdened by heavy expenses, I felt that more modest accommodation was in order. I inspected a neat sign pinned firmly to the north wall of my new room. It read:

Please inform management when your room is on fire.

Making a mental note, I flopped down on my bed, exhausted by the day's events.

Later on, I pressed a handkerchief tightly over my nose and mouth on the way back from watching a thriller at the Regal Cinema. Charles Bronson was a big star in Bombay: posters bore his name and image high above the defiled walls. I walked down Mereweather Road where the sewers were always being unblocked. Dead dog carcasses and all kinds of rubbish were fished up and placed neatly in the gutters. There they continued to decompose — waiting for the right person with a need for a bundle of rotting rags or a dog's carcase to come along, scoop it up, and carry it off with childish glee. In India everything has a use and a value. Torn brown cloth sacks are hauled around from morning till dusk by small boys and old men alike. Some collectors are specialists in maize cobs perhaps, or old tin cans. It sometimes takes a while for the searcher to run down his quarry.

Osman sat in the front passenger seat of the Indian-made Pal taxi. As we wound up Marine Drive, the neon signs of V.I.P. Luggage and Air India flashed on and off. Bombay has a pinkish light which is reflected off the sea as the black polluted waves lap on the shore.

A gang of children were washing amongst broken glass and coconut husks, amid the hoots of rush-hour traffic. Prideep was cross that I was taking a taxi. He asked Osman to explain that he would have preferred me to give him the money and take a bus. Osman was cautious as to what he translated, always eager to ensure that I was happy.

The car turned inwards after Chowpatty Beach as if we were driving to Kemp's Corner. But our destination that morning was the infamous Chor Bazaar: the place where the European antiques change hands. Now with an assistant and interpreter, I felt confident enough to make a direct onslaught on the source of the treasure.

The taxi driver handed me the meter conversion card as usual. The meters in Bombay's taxis are so out-dated that the passenger is obliged to work out the fare that is due, by using a number-filled conversion sheet. As I calculated, the meter ticked and the fare increased. To sit in a stationary taxi was more expensive than if it were moving. The driver said he had no change — a ploy hoping that I would leave the extra money. He sucked harder on his lump of paan, and looked towards the smouldering shrine, dedicated to Ganesh, which sat on the dashboard. I handed over a ten-rupee note and slammed the heavy steel door behind me.

The early activity of Mutton Street is overwhelming. Ten million people live in Bombay and many of them live around

Crawford Market and the Chor Bazaar. Some sleep in gutters, some under the stars.

Ragged tents bulged as the sleeping awoke and started another day foraging for food. Stray dogs chewed on bits of stringy flesh and licked newspapers which had once held food. Mothers breast-fed babies and carefully de-loused their children, who sat obediently still. This fastidiousness always surprised me, for the women practised the ritual even in the most sordid surroundings.

The sounds of ablutions and throat-clearing rivalled those of the traffic. A taxi driver climbed into his machine, propped the horn full on with a piece of stick, and careered into the chaotic bumper race ahead. Ox-carts moved with enormous determination, hauling loads of sugar-cane into the mayhem.

We took tea at the Friendly Guest Tea House, where the owner rubbed his greasy hands together and poured glasses of *chai* slow-boiled all night with milk. The tea was delicious and sweet. Prideep had a toothache and could not drink. Suspecting he had more than one cavity, I wondered how one mouth could be afflicted with such troubled dentistry. He turned a profile to me and looked through the corners of his almond eyes. He knew I was thinking about him. I still hoped that he would prove himself to be a silent paragon like Jeeves.

Flies were swept out with the dust as Osman translated from the daily paper. He loved to talk and took great advantage of the fact that Prideep spoke no English. The two jockeyed for my praise and attention. They hated each other.

Each street corner was loaded heavily with characters who loitered intently. Some were wrapped in blankets, others in lungis, all with thick beards, awaiting the morning's business. These were characters of the underworld. Covered in hideous scars and armed with rusty knives: they were ruthless men who stole to order. But there was a code of honour among them.

Prideep, who was supposed to be the expert middleman

between them and me, was terrified. But Osman was more roused than ever. He lumbered up to a man standing close to seven foot, a Pashtun with a long hennaed beard, and hugged him. The bear hug turned into a spar and the two men wrestled for a moment. Then Osman, who was incredibly strong, dropped his crushed opponent and walked back to me.

'What ever did you do that for?' I stuttered in surprise.

'Have to show your domination over these people or they'll rob you of every paisa you've got.'

We pressed deeper into the bazaar. It stretched for miles and each line of shops was more diverse than the last. My eyes grew wider and wider as I saw things which might normally be displayed in country homes in Dorset or the Cotswolds.

Giant Regency fireplaces, terracota vases, gramophones with fluted brass trumpets, were all around. Belgian crystal chandeliers in blue and pink, five foot across, were stacked up beside oak roll-top writing bureaux, Louis XIV dining chairs, and card tables with faded green baize.

One stall specialised in silver trophies — some for cricket, others for croquet and lawn tennis — all inscribed with the names of generations of English public schoolboys. Cameras complete with bellows, and sixteen millimetre projectors were hidden far inside dark, treasure trove rooms.

Osman clutched an armful of Victorian teddy bears and laughed as he squeezed their necks. Prideep held up an oil painting on a canvas wider than he, depicting a nymph-like nude.

We hurried from stall to stall with the ferment of gold-prospectors at the Klondike. These were all relics of the old days — when the British Raj held the Indian sub-continent in its grip — a time when expatriates were allowed to bring their belongings to the far-flung reaches of the Empire, all expenses paid by the omnipotent Raj.

Everything had a price. Many of the items were very much more expensive than they would have been in Europe. The shop owners were consumed with a passionate greed, the type of which I have only ever seen in India. You could feel it emanate from them, almost like a physical force. They ardently believed that everything — from the greatest battered canvas to the most trivial toy car — was worth a fortune.

A foreigner, even with a humble entourage such as mine, picking his way down the narrow streets, is quoted exorbitant prices. Realising this, I decided to send Osman back another time to spend an afternoon haggling for blue crystal and tin plate.

Bicycle bells rang out and wheels of all sizes collided and crossed. Green parrots strung up by their ankles were on sale for fifty rupees. They squawked in protest and wriggled their toes like amateur escapologists. Carts laden with white collarless shirts were paraded about: the wheels slipping in the sewage, to shouts of '*Panch Rupia*, *Panch Rupia!*' (Five Rupees, Five Rupees!).

Breathing deeply in, I strode onward along a makeshift path, my eyes and nose streaming from the sulphur pollution and stench of poverty. I thought back to duty-free airport lounges with their luxurious chairs and bottles of yellow perfume; it seemed to be the most glorious contrast to Mutton Street's secret world.

The sound of fog-horns grew louder and, I expected a monstrous junction of roads around the corner.

We turned and the golden sunlight blinded us, silhouetting men in turbans and sacred cows. This was the horn bazaar. Any device which could create a hideous noise was here sold or exchanged. Deafening instruments for overland trucks were being prised from their housings and refixed to mopeds. In Bombay, it is far more important to have a sturdy horn than a sound engine.

Osman ambled off and tormented an old toothless wretch for a moment. He returned with a lump of metal wrapped in the *Times of India*, held out at arm's length like a grenade about to explode. Grasping it with some apprehension, I pulled the

The railway station at Gondia, in Central India: the town was once at the heart of Gondwana.

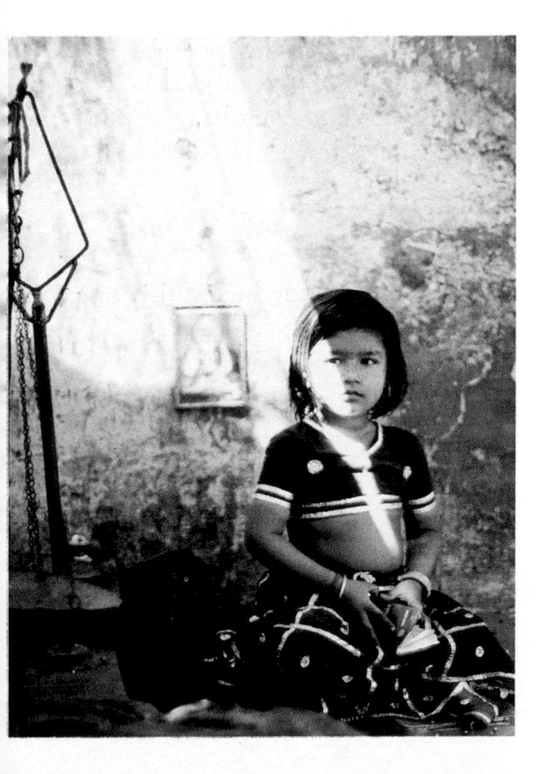

The daughter of a money lender minds the stall near Dadar in North Bombay.

Taxis pause at a traffic light during a break in Bombay's monsoon rains.

Mohammed Ali Road in Bombay, near the Chor Bazaar.

bust of Queen Victoria
aiting to be sold at Bombay's
hor Bazaar – the Thieves
arket.

ameras lined up for sale at the Chor Bazaar.

A street barber in Colaba, Bombay.

The four shoe-makers near Marine Drive, Bombay.

An inlaid figure at the City Palace in Udaipur.

Part of the City Palace, Udaipur.

The curious ceremony near Udaipur.

The Umaid Bhawan Palace, Jodhpur.

A porter in Jaiselmer.

Morning at a bazaar in Peshawar.

An Afghan refugee boy near Peshawar, Pakistan.

A street-side butcher's stall near Peshawar.

sheets apart.

Osman looked away as I held up an antique bicycle horn. It was a touching gift which made me look with growing admiration at this man who had so soon become more than just a translator. He squeezed the rubber bulb between thumb and forefinger with the dainty movement he might use to pick up a teacup in politer society. The demonstration, his expression said, was just in case I should be unfamiliar with the device. 'Now, Sahib, you too are like a bus,' he stammered, before blushing.

I wondered what these words meant, then understood. In Bombay, all the disintegrating red buses (modelled on those in London), have bicycle horns instead of electric instruments. Before the waist-high wheels run over you, you hear a muffled toot. I thanked Osman warmly which only made Prideep scowl harder and longer than before.

* * *

My room at the Chateau Windsor was being spring-cleaned. The commanding lady with the clipboard marched up and down the cell-like box, small though it was, as if it were an army training camp. I decided to take a shower and leave them to it. After spending the day in the Chor Bazaar there is no feeling more invigorating than a freezing Chateau Windsor shower.

The bathroom door was open. An old lady was brushing her teeth inside. She was using *my* toothbrush. It was yellow and had my initials carved on the shaft. Her teeth had seen better days, only a few still clung in the rubbery gums. She looked thrilled as she poked the head with inexperience around the blackened surfaces.

Then, leaning over the basin, she spat out a mouthful of blood, hooting with pain. The once-white bristles were stained red and parted at right angles down the middle: the result of gigantic pressure. I guessed immediately what had happened. What always happened. The contents of my desk were frequently swept into the rubbish bin beneath and eagerly carried off. A process of selective sweeping ensured a wonderful sellable bounty. The servants had the edge because of an incident which had occurred before. I had attempted to throw away a red disposable razor. It did not seem to matter which bin I placed it in, for as if by magic it would always reappear on my bed. Lining up as many figures dressed in khaki shorts as I could find, I had told them that the contents of the rubbish bin could be theirs. I thought that bringing in a factor of personal benefit might solve the problem. How wrong I was.

CHAPTER 3

Too-Feee and Eunuchs

Wrathful then became the Great God,
Called his messenger Narayan,
Said he, 'Bring these Gonds before me —
Outcast wretches! How their stink has
Spread o'er my Dewalgiri.'

A dwarf was walking towards me down Veer Nariman Road. Each of his legs had been amputated at the same height below the knee and the stumps moved quickly on thick leather pads. Somehow they resembled elephants' feet. I wondered for a moment how it came about that both legs were cut off at an identical length. Then he was just another face that blended into the lines of heads which bobbed up and down as they moved away.

While waiting to cross the road behind the Regal Cinema, on the way to visit Mr. Wing Son — the Chinese shoemaker — a sign caught my eye:

Definitely no spitting of paan.

The announcement dripped in bright red saliva, which illuminated the letters. As I stood there, a figure approached me. Her hands piously raised, her gaping mouth revealing lines of ground-down molars. A saree draped across all six foot of the form. Thick black hair sprouted from her nostrils: it had to be a *hijra*, a eunuch. I pulled a folded calendar from my wallet. Indeed, it was Tuesday -- the day Colaba is overrun by men dressed as women — who beg for money and give you luck as a reward for your charity.

Losing my cool, I began to run down Apollo Bunder, past Leopold's and the mystic backpackers; past Wing Son, the Chinese shoemaker, and on.

The eunuchs saw my flight and chased after me: like hounds pursuing a fox. They howled and whooped and pushed back locks of twisted black hair in exultation. Some tripped in their sarees, others pulled them up most ungracefully to reveal knobbly knees. In Mereweather Road I rested on some steps for a moment, regaining my breath. Closing my eyes, I wiped the sweat from my face. There was a tugging at my sleeve. I started up, terrified that the army of castrated men were upon me . . . a turbulent thought indeed. A crouched figure bent over me and croaked,

'Vould you like ears cleaned, Sahib? *Ek rupia* (One rupee).'

As he thrust a pair of tweezers — with a plug of cotton wool on the end — towards me, I ran off yelping like a wounded mongrel. To *them*, I realised, I must have seemed quite mad: to me, they were the insane ones. What was most unnerving was the thought, 'If I stay here long enough, will I become like them?'

* * *

My aunt had airmailed me a bag of toffees from London. They were black and had already begun to melt at the American Express office. I chewed on a lump as I walked past the used clothes stalls and paan sellers, on the way to Chateau Windsor. Memories of leaking packages arriving at my boarding school came to mind. No one else had aunts who even entertained the thought of sending large quantities of pear and apple curry second class through the post. Consequently, they had not been reprimanded for essays like mine: 'My Eccentric Aunt'. My work was branded as a fantasy, though it contained nothing untrue.

Back at the Chateau Windsor there was a rat-like scratching at the door of my room. Vinod, the youngest servant, came in with a soda water. He placed it next to the bag of toffees. Then he watched me read. I was used to being observed reading. Sometimes the room would fill like a railway station at rush hour and I would be expected to cure widespread boredom. Some visitors were complete strangers. This, and their sheer numbers, made me suspect at times that tickets to watch me potter about my room were touted in the corridors when my back was turned.

Vinod edged towards the door but, with one foot still inside, he pointed to the molten lumps of goo in protective plastic:

'Chocolate, Sahib?' He grinned, hoping that I would understand the question.

'They are treacle toffees, from London,' I replied.

'Too-feee?' Something more wonderful than chocolate perhaps.

I handed out a couple of the big black lumps, grease running through my fingers. Vinod skipped off to torment the others.

Later I went to the bathroom to try out my new toothbrush. The locally-made instrument was more suited to painting emulsion over large surfaces, than cleaning the inner reaches of one's mouth. A row of bristles two inches long grated against my gums.

A line of blood ran across the bathroom floor. Not the kind of blood that drips from a cut finger — but lashings of it, as if from a mortal wound. Some of the servants were mopping at the red pools. They looked very worried. When asked what had happened none would say. Only when I questioned harder, one perked forward and broke the silence:

'Sahib, Vinod . . . his teeth pulled from mouth with too-feee.'

The others shuffled backwards as if I was the perpetrator of some atrocity, guilty of supplying a deadly device to pull teeth from the innocent. Another pushed forward and stuttered, 'Vee vere not going to tell you, Sahib.'

Vinod appeared, looking as if he had just axed three men to death. He unclenched a fist to reveal one canine and one incisor. Then he smiled weakly with chess-board gums, and whispered, 'Too-feee.'

* * *

Noises of the night mingled in the darkness. Hindu chants ran down Apollo Bunder with slow melody. A taxi with no lights swerved to miss another. It all seemed like just another Bombay night.

At eight P.M. my Sikh taxi driver lunged at high speed past Chowpatty Beach, accelerating with the intrepidity of a *kamikaze* pilot. The black cab missed meshing with a Mercedes by millimetres, as the driver's turbanned head rocked with laughter.

My parents' friends had invited me as their guest to a neighbour's party. The Bombay socialite crowd would all be there. Since my arrival in India, I had not been accustomed to mixing with the well-to-do.

The party was in a studio flat. The ceiling had been adorned with a sprawling mural by one of the daughters who was artistically inclined. I was taken into the crowded room and introduced to ministers and dancers, producers and businessmen. They looked me up and down and stared with evident and intense distaste at my pleated jacket. It had been pressed by V.V. Gupta, and now resembled a white tennis skirt. I chatted to an English lady who was interested in Afghanistan. Before I was led off to meet some people of importance, she pressed a piece of paper into my palm. Later I read it. The name of a laundry screamed out at me, in block letters.

My gaze strayed to the balcony. There in the moonlight was the most perfect form I had ever seen. She stood tall above most of the guests with the grace of a Nubian warrior, and the poise of a goddess. A solid silver clasp encircled her upper arm. I had to meet her.

Across the room sat a man in Tai Chi shoes and a beret. Feet dodged his crossed legs, which extended into the middle of the floor, but he paid no attention to them. A gaggle of admiring girls clustered around him; he lectured softly, thrilled to have such a glamorous audience. I wandered over and we began to talk.

'Hey man, let me tell you about this place,' he said.

'Please do, I'm new around here.'

He was the first one to avoid questions about my origin, quest, and my jacket's crumpled state. His name was Blake . . . 'D' Blake. A musician of classical persuasion, he had left his native California to travel the world in search of a guru. It was here, after many years, that he had found that man.

The more we talked, the more questions I felt pressed to ask. I was intrigued that a man should leave his native land, then come to live in India, marry an Indian lady, which he had done: and study under a respected master in the suburbs of north Bombay.

A Fulbright scholarship supplied the means to fund Blake's vital research. Such financing fuelled the relationship between pupil and teacher. Blake was devoted to completing a thesis of great magnitude. A topic whose title he imparted in whisper: *The Application of the Electric Guitar in Hindustani Music.*

Blake was *detribalised* — no longer completely American and not quite Indian. An upbringing in the 1960s had shown him many things and given him the basis for a roaming life. He kept repeating 'Yeah man, as long as you're happy that's all that counts.' Then he began to ramble on about my family, of which I had not spoken.

Rivetted, I was eager for him to shed some light on the madness that was Bombay. And, secretly I hoped he could advise about the young lady who had so captured my attention.

* * *

Time began to slip away increasingly quickly as I filled my days with routine matters. Coffee at Gaylord's, tea at Leopold's, checking mail and arranging my laundry, left little time for anything else. One afternoon, as a new batch of crumpled clientele slumped in Leopold's, I was forced to share a table.

The man in the tasselled shoes flicked cigarette ash with a nervous — almost reflex — movement into the top of an empty bottle. His left hand was folded around a copy of E. M. Forster's

A Passage to India. Ah, I thought, the kind of traveller who likes to be immersed in the place. We crossed glances and both frowned at the Australians at the next table. They skulked behind a couple of torn sci-fi paperbacks. The young man at whose table I sat re-contorted his face as his eyes focused on Forster's words once again.

Waiter number sixteen weaved back and forth, bringing endless cups of coffee to the man: who drank them black and in one gulp. After every second earthenware cup had been drained he would stride off to relieve himself. Two hours passed and we sat in silence throughout. Then I was caught reading at right angles the blurb on Forster's genius: and the ice was broken.

Another Rothman cigarette began to smoke as a dulled Zippo clicked shut and was slid into the man's shirt pocket. He introduced himself as Hugh Randolph Hamilton-Waite.

Hamilton-Waite had travelled widely. His father's diplomatic rank had necessitated such upheaval. He lived in Paris; and moved about on his wicker-based chair with a definite delicacy. I drew backwards towards the window, keeping my distance, but at the same time was intrigued. I asked what he did.

'Nothing,' was the brief and disconcerting reply. Which left me grappling with a chap of perhaps thirty who had seen the world but seemed uncomfortable within it. He repeated many times: 'I have been so terribly, terribly ill,' the voice deepening with dramatic emphasis.

I felt sorry for him, quite out of place in Bombay, yet he somehow fitted into Leopold's as everyone does. Making polite conversation, I declared that Gaylord's was the only sensible place to dine in Bombay, and across from it, the infamous Chateau Windsor.

Stretching out a hand for him to shake, he gripped it as an elderly aunt might do — clasping the fingers just short of the knuckles and holding on for a moment weakly. I left Hamilton-Waite to his coffee and duty-free Rothmans and wondered what his future might be.

Nights spent worrying over my two assistants, and their lack of success in finding treasure, had put my sleep-pattern off its usual orderly track. I had decided to go to a chemist to buy some sleeping tablets. The pharmacist held up a shimmering pack of Diazepam, explaining that a prescription was necessary from a doctor.

A moment later I was round the corner at the rubber stamp bazaar. There I commissioned a stamp to be designed and constructed. It was to read:

DR. TAHIR SHAH
PHYSICIAN & SURGEON TO THE KING.

An apprentice took my order and set to work immediately. Flowers were cut out and placed around the words, somehow emphasising their authority. I left a twenty-rupee note and returned to the chemist, stamp in hand. He produced a sheet of paper and an inkpad at my request. Pressing the block down — it was certainly ornate — I wrote out a prescription for ten Diazepam.

'I am now a doctor,' I said audaciously.

There was no dispute. The stamp was my passport into the world of medicine.

As the chemist admired the fine workmanship that had created such a superior credential, he passed me a sheet of chalky-white pills. There had been no discussion how a layman could in twenty minutes not only become a doctor, but a surgeon too, and to *The King*. I was learning how to behave.

As I strolled back to Chateau Windsor, I remember my head spinning at the advantages of the system. Great things could be achieved, nothing could stop me now.

At ten forty-five P.M. there was a knock at my door. Vinod pulled me to the telephone in the hall. A voice crackled in the distance. It was the manager of Gaylord's, who said that a gentleman was requesting my company and inviting me to dine. I went down to Gaylord's.

Great activity surrounded one table on the veranda. Waiters were bobbing and weaving about. Some loitered, expecting instructions, and the manager poured from a bottle of Omar Khayyam, Indian-made champagne, wrapped in a towel. The table top had been covered with a gingham cloth, and beside it was stood the champagne bottle in a cooler.

Hamilton-Waite sat resplendent in a cravat and double-breasted jacket. He sipped from a fluted glass with a degree of grace and, in his theatrical manner, he spoke of his travels . The manager circled the table like a shark awaiting its prey. He wanted to be introduced. I was worried that my reputation would be ruined and I would never be able to eat there again.

Hamilton-Waite spoke at length about his life as an ambassador's son, and how his friends knew him as H.R.H. He removed his jacket and I automatically drew my feet under my chair.

As before, he drank many cups of black coffee, this time diluted with imported brandy. Again he spoke of his mysterious illness. I plucked up courage and politely asked what exactly the condition had been. 'It's mental,' was the reply. He hated life and was useless for it, showing no understanding of my exhilaration for living. He was despondent. A man rich enough not to work, and poor enough in spirit to do nothing.

Hamilton-Waite left six hundred rupees, about twelve pounds sterling, as a tip — many weeks' income in the eyes of millions of Indians. We moved out into the street to hail him a cab. Deformed bodies lay strewn across the pavement, huddled against railings in rags. Their absolute will and ardent determination to survive — the opposite of their supposed fatalism — contrasted with Hamilton-Waite's lethargy. I felt both sympathy and condemnation for him. In his society such weakness and irresolution were sure to survive. It is an unjust world.

* * *

The concrete benches in the gardens of the Prince of Wales Museum were newly painted and very comfortable indeed. One Thursday afternoon, as I basked in the absolute humidity on bench number three, a tall man, with a pencil-line moustache and greased-back hair, sidled up. Tweaking the big toe on my right foot, he asked,

'One rupee for a blind dwarf?'

'You don't look blind to me,' I replied, noticing that the rather well-dressed man — who stood close to six foot —had a neatly furled newspaper under one arm.

'The rupee is for my blind brother,' said the giant, 'he is a dwarf.'

'Go away and leave me alone!' I called, eager to be left to slumber on the cool white concrete. I shut my eyes firmly, but sensed that the chill shadow of the man had not yet moved on.

'Your sister Safia would want you to give me a rupee!' grunted the figure as I was dozing off again.

How did he know my sister's name?

'I know other things,' continued the giant boldly as if reading my thoughts, 'I know everything about you.'

The man opened his mouth and scraped his tongue. A newspaper editorial the week before had instructed the denizens of Bombay to shun mind-readers. It had claimed that phenomenal feats of the mind, which were quite possible to genuine mystics and resulted from extensive meditation, were nothing more than a cheap stunt when carried out for money. Nevertheless, I was prepared to conduct my own investigation.

'All right, then tell me about myself!' I said.

'You were born on 16th November 1966,' began the giant firmly.

'Well, anyone could know that,' I snapped.

'You are allergic to shellfish and your family comes from Paghman in Afghanistan,' he continued.

'Go on, tell me more,' I said, intrigued by the man's information.

'The second book you edited was called *Cultural Research*,' he continued . . . 'Your blood group is O-negative, and you had your tonsils out last year.'

Fishing a single rupee coin from my pocket, I handed it to the giant.

'Take this for your trouble and now leave me in peace!'

But as I nuzzled back to sleep the deep voice came again.

'My brother has talents even more unusual than mine.'

'Ah,' I remembered, 'the blind dwarf . . . give him the rupee and my greetings. Now if you will excuse me I really have to get back to sleep.'

But the giant was not ready to leave.

'He may have physical handicaps, but my brother's mind can see through walls . . . his skills can turn your desires into reality . . . for he is a white swami.' The ease with which the sentence flowed from the giant's mouth made me suspicious. I sensed that the routine had been acted out many times before. Indeed, perhaps many times that day alone.

Just what led me to seek the blind dwarf's guidance I do not know. But within minutes of hearing of his curious mental powers, I was bumping along in the back of a taxicab, bound for a rendezvous with the white swami.

In a suburb of a suburb in north Bombay the taxi slid to a halt. It had become embedded in mud. The driver glanced at the photocopied map — which had been efficiently supplied by the slick clairvoyant — and pointed to a corrugated iron shack in the distance. A sign, nailed to the exterior of the building, advertised in several languages:

PALACE OF THE WHITE SWAMI:
Fortunes Told
Secrets Revealed
See Through Stone
Become Invisible

As I was about to rap on the door, it was swung open by an

elderly women who was wailing with grief. She left, and I entered the Palace of the White Swami.

The dusty wreck of a room was bisected by a shaft of bright sunlight which sliced through a hole in the roof. Sitting on a mattress, amid a clutter of peculiar medicinal odds and ends, was an apparently blind dwarf.

'Welcome!' he growled menacingly.

'Your brother said that you would tell me . . .' Cutting me off in mid-sentence, the dwarf said,

'I know what you want to know.' He picked up a dark brown earthenware jar and held it out towards me at arm's length. On the side was scrawled in white paint, *100 RUPEES PLEASE.*

The jar was rattled imperiously. I dropped a fifty-rupee note into the container, hoping the blind dwarf would not notice the lesser sum. Without a word, the white swami waved the jar once again. And, when I had deposited a further fifty rupees, he prepared to solve my case.

First, a thread was drawn from the pile of a tattered grey rug. Dividing it in two with a long, blunt *talwar* — an Indian sword — the blind dwarf tied one half around my left wrist, and placed the second portion under the mattress on which we both now sat. Then, foraging about, he picked up a dry white bone — probably the thigh bone of a sheep or goat. A pinch of red powder, taken from a carved wooden box, was pressed onto the bone. And, as a cloud blocked the sunlight for a moment, the swami lit a stick of incense, and proceeded to wave it in circles around his head. As the trail of scent revolved rhythmically around him, the seer began to babble the sounds of a language which sounded extremely unusual to me.

The ritual continued for almost half an hour. The white swami, who moved through familiar motions, retrieved the grey thread from beneath the mattress, tying with it the remains of the incense to the thigh bone. An old toothbrush which had been brought out was used to scrub the palms of my hands with a little water from the kettle. I began to sense, from his expression and movements, that the dwarf was acting on autopilot.

But, just as I was about to announce my boredom, the ritual came to a sudden stop. The blind swami put away the toothbrush. Then, smoothing back his jet-black hair, he said,

'I can only help you if the spirits would like you to be helped. They say that you do not deserve their time, and so I must now ask you to leave instantly and immediately!'

The blind dwarf turned away and began to fumble through a heap of bleached white animal bones, as if reverting to urgent business. Feeling rather despondent, and too unhappy even to demand the return of my hundred rupees, I slunk away.

I had feared from the start that my quest for antiques would not be an easy one to complete. But the new and unwelcome news, that the spirit world was now against me, had made the task harder to bear than ever.

Reeling from my experience with the mind-reader and his brother, the swami, I began to devote a great deal of time pondering their singular abilities. Most people I consulted thought my questions had no grounds. One man, who was hawking bath-towels stolen from the Oberoi Hotel, shook his head vigorously from side to side when I told him of the mind-reader's talent. 'Is that all he could do?' he asked in disappointment.

Only when I had quizzed several dozen people, did I get an answer which seemed satisfactory. A street-barber, squatting outside Churchgate Station, was only too delighted to discuss the matter while shaving an elderly client's head. As he moved the cut-throat razor over the stubble, he explained: 'You must understand something. These mind-readers and swami types are very clever folk. For weeks they study their prey, learning all about them and tracking their movements. They hire researchers — even sometimes engaging spies abroad — and only when they believe that they know everything about you, they move in for the kill.'

Later, I emptied out my wallet to look for a telephone number. And, as I hunted through the mass of ticket stubs and scraps of crushed paper, I realised that it contained all the information revealed to me by the giant mind-reader. I recalled the continuous stream of people who invaded my room. Perhaps the street-barber had been right.

Wing Son, the Chinese shoemaker, sat on the bare floor of his shop and pulled stitches through an old black riding boot. He removed a shoe from the display, and pointed out the quality as he did so. His features had been softened by time, and a pair of pupils — frosted with age — hid behind spectacles as thick as milk-bottle glass. His father had come to Bombay as a refugee in the 1920s from Canton, setting up business in the same shop.

Wing ran his fingers over the wooden last for a lady's shoe.

'My father loved this one,' he said squinting with magnified eyes. 'You just can't get them any more; there have been problems in Agra.'

Wing Son seemed to be a man who understood how the city worked. Himself an immigrant to Bombay, he might, I thought, have a tip or two for a treasure-seeker such as myself. I explained what I was searching for. He glanced around his shop: taking in the old tattered lasts, the bundles of thread, and the heap of worn-out shoes he was to repair.

'If I knew where a great treasure was,' he said shrewdly, 'would you expect me to be working here day in, day out, as I do?'

'Well do you have *any* advice to give me?'

Wing Son thought for a moment.

'If you want to find fantastic riches,' he said in a silky voice, 'you will need a pair of Chinese shoes.'

So, taking Wing Son's advice, I placed an order for two pairs of brogues, one black and the other in brown suede. A piece of string with inches marked in ball-point pen was slid around the arches of my feet. Wing Son read off the scale in Cantonese and noted numbers in the order book. His eyes glazed over as he spoke with slow dignity.

'I have people all over world who come to me,' he said. 'They always remember Wing Son.'

* * *

There were problems moving around the city at night. For a fortune in notes of several currencies was strapped tightly to my waist. After weeks of flattering high officials, and coaxing their servile deputies, I managed to open a bank account. First, I had chosen a backstreet bank in Colaba. The director of new accounts was so overjoyed to have a customer with cash that he treated me to a slap-up lunch.

We chewed at chicken bones in his office and wiped the grease on figure-covered sheets of paper. It was all very satisfactory. I thought it a good moment to tackle the question of a safe deposit box in the vault. Could I have one? Certainly, of course I could. Stamps with crests and tigers' heads were dug out of drawers and licked. They covered my signature which had been etched into quadruplicate sheets.

'Can I deposit the money in the box this afternoon?'

'It might be a little longer than that,' was the vague reply.

'Could I see your vault?'

I expected to be led to an underground strong-room. The director clapped his hands and a stooping accountant beckoned me to follow. He walked around chairs and desks taking a distinctly indirect route. Then he stopped in front of a filing cabinet and hovered with unease.

The bottom drawer was missing and a dabba box had been stowed in its place. The smell of curry and lentils wafted upwards. I weaved my way back across the room around the stacks of papers and waiting regulars.

'Wonderful!' I exclaimed nervously. 'Would you expect that I could get a box tomorrow?.'

'Perhaps,' said the director as he sucked at the ball joint of a chicken's leg.

'What exactly does the availability depend upon?' I was determined to get fundamental answers to basic questions, and cut through the layers of uncertainty.

'It all depends if someone dies.'

I slid a fifty-rupee note — known throughout India as Inkpot Money — under the desk blotter and pretended to tie my shoelace. I could just see a hand digging for the note from the other side of the desk. It foraged with mole-like experience. Then I directed a simple question,

'In your estimation, is a client likely to pass away today, Sir?'

'Positively if not certainly!' were his words, his head wobbling from one side to the other as he spoke.

But my efforts had been in vain. The manager of the branch had heard that a foreigner was trying to keep his money within his establishment. He drew a deep unbribable breath and boomed from his office:

'There are no provisions for such a situation to exist. You must close your account immediately!'

I was more demoralised than ever. Prideep and Osman insisted on hanging around me like flies around butter. They just wanted, following true eastern tradition, to make me happy. Osman began to tell jokes. The punchlines were obscured by indirect and terrible translating. Even Prideep frequently fell to the ground, cackling with hideous laughter.

I was getting a little nervous that both assistants might become reconciled and unite against me: was a possible mutiny underway?

I began to track down a vault with lockers to rent. Osman had a plan. He had a distant cousin who worked at a bank near Akbarally's Department Store. The relative cleaned all the offices and would be able secretly to pencil in an appointment for me with the manager. It seemed a cunning ruse and I sent Osman off to contact the cousin. Alas, it turned out that the man had been laid off because of restructuring and decorations.

I was inspired by Osman nonetheless. Handing Prideep a tie, I swung my pleated jacket over my shoulders with the aplomb of a ring-master. With Osman towering on my left and Prideep scurrying like a mouse to keep up on the right, we stormed into the building and I strode into the manager's office — pretending to be an old friend.

My assistants waited outside the door with crossed arms and straight backs. I had told them to look intimidating. Osman pulled faces and showed his teeth. The manager greeted me so warmly that I thought for a moment that we had met before. He presented me with six forms to complete and promised me a box in the strong-room in one week's time.

By then a shining new key had been cut for box number 88. It was passed to me in a small green envelope and I turned it in the lock for the first time. There is nothing so satisfyingly perfect as the click of a well-fitting key in a steel lock.

The vault was the most idyllic place in Bombay. There was a certain smell of documents and industrial detergent. In its cool and dehumidified atmosphere I felt secure and hidden from the world.

Prideep and Osman became used to finding me in the vault where I would sit for hours and read or sleep. In London one might look upon someone who habitually snoozes against the back wall of a steel-lined vault as eccentric. In Bombay it seemed a perfectly normal way to behave. The bankers were delighted that I made such complete use of their facilities.

On one such day I was taking a nap in front of my locker. There was a thumping of feet and Osman bounded into the strong-room. His cries echoed about the chamber like those around a tomb.

'He wants to meet you! He wants to meet you!'

I resented being woken so suddenly.

'What are you on about, Osman? *Who* wants to meet me?'

'The Dervish does.'

CHAPTER 4

Send the Fool Another Mile

Some took sticks and some took stones,
Some took clods, and off they scurried
After Warche, King of Squirrels,
Hip-cloths streaming out behind them.

Lines of black taxicabs with yellow roofs waited opposite the Opera House. Each driver had turned his engine off and was jamming down his horn in the hope that it might clear the way. An electric bugle sound radiated from under the bonnet of our taxi. The driver had just been to the horn bazaar and picked up the latest little number in public harassment.

The Opera building must once have been a wonderful sight. I wound down my window to take a better look. A hand brushed across my face and poked about inside the taxi. With no fingers, just concave stumps, it was attached to a blind *baba*, led by a young lad. It is common to see old men with advanced eye conditions being led about. The couples have a symbiotic relationship, each compensating for the other's weakness. Before I had a chance to produce a coin, the blockage cleared and we sped on towards Foras Road and our appointment with the Dervish.

Foras Road has a sordid reputation. It is the red light area of Bombay. The taxi driver had chortled when Osman, Prideep and I leapt in and told him to hurry. Although it was still early morning there was enormous activity around the lodging houses.

Children carried pots on their heads, and water sloshed over the sides. A two-year-old would scrub at a baby's back, and her sister would, in turn, pour buckets of brown water over her. Old crones sat in doorways, while their daughters were pushed out to earn money. It is intriguing that a society which is very covert with sexuality should be so straightforward about prostitution.

Leaving the taxi, we stumbled deeper into the filth and I felt ashamed for complaining about my life and conditions. A boy had fashioned a blade of sorts from a tin can's edge. He was sawing at the horn of a dead goat which seemed to have been killed by a passing vehicle. The boy screwed up his face with effort and began to jump on the horn, trying to make it snap.

The community existed by selling reused goods. All the plastic bottles and cardboard boxes from uptown homes served new purposes. On Foras Road it did not matter what something had been, only what it could be used for now.

Pimps surrounded us and offered us girls. 'You want a young one, real pretty?' Osman was getting very agitated and I was nervous he would attack the next pimp who bothered him. A child of about twelve called to Prideep, her face had been bleached and was white as snow. But her neck and hands were dark brown, and they moved from side to side hoping to coax Prideep to join her.

Osman had been given orders that we were to contact the Dervish through the manager of the underground bar somewhere in the locality. We walked up and down asking all types of people where exactly the bar was hidden. Some pointed left and others shook their heads dolefully. Did it mean they did not know, or that our quest was dangerous?

Osman plucked up a shoeless lad, and dropped him onto his shoulders. Squinting with Nepalese almond eyes, the boy had assured us he could show the way to the bar. He laughed so loudly at Osman's jokes that his face seemed to split in two. Steps led down from the street into a subterranean cavern. We descended. Girls with elaborate costumes and ankle bells danced to the tune of a *sitar* with the grace of ancient styles. Prideep was happy and began to twitch. He always twitched when he was happy. Yet I was nervous of the revolving red lights and anxious for the impending rendezvous.

A waiter took our orders and said the middleman would be along shortly. An hour passed. Another hour passed. I was getting tired of the dancing.

Just as I was about to storm off, a hunchback with a shaven head appeared, and told me to follow him. My colleagues would not be allowed to meet the Dervish, but they could drink tea with his guards.

We moved through alleys and down passages between kiosks where clients were already being entertained. My heart was thumping and I must have looked worried. Osman put a hand on my shoulder and smiled as I turned back to see his expression.

In one alley, which was darker than the rest, a door within a door opened. We entered a courtyard and I was led away from Osman and Prideep.

Guards loitered, toying with the triggers of Chinese-made Kalashnikovs. I tried to look serious and not as frightened as the situation warranted. A glass of tea was poured and passed to me. Grains of cardamom settled down at the bottom. Some sultanas — mixed with pine kernels — were placed next to my right hand: in Afghanistan known as *kishmish*. Who was the Dervish? For cardamom tea is also a favoured drink in Afghanistan.

I waited. Then the door swung open and a huge figure approached me with outstretched arms. Everything about him was big. His strides were long and full, and his limbs seemed double the size of those of any normal man.

My fingers were crushed in his grasp, and it was as if I were being greeted by my oldest friend.

'How kind of you to find me here. I am Yusuf Jahan. Some call me the Dervish.'

He spoke with slow deliberation in very good English, in an unusual, courteous voice which somehow made one feel warm and distinguished. A thick black beard reached to the second button of his shirt. He was dressed in camouflage army fatigues. A straight-bladed dagger — a Khyber knife with a bone handle — poked from just beneath his belt. The instrument and the man were most definitely from the wild lands of the Hindu Kush. What was an Afghan doing here in India?

Choosing my words carefully, I addressed him,

'*Aga*, forgive me,' I said, 'but you seem to be a man from the north-west of this land, perhaps from the country of my own ancestors: Afghanistan?'

The Dervish smiled with pursed lips and nodded as if I had answered a puzzle and pleased him.

'I am from Jalalabad,' he said. 'I heard that *Tahir Shah* was looking to buy certain items in Bombay, the name sounded Afghan and so I sent to meet you. But *Shah* in our country is a title, what is the name of your family?'

'We are of the Hashimite family. We come from Paghman. Alas, because of the war I have been unable to live in Afghanistan. I was educated in the West and have lived there most of my life.'

'You must be proud of your homeland, then it will be proud to have you as a son,' began the Dervish. 'I left Jalalabad when the KHAD, Afghan secret police, offered a reward for my arrest. I had wanted to journey south for many years, and so made for India with some of my men to live amongst these Hindus. With the end of the war in our country, and the end of KHAD, we will soon go home!

'I am like the fat which never mixes with the tea . . . our customs and society can never be reconciled with those of India. I had hoped to come here and teach them to be like us. Now I realise that they are happy in their ignorance. You can put a fleece on the back of a wolf but it will never take root.'

Though I felt a kinship with the Dervish, I decided to cut through the pleasantries to see what assistance he could be to me. The Pashtun anticipated me.

'I hear that you are looking for old things. What old things do you need?'

I explained that I wanted to purchase both Indian and European antiques. But until now I had found little to satisfy my interests. The Dervish listened, nodding gently. He only began to speak when he was sure that I was drained of words.

'I shall see what I can do. Are you looking for any other products? I have many friends and could be of great help to you.'

What exactly was he aiming at?

I asked: 'Is there anything in particular which you think might be of interest to me?'

He looked at me directly. Black eyes burned from his face and his Pashtun nose hooked at the air.

'I have a quantity of Dragunov sniper rifles. Seven point six two millimetre SVD. Capable of firing twenty rounds per minute, 830 metres a second. They are enormously accurate, and are in excellent condition. At this moment available to be exported.'

So, he was in the arms business . . .

'Well, Sir, for the moment it is not exactly what I had in mind. That is to say I don't have orders for such merchandise.' I stuttered, my thoughts floundering.

'Well what about SA-7 Grail hand-held anti-aircraft missiles? Six mile range, highest Russian technology. I have a contact who is willing to supply.'

There was silence. The Dervish looked displeased and scratched his forehead with a set of manicured nails. I gulped my tea which was cold, and agreed to notify him if and when I was ever in need of a Grail Missile. He passed me a silver bowl of sugar-coated almonds. I praised their taste, he was pleased that I liked them.

'I have them sent from Kabul every month. It would be unbearable here without certain luxuries. You must see what else I brought with me to this heathen land.'

We both stood up and went to a stable, guarded by a lad who was armed to the teeth. Inside were two ponies.

'They are trained for *Buz Kashi*, the Afghan national sport,' said the Dervish. Images of this most extraordinary game came to mind. It is the sport — said to be the forefather of modern polo — played on horseback by anything up to a thousand players. A stuffed goatskin is fought over by the mounted horsemen, with the aim of positioning it within a circle on the field. Fabled as being one of the roughest sports ever devised, the horses are at times trained to bite each other.

The Dervish shouted out, 'Do you play?'

'I haven't ridden for years, but next time you have a game perhaps I could watch.'

'You will be the guest of honour. If I have any information before then I shall send for you. Now I am sure your friends wonder where you are.'

We shook hands and I left the Dervish with his ponies.

Osman was relieved to see me. He had been trying to teach Prideep and the guards a game like bowls, only played with small pebbles which do not roll. I did not mention what the conversation had been about. Strangely they were not curious at all. We left by the door within a door and started to look for a taxi.

* * *

There was a need to talk to someone who might understand. I remembered the American, sitting advising people that day at the party: D. Blake. I telephoned him. His words mingled with other voices on the line, which crackled in dialects, spreading gossip and news from one mouth to the next.

'Yo man, just ride on up here and we'll chew some fat. Tell the cab driver you want to go to King's Circle. Get off at the Aurora Cinema. Ask for the American, this is a small neighbourhood. See ya later.'

The drive was longer than I had expected. The first four taxi drivers I had asked refused to take me. One scowled and berated me in Punjabi — saying that after taking me once before he had declared war on all westerners. I was secretly chuffed to have acquired a reputation of sorts, even if a bad one. There must be five thousand taxis in the city: making the odds extremely small of getting the same one twice. Bombay is like New York when it comes to taxicabs. The drivers have seen everything. They cannot be impressed. Sometimes I rambled on, telling tall tales of great fortunes. Not a single one even raised an eyebrow.

A tear-shaped bottle of imported iced tea sat on my lap. It jerked about as we swerved around blind bends, up and down hills. The jaunt seemed to encompass all the life that India has to offer, perhaps all that is human.

We sped on like the wind through suburbs and outskirts where wealth and indigence meet. Rows of lights twinkled in the twilight, as millions of feet dodged through chaos, and holy cows became traffic islands at their will.

The taxi stopped to let a group of oxen rearrange their form. A man with mutilated legs, riding on a primitive skateboard, grabbed hold of the rear bumper: he was propelled at what must have seemed the speed of light. His mouth burst open and snapped for air. The wheels were in danger of melting as they spun round and around. Then the board hit a bump. The form's rags were swept back with aerodynamic precision: he curled into a ball and braced for the shock as he became airborne. I heard muffled cries and saw a pair of twig-like limbs revolving into the night.

Blake was training a flock of vultures to take chillies from his palm. They squawked like badly-behaved school children as they stomped about, refusing to respect his command.

'This is just the first step,' said Blake, enthused to have an audience on his rooftop. 'They prefer chapaties, but I read that green parrots like chillies: they're all birds. In the afternoon they sit around and preen each other. That's when they love to hear my bongos.'

He beat out a tune on a hide-covered drum. The vultures flew off to a faraway tree. 'They only like it in the afternoon, you understand.'

The roof was concealed behind numerous sets of railway tracks, across from a six-lane highway, and at the exact point above which three glide-paths crossed. Yet somehow there was silence.

We sat on silk cushions, sipping brownish tamarind juice and watching geckos watch us with an air of psychopathic derangement.

'When the vultures have been tamed I'm going get those gecko suckers to walk on a leash . . . just wait and see,' said Blake.

He would lurch forward with anticipation and passion at the telling of a story, and his bright green eyes would flash with his excitement for another tale.

Before settling in India, Blake had taken Priti, his wife, to West Africa, in search of a spiritual director. Whilst living there he had studied West African magical sciences. As we spoke, he brought up one of the most sinister areas of study, whose practices seemed bewildering.

The belief is known as *Macumba*. It was almost as if Blake had to fight himself to conceal what he had learnt. He seemed desperate to tell me of this curious art, yet when I began to question him, he forced me to drop the matter, which I did.

My interest in West African witchcraft had come long before with the letters of a friend, who had ultimately gone to study in Freetown, Sierra Leone. I intended to visit him and learn more of his efforts to learn about ju-ju. But Blake had mentioned another dark science — *Macumba*. Although African in origin, it was developed in Brazil. Known to have roots in many societies and cultures, it has taken symbols and rites from many nations and religious groups, including Hinduism.

Blake did not realise it, but in refusing to tell me more of what he knew, he had made me all the more determined to pursue the matter alone.

He could see I was thinking hard and he changed the subject:

'You're too goofy to go into the antiques or any other business,' he exclaimed, sprawling back on a wicker sofa. 'Man, people in this place will rip you for every paisa, they don't care about long-term deals . . . they all want to make a buck. Just one buck and that's fine for them. Look at all the corner stands from here to Churchgate: those guys are just treading water trying to survive. Okay, some of them have crawled this far and consider a news-stand as fulfilling a life's ambition, but for most of those dudes there isn't a hope in hell.

'Those bastards in the West go on moaning about their misfortune: I just want to show one of them North Bombay! That'd keep them quiet and give them something to think about. Man, I don't even like to go downtown to Churchgate; it's full of snobs in taxi lines who couldn't give a damn. They have their boots cleaned and never even take a look at the guy who's doing the job.'

Blake had married Priti eight years before. The more time I spent in Bombay, the more I came to realise what a famous wife he had. She was well known in advertising and graphic design.

'It wasn't easy for my parents when I married Blake,' she said. 'We met in the States; I was just travelling around. Then we went to West Africa where he was in search of his guru. Six months later I persuaded him to come here. I think my parents must be very special people to have accepted the situation so readily.'

I could see that they were very much in love. Blake and Priti were the first educated people I had met in Bombay who were not trying to impress or astound me with their intelligence. Priti spoke demurely and behaved with great elegance.

'I'm really happy that we are living here,' she said: 'I liked the States: it has advantages for a woman who wants to get serious work done. People accept it there, more than in Bombay where so many men are in my field. I wouldn't like to live in the States for a long time, though. Once, Blake's oldest friend invited us to dinner. He cooked spaghetti, and when Blake began to help himself to more, it was pulled away. The host took it for himself! In the East a guest is treated as if he were God.

'Some Americans tend to be superficial. When I first went there I was visiting my brother in Kentucky. We were invited to a belly-dancing competition in a tiny town, in the middle of nowhere. I couldn't believe my eyes: all these fat American women wrapped in sheets swaying their waists and shaking their heads from side to side. People kept giving me uneasy looks when I said my name. When I told one guy, 'Hi, I'm Priti,' he rolled his eyes and said, "Do you really think so?" '

I asked Blake who the beautiful girl had been at the party where we first met. She was, he explained, the daughter of the host that night. Was there any chance of meeting her? Blake chuckled and rubbed his fingers across each other and spoke.

'I can arrange to introduce you. But it will involve your becoming my pupil and doing all that I say. If you put your trust in me all will go well. To show that I am your guruji you must bring me a garland of flowers and a coconut. This is tradition.'

I agreed and the subject was dropped. It was decided that I should be introduced to Blake's own guru. He was an aging teacher of music, the finest there was: a man who had grasped the very mechanics of Hindustani rhythm and lilt. I picked up a six-inch spool tape, sitting next to the peanuts. Blake started up from his upside-down slump:

'Hey man, be careful! That's weeks of work you're holding right there.'

'Wow! What is it, some new sitar track or what?'

'No man, it's for a great new Hindi movie. It's *atmos*.'

'Atmos?'

'I recorded twenty-four hours of it. It's fantastic aphony, man. I'm really happy with the way it turned out. You see, movie tracks must have atmos dubbed in, otherwise you just hear the projectors rolling.'

I knew that there was so much for me to learn, it seemed having Blake as a guru might help me understand more of India and its unconventional customs. We spoke some more, then I left D. Blake and Priti to tame the vultures on their rooftop in the middle of nowhere — which was somehow so central all the same.

* * *

'The Town Hall's where you'll find it.' Everyone assured me that this legendary site was the solution for everything and anything. Sometimes strangers stopped me in the street, muttering 'Town Hall', as if it were a secret curse or code they were desperate to pass on.

One day I was so curious to see what I had been missing that I jumped into a taxi.

'The Town Hall please,' I said.

'Round ball? Vat round ball?' came the confused reply in a heavy Gujarati accent.

'Not a round ball, but the Town Hall. It is very famous, everyone knows where it is.'

'Vere is it then, Sahib?'

'I don't know, you're the driver. You must have gone there before.'

'I vill take you to Haji Ali's Tomb. It is nice place. You like it.'

'Are you crazy? If I wanted to go to Haji Ali's Tomb or to a round ball I'd say so.'

The driver looked at me in the rearview mirror, his face drawn with worry. He unwound the window and opened the door from the outside. There were shouts in Gujarati, Tamil and Punjabi. Everyone was baffled.

'It must be a big old building,' I chirped.

Then a bear-like driver laughed and pointed to the back seat of his cab. He, apparently, knew the way. There were problems because the first driver had made me pay the fare in advance so he could buy some petrol. Couldn't the one who knew tell the other? No, that would never do, for the one who had the knowledge was suddenly unable to recollect the names of any of the roads. They tried to draw a map in the red dirt. The finger which was poking about unearthed a one-rupee coin. A brawl began as the drivers debated who owned the rupee. Snatching the coin, I decreed that anyone who could take me to the Town Hall would get one rupee extra. It was decided that they would take it in turns to drive me. But the bear of a man pushed me into the back of his cab and we screeched away.

I have a very bad sense of direction. But it seemed to me we were going out of the town. An hour passed and I was pretty sure the Town Hall was not twenty miles out of Bombay.

'Where the hell are you going?' I screamed. 'Stop right now and take me back to town.'

'No, vee going to Town Halls, Sahib . . . *ek* minute.'

I sat back, knowing that I would be the only casualty. Ideas ran through my mind. Perhaps the whole business of the Town Hall was one enormous joke. Like the village idiot who had a prankster's note pinned to his back, reading 'Send the fool another mile', I was being passed from one to the next.

I could hear aeroplanes above the yellow-topped taxi. A large white sign depicted a bowing Maharaja — the symbol of Air India. Now I knew where we were. It was not the Town Hall but the airport.

'Why the hell did you spend an hour bringing me here? You're an idiot!' The driver beamed with satisfaction.

'No, Sahib, I bring you to the Town Halls. Look there it is.'

A bony finger stretched out and I stared in astonishment at the control tower to which he was pointing with pride. He mumbled:

'I vas not understanding at the beginning. You see most people are not vanting to come here. That will be two hundred rupees, plus the bonus one rupees makes two hundred and one rupees, Sahib.'

I faced the fact that I had been beaten yet again.

Another week passed and I asked Prideep and Osman to try and find out if there was a Town Hall in Bombay. They both thought, however, that it was totally logical to be taken to the control tower of an airport when asking for the main building of public affairs. I began to get to grips with the fact that it might be me who was going insane. I looked in a mirror at the Chateau Windsor to see if my eyeballs were twitching. Staring deeply at my reflection, I sensed an unfocused row of servants cackling behind. Then, I pulled Vinod to one side, and put it to him straight:

'Do you see me doing anything unusual? I want you to watch out and tell me. I can take it, don't worry. Do you think I'm a bit mad?'

He looked squarely into my eyes — which had indeed begun to twitch and cross uncontrollably — they blinked and flashed and I felt like barking out loud. 'Do I look cuckoo to you Vinod?'

'Sahib, you not a cloo-koo.'

'Not a raving lunatic: a screwball, an aberrating corybantic?!'

Vinod was openly nervous of my behaviour. He shuffled his bare feet in circles and said comforting things:

'Sahib, you are not mad. You will know if you are when your ears turn green.'

I thanked Vinod for his words of support and went to my room, pondering what he had said. There I lay on the bed. My head spun and for the first time I succumbed to it. I was in a country where everyone was a little peculiar — a bit off the norm. It was one against nine hundred million: a population who will say exactly what they think you wish to hear. My only fear was for those in the mental hospitals. Were they, by my standards, completely sane?

Osman pounded at my door. We had a rule that he could only report when I gave the word. He stood straight-backed, fidgeting up and down like a schoolboy who needs permission to be excused.

'All right, what do you have to report?'

'We found it! We found it! The Town Hall! And I know why you could never find it.'

'Why? What are the secret directions?'

'You have to ask for Akbarally's Departmental Store, of course! It's right behind Akbarally's.'

I leapt up. We would go at once.

A botanical garden led to the Town Hall and was home to what looked like a battlefield of bodies. Children crept about, picking the pockets of the sleeping and playing marbles in the afternoon heat. Akbarally's was indeed the landmark. It was surprising that no one seemed to know where the fabled municipal building stands. The desire to tell all the cab drivers of my discovery gripped me. The one stipulation to be a taxi driver in Bombay seems that you must have no knowledge of the city's geography and layout.

A wrought-iron gate swung open. We crossed a street and climbed up a wide set of steps. Constructed in 1833, the building was like a grand pavilion; white, with canopies over the windows. Corinthian columns supported the roof, and marble statues lurked in corners. An odour of bureaucracy persisted, as if we were entering a warehouse of partially processed, stored information. This was a place where data with no constructive use to anyone were protected and pored over by an army of what are known in democracies as public servants.

The floor creaked as I tiptoed up to a large south Indian woman dressed in a sparkling white saree.

'Excuse me, I'm interested in membership of the library.'

'Do you want temporary or permanent membership?' she asked.

'Temporary would do fine.'

Thrusting her right arm in the air, she announced with crushing authority:

'There *is* no temporary membership!'

I coaxed her for half an hour - and was promised an assistant who would help me choose three books. It was forbidden to tip the servant and to spit paan on the floor. I would obey all the rules.

The lady in radiant white was pleased, and clicked her fingers. No one came. It was then that I realised that this woman who had been dealing with me was not employed by the library at all.

Within minutes the real librarian arrived and arranged for an assistant to help me.

A pair of feet in bedroom slippers dragged across the unpolished parquet floor, making it creak and bend. The servant showed no enthusiasm for life. Osman was concerned that a man should be so sad. The character stared up at me like a dog which had been tormented with a bone, but no longer had the energy to care if he got it or not. His face was deformed and one ear was badly torn.

We staggered round and round, taking short cuts through the alleyways between the stacks . . . round and round. I gained a certain feeling for the geography of the room. Still Osman and I followed one step behind the servant, digging our metal heel studs into the parquet. Osman cackled uncontrollably, ecstatic that he could be so tormenting. The servant was not in the least intimidated: he trudged on and on around the stacks as if in a trance, his bedroom slippers sliding with a muffled grating sound.

Osman's feet had developed blisters, so we paused to sit on a wide blue vinyl-covered couch. He removed his shoes and stuck his thumb in his left ear. Fishing out a lump of beige wax, he rubbed it over the blisters. Then, he smiled and his spirits were rejuvenated. The assistant paced on with time-measured steps. Four hours passed and I had almost given up hope of ever seeing the three books I had ordered.

Shuffling feet moved among the blackness of bureaucratic papers. A sign fell to the ground and Osman picked it up and read the words: *No book is for sale.*

Volumes were piled in every corner, covered with black dust, some were backwards or upside down. Ladders with broken rungs led to galleries where carved ebony lions sat guard. Monastic methodical silence, not even disturbed by ticking from the wall clocks — those had stopped, probably many years before. A young clerk slouched over a heap of disintegrating newspapers, labelling with careful precision. He appeared resigned to a lifetime of sitting, in devotion to routine. The books he guarded were too precious, his glance and posture said, to be touched by the hands of infidels.

The assistant trod on, clutching my order close to his chest. Osman and I wandered away. The statues stared as if to recognise our failure. The taxi drivers could rest in their ignorance of such a legendary place.

* * *

That evening, as I clasped my head in my hands in defeat, a call from Blake was announced,

'Yo man, I told you to leave it all to me! I've fixed it all up. You can relax and let the wheels turn smoothly,' he said.

'Blake, what are you on about? What did you *fix* up?'

'Man, I hope you appreciate it, after I put in all that sweet talking and sliming.'

'What *are* you on about, Blake?!'

'I got you a date with Himala tonight. You have to pick her up at eight-thirty. This is the address. Don't be late.'

I ran about the hotel wondering what to wear, what to say? Where I should take her? Vinod had let himself into my room. He had learnt to whistle through the new gaps between his teeth, and had come to demonstrate his new talent. As he whistled he swung his head from side to side, splattering saliva across the walls.

The door vibrated as fingertips clawed down its outer surface. I opened it to find a tidy procession of servants. One carried clean towels, one a bar of soap, another a shoe-cleaning kit and, the last, an iron. The first reported:

'Sahib, Anan the telephone operator said to bring you these things. Where is the shirt you will be wearing on this very special evening?'

I had always suspected that my conversations were monitored. My suspicious were at last confirmed. News of the impending occasion had spread like wildfire. I went to see V. V. Gupta, who worked miles from Churchgate. After handing me a stack of multi-coloured boxer shorts, he nudged me in the ribs and giggled:

'My wife says you should wear the yellow silk panties this evening. I think better to put on the pink ones as it's the first time you're with her.'

How did *he* know about Himala?

Prideep and Osman had also heard of my date and dropped by, to give me some tips on Indian girls. They would not leave until I had repeated all they had said. Osman made notes in calligraphic script (which he had learnt at *The Embassy* while mastering his trade as a janitor). Prideep forced Osman to translate all that he had to say:

'You must remember always to tickle her under the chin and to blow in her ears — girls like that, you know. If you want her to fall in love with you, you must have her serenaded by my cousin's *sitar* band. They are available tonight, I already made sure. They can be here by eight and come with you. Their charges are reasonable.'

Osman pushed Prideep out of the way and stopped translating his words.

'No, no, no! Prideep's all wrong. To win her heart there is but one sure way.' His voice lowered and I bent forward so as not to miss the words of great wisdom. 'You must take her to *Ali Hussain's Halal Meat Chop House*, when you get there mention my name and ask for the *special Chinese soup*. As soon as the first spoonful touches her lips she will follow you to the end of the world. I have already told Ali Hussain to make room for you. He owes me a favour.'

I was moved by their concern and unbridled gladness for my evening with Himala. Osman handed me a sheet of paper with their combined notes laid down in neat italic script.

As I handed my key in at the desk the manager turned and wished me luck. The corridors were lined with double rows of saluting servants. It felt as if I were going to collect a gallantry medal.

Having taken a taxi past Kemp's Corner, I waited outside the apartment because I was ten minutes early. I seemed invisible to the hordes of commuters who rushed past.

Himala's mother opened the door to the apartment. She was straight-backed, correct and very elegant. All eyes were on me as I crossed the room.

Trying to avoid the microscopic scrutiny, I slunk into a chair and attempted to disappear myself by mental effort into the surroundings. The family was having the customary evening discussion: deep in debate as to whether it was better to be good or to be bright. I steered diplomatically around the argument, trying not to take sides and thus to avoid making enemies. Himala's mother peered at me from above her white-framed bifocals and suggested that we leave.

Blake had done very well indeed to cajole such a formidable matriarch into allowing me to take her daughter out without a chaperon. I wondered exactly what he had said to win her trust. My coconut and garland had not been wasted.

Mosquitos and flying beetles buzzed around fluorescent lamps outside the Roxy cinema. Pineapple and melon was being cut into mouth-sized lumps and put on green plastic plates. I queued up and bought two tickets for *Tridev*, one of the great epics of Bombay's movie industry, which Prideep had recommended.

We took our seats upstairs in row D1. Giant lights, suspended from the ceiling, flickered. Arabesque scenes hung from the walls around us — like tortured prisoners in an eternal captivity. The seats squeaked and were hard and uncomfortable.

A quarter of the screen began to reflect an ancient advertising film in blue and white. The virtues of Uttar Pradesh Province were explained by unsynchronised mouths, strobed with thread lines and the neat silhouette of the sound recordist's head. Suddenly — without warning — the epic began.

Like a convict facing a life sentence in solitude, I considered how I would ever emerge sane after three hours. The plot was hard to follow, especially as I understood very little Hindi. I pressed Himala to translate every line.

Villains framed a man for murdering someone; they kidnapped another taking him to their fantastic castle, perched on top of a waterfall. A group of three Indian musketeers united against the bad men and penetrated the castle's perimeter. Battle scenes became love scenes as the audience gasped and cheered in unison.

As minutes turned into hours, I sensed water dripping onto my neck. There was a crackle of food wrappers and I swivelled in my seat to tell the weeper to back off. As I turned, my eyes bulged in horror. Osman and Prideep gaped at me adoringly.

Osman was crying like a baby, and Prideep pushed a bag of miniature samosas into my face. I yelled at them, shocked that they would stoop to spying, then shouted that they should leave. Himala and the audience looked eagerly to see what the commotion was about. The pair stood up to leave. As tears slipped from Osman's eyes, he chirped:

'Don't forget to blow in her ears and remember Ali Hussain's soup'!

A man stumbled through the aisles juggling a tray. 'Tea in a tray, tea in a tray!' There were shouts and hisses as his head was profiled on the screen. I tried to get back to the plot.

The villains' kingdom had, for some reason, burst into flames and heads were rolling on the ground. Swords flashed as they sliced through the air and, in the middle of the final battle, a tumultuous chorus of the theme song began, 'Oye-oye, Oye-oye!'

Continuity is unimportant in Indian film-making. Characters can appear in fresh costumes half way through a speech; or a murder scene can be interrupted with a song which involves the whole cast (whether they have already been killed or not).

Three hours after arriving, I left the Roxy exhausted — with Himala linking her arm through mine — and we took a taxi to the Ambassador Hotel to eat in the revolving rooftop restaurant.

The manager showed us to a table which overlooked Marine Drive.

V.I.P. Luggage flashed on and off, the letters reflecting off the black water. The street lights, which lit up the peanut sellers and prostitutes, looked like an elegant string of pearls. Himala sat opposite me and smiled demurely. She seemed thrilled to have escaped her mother's clutches.

Marine Drive became Flora Fountain as the floor moved, revealing Bombay's high spots. The roads were deserted. Now and then the odd yellow-topped taxi or white Pal car passed, flashing ambers, and an occasional working headlight.

A waiter appeared with arms covered in plates: fish and fettucini and iced mango juice. The evening was idyllic. We drank to Blake and Priti's health. My mentor had done very well.

The silence was broken by shouts at the next table.

'Is this steak sacred? Am I eating *holy* cow?' The cries of a severely overweight gentleman — with a Central European accent — echoed around the revolving dining room.

The waiter was shifting uneasily from one foot to the other, obviously concerned by the notion that something he worshipped was being eaten by a foreigner.

'Ludwig! Ludwig! Leave zie nice vaitor man alone,' croaked his wife, as she continued to smoke a miniature Havana cigar, in a gold holder. Her chest, which was richly adorned with Egyptian tourist ornaments, rattled when she spoke. On noticing my interest in her husband's outburst, she turned to Himala and me:

'India ees so mystical, vee love it here,' she said sternly narrowing her eyes, 'You are very lucky to have such a country such as zis.'

Thanking the lady, I tried to draw her conversation to an end. One would often see westerners in Colaba, dressed like the couple at the next table. They would never venture more than one block from the Taj Hotel, immaculate in Givenchy suits and Banana Republic jackets, leading beggar children around by the hand. I would watch with interest. They never gave a single coin to those children — let alone clothed or educated them. Instamatic cameras would record the 'mixing with the natives' for posterity; and the party in broad-brimmed explorers' hats would return to sip tea in the gardens of the Taj.

Down below, Gaylord's was turning through the window pane. The wise old manager, always immaculately dressed, would be down there pleasing his customers.

Himala held her hands across the table. I noticed a dull silver ring on her left hand. 'Who gave you that?' I asked.

'It's a toe ring.' She turned it round, revealing a tiny flower on the inside. 'My sister wears the other, she bought them when she went away to study.'

'Why don't you wear it on your toe?'

She giggled and replied, 'That would just *not* be done.'

It was late when we left the Ambassador Hotel. We strolled down to Marine Drive and walked for a few minutes. Street sellers were still offering their wares. 'Rubber gloves, rubber gloves, peanuts, shoe shine?' Bedding was being laid down and bodies were hunched up against the sea wall. An old man called out to us. I looked down. On a rag he had placed two combs: one yellow, one red. Fishing boats roamed out into the darkness towards the horizon. Himala breathed deeply. She said,

'I am really happy here. I never want to live anywhere else.'

I thought about her words and Bombay. I thought about the garbage and the heat, the smells and the millions of people.

'You're right,' I said, 'This is a very special place.'

* * *

Wing Son saw me enter his shop, tucked behind the Regal Cinema, and climbed down the narrow ladder from the attic workshop. He seemed pleased and I knew that it meant the shoes had been finished. He walked to greet me with a nervous smile, chewing at the corner of his mouth, waiting expectantly for my praise.

Two packages were produced, wrapped in paper printed in large Hindi script, tied with string and bows. I drew the leaves apart and held each shoe in turn, admiring the stitches and wonderful quality of the calf's leather.

'Put them on your feet . . .,' he said, 'See how they fit; I made the soles extra thick like you asked.'

Wing fidgeted as I tried on each shoe in turn. They were sculpted perfectly to my feet.

'These are the most wonderful shoes I have ever worn. I shall always be proud of them,' I said.

Wing Son, the son of Wing Son, smiled like a Cheshire cat, the contours of his face curved and blossomed into the greatest expression of pleasure that I have ever seen.

Barefoot bearers who knew no other life weaved through the meshed traffic carrying dabba boxes on their heads. There was a smell of chapati flour and mutton curry, of sesame seeds and pumpkin chutney. Feet moved in all directions. Four hundred people lined up at a bus stop: in Bombay it can take nearly a whole day to get to work.

Weaving my way back to the Chateau Windsor, around sets of mutated toes, I thought for a moment about how no one moved in a mainstream way. Millions of people walked about bumping into all around them. Everyone behaved independently from the rest. There was no unison or continuity of movement, just random bombardment, like billiard balls colliding in a box.

At the Chateau, a telegram had arrived. It was from Blake. It read:

HEY MAN CANT GET THROUGH BY PHONE MY GURUJI PLAYS TONITE MEET YOU GAYLORDS 7PM BLAKE.

Midday chimed as usual twenty-three minutes early. The Chateau Windsor was on its own time, five hours and seven minutes east of Greenwich. I lay on my bed and felt the resonance of bells. The Chateau, as it was locally known, had a certain quality which made one feel impregnable and warm.

The yellow-flowered wallpaper watched me dress. I was sure it moved around when I turned my back, swanning about like a gigantic triffid. Switching off the light, I went down to Gaylord's. The foliage could play in the darkness until my return.

Sunday night was always packed at Gaylord's. Large, bulging mothers sidled about in tight shoes. Their coloured glass bangles tinkled in the evening air as they struggled to place one enormous limb in front of the first. Only by such burdened mathematical precision were they able to move. In India the rich die of heart-failure from obesity, the poor from starvation.

A blind man passed. He also moved one foot in front of the other with the same delicate mathematics. A stick with a bicycle bell attached to the handle was his guide. He sauntered forward cautiously, ringing the bell. Sarees were pulled tighter to conceal the fleshy reams of fat surrounding Bombay's wealthy.

Blake came an hour late. I poured him a cup of tea with lemon. He added milk and the liquid curdled, but he insisted on drinking it.

The restaurant's manager circulated, ensuring that we and the other clients were content. And, when my guest went to wash his hands, he offered to buy my watch. I refused for the hundredth time — in a bargaining routine which was enacted twice daily — regretting as usual that it had been a gift. The old manager smiled with a mouth which bore the scars of immeasurable quantities of paan, and drifted away.

Blake was eager to know the details of my date. He had acquired a general report from the vegetable bazaar that morning. Apparently everyone was talking about the events of the night before. It was something which I did not doubt for a moment, for Bombay is a city where gossip is treated as a commodity. Praising Blake, I assured him that his tutelage had already brought results.

'Well, now you must meet the teacher of the teacher: my guruji,' he said.

* * *

A chord was struck and the guru began to hum. His eyes were closed, palms upturned and open. Two giant *tanpura* — instruments like sitars made from gourds — produced a droning sound, almost a stage on which the guru performed.

We all sat cross-legged and obedient on the floor of St. Xavier's college. Long faces with deep black beards stared down from their mahogany frames. F. Dreckman, former headmaster, watched in amazement from the confines of his frame, listening to the wailing sounds which were now being emitted from the guru's mouth.

The teacher was a refined, white-haired man of perhaps seventy. His skin had no wrinkles, his hair was wetted down and combed. A bow ran across a *serengi*'s strings and the vibrations echoed about the Gothic hall.

A little girl stood up and dragged her rag doll across the floor. She passed a row of ancient pupils, with white sticks and swollen eyes; her ponytail swung from side to side as she ran off into the courtyard.

The teacher controlled one sound, taming it with his lips and balancing upon it like a tightrope-walker. A man with headphones began to weep; a lady's body quivered ecstatically, as she tugged fitfully at her hair. Blake and I watched, hypnotised by the sounds enclosing us.

Three hours elapsed and I was numb from the waist down.

The guru suddenly stood up and left. The audience sat transfixed and motionless. Blake turned to me and whispered with deep pride:

'That was *my* teacher.'

CHAPTER 5

The Alchemist's Assistant

Purest water may be stained;
Stainless all and pure was Lingo.
Diamond sparkled on his navel;
On his forehead beamed the Tika.

Osman and Prideep had been in my employment for some weeks. Every Friday I would take them to lunch. It was the high point of their calender. During the meal I would harangue them as a reminder of what they had been hired for: but my orations never seemed to increase their output. I realised later that, in the East, a commitment to produce does not automatically accompany employment.

To stimulate the ambitions of my team, I offered large bonuses and rewards upon our success in finding bounty. They seemed unimpressed.

One Friday they turned up as usual, expecting to be fed. The shadows of the two — who were lurking in the hallway — were visible through the gap under my door. Prideep was practising his English loudly, with Osman instructing. They hoped that I would hear their voices and come out.

'Come on Prideep, you must try counting again.' Osman spoke with self-consciously amplified words. Then Prideep began, 'Wone, toe, flee, fooer, seeks, nine . . .'

'Well done, that was much better, Prideep.' Osman paused, waiting for me to open the door. He was teaching his colleague to count wrongly, I realised, so that he would himself never be replaced.

'Maybe Tahir Sahib wants to be left alone today,' said Osman sadly. I heard a slap, Prideep had evidently forgotten his cue. He yelped pitifully.

'I don't know what we should do with this letter that has come from . . . who is it from, Prideep?' There were whispers in Hindi and Prideep stammered, 'Day-wi-ss-hah!' Running the sounds through my brain, I decoded them to make *Dervish*. Then, pulling open the door, I grabbed the letter from Prideep's fingers.

The brown manila envelope was too thin to be a bomb, so I sliced the top off with a scalpel. Inside was a hand-written note. Thumb prints obscured many of the words, but I made out:

To the Presence of: Tahir El Hashimi,

Insha Allah you are well and your men are healthy also. I fear that soon I shall have to return to our own land, for these infidels make my blood too warm. I have been unable to find your old things in Bombay, but have contacted a Muslim who lives west from here. You must go to meet him in the Great Thar Desert. He awaits you and keeps the treasure hidden. Go first to Jaisalmer in Rajasthan and use the instructions on the back of this paper. His name is Abdul Rachid Mohommedi. His friends call him *Abdul the Warrior.*

DERVISH.'

It all seemed too wonderful to be true. I read the letter several times, almost choking with anticipation. Prideep and Osman gazed at me: they felt left out. Besides, they had not been fed yet, as tradition decreed. I waved the letter in the air and shouted:

'We are going to Rajasthan!'

* * *

Arrangements were made to leave Bombay in two days. V.V. Gupta handed me another stack of silk boxer shorts — large enough to fit a hippo — and wished me well. He was a kind-hearted man, although enormously slow in his craft.

At Chateau Windsor, sixty servants knew that I had paid the bill, and they all loitered outside my door waiting for my departure. Some pretended to be polishing, others mopping the walls or straightening pictures. An air of expectancy filled the corridors. I went to the bathroom to shave. When I tried to get out into the hallway I was knocked back by a wave of small men in khaki shorts, all of whom wanted to be the first to be tipped.

In a moment of exultation I had decided to take Osman and Prideep along. After all, this was to be a great expedition and an entourage was most definitely in order. The team turned up three hours early. Prideep had never left Bombay before. He had heard, though, of the palaces and castles of Rajasthan. Osman was for the most part the perpetrator of these glorious tales. When he was working at the American Embassy in New Delhi he had once been sent to Gwalior to fetch some cleaning fluids. I often wondered what the cleaning fluids were doing in Gwalior in the first place. I had not asked, however: in India an explanation is often more confusing than what prompted it.

Osman led Prideep past the rows of servants — who lurked like vultures in wait for their prey to die. Sixty heads were drooped in respect and anticipation when they saw me, in much the same way that vultures cower.

Osman had packed a battered leather case which was covered with labels of many destinations. He attempted to convince me that he had escorted the case to the places advertised on its exterior: on secret diplomatic business. A couple of shirts and a tie with spots moved about inside. I handed him a compass to wear around his neck at all times. He demanded a short lecture on its use. After that there was no holding him. His eyes lit up and he read off bearings, pointing the instrument like a water diviner around the room.

Prideep had become jealous that Osman should be so favoured. I passed him a portable stove and said that he was in charge of making soup. Osman translated my words, punctuating them with bearings generated by his new toy. Everyone was happy.

The lift was summoned. Sixty mouths smiled. We walked to the contraption. Toes trod on toes in our wake and I heard my rubbish bin being torn apart. I had left a couple of old paperbacks and a half-used bottle of shampoo. Two pairs of feet rushed past me and ran down the stairs. The lift came and I handed a hundred-rupee note to the manager. He promised to divide it up amongst all the employees. Osman hailed a taxi to take us to Bombay Central Station. As the bags were loaded into the cab I noticed my paperbacks staring up at me: for sale on a street stall at ten rupees each.

Bombay Central is like a cavernous aircraft hangar. Its immensity sends shivers down one's spine. We slipped into the building though a side entrance. Everyone seemed to have a well-defined role, a purpose for their presence. Sacks of flour were being dumped into the middle of the place. Guards in worn-out quasi-military uniforms, and decorated with twisted moustachios, brandished shotguns and looked as menacing as they possibly could. Osman fought off the army of red-shirted porters, who had brass number bands on their arms.

Prideep had put on his best shirt, which had electric blue diagonal lines running across it. I had never seen him look so neat. The other shirt he possessed, the one he usually wore, was folded up and stuffed into his trouser pocket. He had no bag.

Osman began to read out bearings, assuring me that the practice might be welcome in case there were trying times ahead.

Extended families lived in isolated groups in the middle of the floor, amidst the paan spit and sacks of flour. A machine, with flashing beacons and grinding cogs, would tell one's weight and fortune for 50 paisa. Fishing out a coin, I inserted the money in the slot and stood on the platform provided. Whistles sounded, sirens roared, cymbals crashed and, as a brace of revolving lights spewed colour through the bleak surroundings, a rectangular chip of cardboard was thrust from an aperture towards my face. Having caught the card with my teeth, by some remarkable reflex action, I inspected it closely. On the front was written my weight. And, on the back, was a sinister warning. It said: *Spit into the spittoons only. Travel may be imminent. Be Prepared!*

Lists of names, pinned to a board, indicated where we would sleep. The journey to meet the Warrior was complicated to say the least, and entailed changing trains several times. Firstly, we would have to take a train to Vadodara, an important city in Gujarat. Osman assumed control, which only seemed natural as he had the compass.

We climbed aboard. Every door and window was left wide open, to cool us in the night. The fans were paralysed and looked as if they had not revolved in many years. A clicking of iron on iron filled the carriage as it pulled out from Bombay Central.

As we passed Dadar and the suburbs, I imagined Blake watching from his rooftop. The tracks cut through the city dirt and took us far out into the countryside. Buffaloes bathed in flooded pools and young women worked in the paddy fields. The horizon grew black and fireflies jostled in patterns as the night approached.

Prideep pointed to the flames of paraffin lamps as they came alive in the distance and cackled in awe at the experience. He was happier than I had ever seen him. He lit the portable stove and made some soup. I was to discover that making tasty soup with one carrot, ten peas and a little dishwater, was his greatest skill. One wondered what the man would be capable of creating with a blender and a non-stick frying-pan.

The train tended to screech to a halt every few minutes. While it was stationary for a moment, I opened my mouth and it filled with mosquitos. There was a sudden infestation of gnat-like insects. The light above my bunk was obscured with fleas which formed one solid layer. The air buzzed with life as arms waved around troubled heads. It was at this moment that a fortune-teller arrived.

He had nowhere to sit and so Osman invited him to stay with us a while and share some dishwater soup. The strangest thing happened: all the bugs and grubs and moving specks disappeared. We could all breathe easily again. The man who came and sat wore a blue coat which was visibly infested with parasites. Prideep tore a few chapaties and passed around a pot of thin pea soup. Our guest began to speak in perfect, if individualistic, English.

'My business is to tell the future,' he said. 'There are many things which I can see and feelings which enwrap my bones.' He brushed back his long white hair with the palm of his hand and paused for a moment or two. 'I should like to be of help to you, Sir, and your party.'

He had no crystal ball or magic cap, just a wrinkled face with long, prominent ears, and a pair of slippers with curly toes. His words were those of an actor, spoken with theatrical flair.

Osman pointed at Prideep who was probing around his mouth with the end of a spoon. With a smile he said:

'Why doesn't he tell Prideep's future?'

Prideep heard his name spoken and looked up, hoping that it meant good things.

The seer nodded and closed his black eyes. Taking Prideep's left hand in his bony fingers, he swaggered about, moaning wildly. The other passengers turned and watched. Mothers paused from feeding infants and a group of city men dropped their playing-cards. At first, Osman and I suspected it was all a big joke. Prideep did not know what was happening and looked terrified. He tried to pull his hand away, but it was gripped too firmly.

The seer dropped Prideep's fingers and jumped up so suddenly — as if he had received an electric shock — that Osman and I shouted: 'What is it? What did you see?'

Prideep had understood nothing of the episode and went back to drinking his soup. The fortune-teller clasped his hands together and mouthed a short prayer.

'This boy is cursed!' he said simply. Osman and I stared at each other and then at the old man.

'What're you talking about? That's Prideep, he's all right,' Osman said.

'He has a deadly curse cloaking his existence. You must keep away from him. It was placed upon him as a child.'

'Can it ever be removed?' I asked.

'Removed? See how he waves his head about and his tongue beats in his mouth! He is mad and dangerous!'

Prideep had burnt his tongue and gums on the boiling pea soup and had begun to choke. As he yelped, Osman thumped him on the back, thinking that it might clear the blockage. I turned to the great mystic and explained, 'My friend, he is not cursed, he just burnt his mouth. The soup is very hot you know.'

The wrinkled lips parted,

'I have seen his future. I have witnessed many things.'

'What have you seen? Tell us!'

The prospect of knowing Prideep's future was somehow fascinating. We were prepared to listen, if only for cynical entertainment. Prideep could not understand the conversation, if there was anything he should know, Osman could translate. The soothsayer began,

'What I have witnessed is unpleasant, I will reveal in the hope that the future's events may be changed, and that one particular incident may be avoided.'

'What are you trying to say?' The conversation suddenly took on a rather more serious tone. Osman and I listened, as Prideep began to clean the stove, absorbed in the operation.

'Your friend will some time from now — in some place from here be working in an office — his mind deep in his work as it is now. He hears screams from the building opposite, the cries of a little girl. He runs out of the door and sees flames consuming the house. The child is trapped inside. He puts his arms around his head and rushes to help her. The roof collapses. No one leaves the building.'

Osman had tears in his eyes. Prideep sensed that something was bothering us. He looked up and we all tried to smile.

'Your friend is cursed,' the sage repeated.

Osman addressed him, his words shaky and carefully phrased: 'Wise man, what can we do to defend our dear friend?'

'Such a strong curse is hard to deal with,' said the fortune-teller.

'But you must know of some solution,' persisted Osman.

'Well,' began the sage, almost reluctantly, 'there is one thing that may protect him. In Vadodara my cousin lives. He is the alchemist's assistant . . . he can make a talisman which, if your friend wears it, will protect him always. Go and ask for *Bhindu*.'

Osman inscribed the details on my white note-tablet. I handed the seer a few coins. Wishing us a comfortable night, he left to ply his trade in another carriage. As his blue coat moved away, the light was obscured again with fleas, flies and crawling things. Then, jumping up onto my bunk, using my camera as a pillow, I tried to sleep.

Prideep shook my arm as I slept late and handed me a cup of sweet tea. The train had been delayed for three hours during the night. We went to the lavatory in turns. The floor was slippery and covered in mud. Paan juice had been spat across the walls from many misjudging mouths.

Vadodara was to entertain us for one day, then in the evening we were to catch a train to Udaipur. The sun shone brightly but had not yet begun to warm the air. My body was red and sore from a thousand insect bites. We had breakfast at the Hotel Aditi. Macaroni cheese came sweet, with a runny white sauce. I had encouraged Osman to order the macaroni, saying that it was very European. Disgusted by the sauce, he had requested for the pasta be taken away and rinsed. Osman never had very much good to say about the Europeans. He jumped at the fact that the British almost certainly renamed Vadodara, their own 'Baroda' because they could not pronounce the real name. Nowadays the two names coexist.

We took a walk around the town.

Vadodara was not, as many now think, anglified by the British, but by its own Maharajas; for it was the capital of a state, rather than part of British India. Nevertheless there are Devonshire cottages, great institutes dedicated to Queen Victoria, street lamps and four-faced clocks. Unfortunately, when the Maharajas lost their authority, all they had created fell into a general state of Indian dilapidation. The paving stones were cracked and the clocks' hands long removed. Whatever the former rulers had tried to create had been replaced by a more peaceful Indian way of life.

We strolled into the grounds of Maharaja Gaekwar and viewed, for one rupee, the paintings in his gallery. He had a European collection which would make many museum curators in the West envious. Prideep and Osman cackled away together in low voices, laughing freely at what I had been educated to respect. In Bombay, I recalled, I had met an Indian lady artist who told me about the French Festival in India. She reported that several priceless paintings by Europeans, such as Monet and Manet, had been transported to Delhi and hung there for a few weeks. The French guardians of the masterpieces were horrified when Indian visitors to the exhibition ran their grubby fingers over the canvases. They insisted on *feeling* the workmanship.

* * *

The floor of the bazaar was covered in life and moving limbs. Naked children filled Thums-Up cola bottles with dust and chewed on bits of glass. They pointed at us, their noses running and their hair matted with dirt. A boy was pulling himself along the ground. His legs, wrapped in linen bandages, were totally concealed. One leg stretched forward, the other backwards: he was doing the splits. I stared in fascination and pity, for the child was still moving although attached to a pair of dead legs. He put out a hand, but only I saw his attempts to reach out to the world above him.

We walked into the blue smoke of peanut burners; my eyes darted about, taking in people living like spiders sprawled across a web of absolute poverty.

Osman was miserable. He had stopped reading out compass-points and was the picture of dejection. I was astounded that his feelings for Prideep were suddenly so strong, when until recently they had hated each other. Osman dropped hints continually that we should seek the alchemist's assistant and get him to protect Prideep from the eternal curse.

'Do you really think it'll make a difference?' I asked Osman as we trudged along. 'All that performance last night by the fortune-teller might have been a ruse to increase his cousin's business. Alchemy isn't as productive as is widely believed.'

But Osman insisted:

'You heard what the wise Baba said, and you saw his manner when he said it; his voice trembled and he didn't want to reveal the future at first. It is our responsibility, as Prideep's guardians, to help.'

Having agreed that the visit might be interesting, Osman pulled out the directions that he had made, and we set off.

The rickshaw laboured under the weight of its driver, three passengers, and our luggage. After careering for several miles away from Vadodara, it turned onto a road obviously used mostly by oxen. Osman and I looked at each other as if to note that the rickshaw was lost: a very usual occurrence. Prideep was humming the song from Tridev; he clasped the portable stove and sighed as we bumped along. His seemed to be the only mind that was at rest.

The rickshaw came to an abrupt halt and we were required to pay twelve rupees. Prideep had become friends with the driver and offered to make him some carrot soup. The two men crouched over the paraffin Primus: one shielding it from the breeze, the other pumping the handle.

Grinding sounds and cries in Gujarati radiated from a black hut some thirty feet from where the rickshaw had stopped. Was it the alchemist at work? Would we see molten gold produced? We knocked. There was no answer. Osman pushed the door open and called to a boy who was sharpening knives. The child ran off. A man, whom I assumed to be his father, appeared, and motioned us to enter.

The interior of the hut was dark, smoke-filled, and smelt of sulphur. In one corner six grey sacks were piled up on each other; in another had been placed a miniature cage in which a brown rat was scurrying. Much of the hut's main room was taken up by a large homemade workbench. Cluttered with odds and ends, the surface of the bench was sprinkled with a kind of fine black sand. And, at the far edge of the counter was a sinister apparatus, festooned in cobwebs and dirt. A mess of beakers, tripods, burners and primitive condensing-tubes, I suspected that the contraption might once have been the alchemist's tool.

The alchemist's assistant was a very average-looking man, dressed in a white loincloth and the remains of a string vest. Osman began to speak to him in Hindi. There was no communication. He tried English; our host replied in Shakespearian English. I explained that we had met a fortune-teller on a train and we were to ask for 'Bhindu'. He was Bhindu. Could he produce an amulet to protect Prideep from his fateful future? He, and only he had that skill, we could be assured. Osman smiled and asked how long it might take to make such a powerful charm. Two hours, and it would cost one hundred rupees. The whole procedure seemed rather commercial; I had a nagging feeling at the back of my mind that we were being exploited.

With the smoke blinding us, and the stench of sulphur unbearable, we went out into the sunshine to allow the master to craft the charm.

The carrot soup was very tasty. Prideep had gathered some wild herbs and seasoned the carrots and water with them. Osman paced up and down. In the black hut, magical spells were being cast. Fantastic words and sounds escaped through the broken window pane. We waited. The driver fell asleep. A goat came and went.

Then the alchemist's assistant opened the door and beckoned us forward. He held in his hand a rust-coloured talisman, one inch square. A leather thong passed through an eye at the top. It bore a single sign rather like an asterisk in the centre of three concentric circles. I handed a note to Bhindu, who stood in the doorway, he tucked it deep into his lungi. I asked if he still practised alchemy.

'Alchemy, not now. The master hath died.'

'How did you learn such fine English?'

'From the *teach-book*.' He went and delved deep in the back of the hut, returning with a leatherbound volume. I read the words from the first page:

'*A Practical Grammar of the English Language, by John Burn, Printed Glasgow, 1766.*'

We thanked the alchemist's assistant and went back to the rickshaw. Osman called Prideep to him. He spoke slowly in Hindi. I could just understand what he said.

'I want you to promise me one thing. Can you do that?' Prideep nodded and waited for Osman to continue.

'Will you promise to wear this amulet around your neck always?'

Prideep frowned but agreed that he would, if only to make his friend happy.

Osman tied it around Prideep's thin neck and spoke. 'My friend, you must not question this ever or fail me. You are bound by a promise. Never cut the thong and I pray that God shall always love you.'

Vadodara passed from under the railway tracks and we left Gujarat, India's only dry state, behind. Osman read numbers off the compass and coal smoke churned in our wake. My heart beat in time with the sound of the steam-engine chugging along. A feeling that life in the world was idyllic pervaded. Images of the bazaar and the boy with dead legs seemed to be but phantoms as we prepared our minds for the journey that lay ahead.

The train stopped at a station a couple of hours from Udaipur. It was called Zawa. Rain poured from the sky and the population of Zawa — some two hundred people — loitered on the platform watching our arrival. Many were sheltering from the sheets of water under moth-eaten black umbrellas. When I climbed down to stretch my legs, I met a young man with deep-set eyes and straggly moustache, who was hawking oranges. He lamented that no one ate oranges when it rained, and said that the people of Zawa always trooped out to watch the train pass through their village. It was tradition.

Leaving the orange-seller to his trade, I climbed back into the carriage. And there we lay on our bunks waiting for the iron wheels to move. They did not, for what seemed like days. Then it was announced that we would depart at three o'clock. The driver climbed down from the locomotive, and lay on a bench. He fell asleep, the stoker at his feet. Groups of old men crouched about, smoking biris, and wrapped in blankets against the chill. Goats chewed on reeds, or ambled about eyeing the black umbrellas as if they were delicacies of some mouth-watering cuisine.

At Udaipur, a rickshaw laden with our bedraggled group left Udaipur City station behind. The journey had been seriously delayed, largely due to the apparent lack of enthusiasm by the driver for his career.

The first rays of light were reflected as pink rings in Prideep's eyes. We jerked up and down as the rickshaw capered from one pot-hole to the next. It laboured up narrow streets, making the sound of a Spitfire. The ground was knee-deep in rain water. Suddenly a surging undercurrent caught the floundering black rickshaw, transforming her into a makeshift raft.

None but a sacred cow bore witness to the driver's pleas for help. Every hotel and guest house in Udaipur seemed to be full. The driver beached the craft on the steps of a great temple. We abandoned the rickshaw and pressed on through the dark waters in search of a room.

Osman thumped at a giant Mughal door within a courtyard, sensing that the building might provide accommodation. There was no reply. Just as we were about to leave, a bolt was slid back and a cloaked figure welcomed us. We had arrived at Bada Haveli. The host was Lala, a man of exquisite bearing, gentle features and grey-green eyes.

Lala greeted us, his hands with palms placed together and fingers at a point,

'*Namaste*,' he said bowing his head and placing his palms together. 'You are very welcome to stay here for as long as you wish. This is a traditional house, there are few of the modern conveniences which other hotels offer.'

The Bada Haveli lay amidst a network of chambers. Courtyards opened into secret gardens and steps led to upper levels. A *haveli* is a house built for a nobleman, a gentleman of standing. We were taken by Lala to our rooms. My bedroom had an antechamber — three feet wide and four feet long — which Lala referred to as a 'breakfasting room'. The windows had no glass, but neat-fitting wooden shutters with filled pointed arches in the classical Mughal style. The bed was a marble slab with a sheet on top, and a bolster at one end. It was very hard. The floor was stone and decorated by drips of multi-coloured candle wax.

Lala rushed about tending to our needs. He brought a cake of red soap that another guest, he said, had left behind.

Osman and Prideep took the room next door. Stained-glass

panels had been set into one wall. When the sun shone, its pink light was tinted in greens and blues. Prideep's face glowed with the sort of excitement children feel at Christmas. Amongst the green and blue rays were columns decorated with mythical scenes. Lala smiled, acknowledging our obvious delight that the lodgings were so bewitching.

On the second level was a garden where squirrels played, darting about after each other. We climbed up onto the rooftop. Steps protruded from the walls — an advantage of 'afterthought' architecture. There we sat for two hours gazing out across the city as it woke and came alive. Women were preparing their homes for the day, feeding children and hanging bundles of clothes to dry. Shopkeepers began to put their wares on display as the narrow streets of Udaipur bustled with the frenzied activity of the morn.

The architecture, the colour of the light, the smell and sounds of the city as it woke, intoxicated us all.

Lala brought a tray of peanut balls, honey and a loaf of fresh coarse bread. He was fasting, but looked on with no sign of temptation as we feasted in his presence.

This was an extraordinary man. It was a delight to meet a person so eminently charming and kind. We were grateful that such civilised courtesy should be showered upon us; especially since we had only just met.

Lala spoke softly with a dignity that captivated his audience:

'My family were the official astronomers to the Maharajas for many generations,' he said. 'Being of that status allowed us to build a house on the third highest site in Udaipur. When my father died, I had no choice but to rent out parts of the building to guests. I have not had the means to develop amenities as yet. But in the future I hope that more tourists will come.'

'Do many foreigners come and stay here?'

'The problem is that I refuse to pay the unreasonable demands of the rickshaw drivers who bring people from the station. They want half the rent money. That is too much, so they take tourists to the other hotels.'

Rex was the only other guest at Bada Haveli. Aged about forty, he wore wire-rimmed spectacles, and was dressed in Bermuda shorts and a sunflower shirt. A strong Afrikaans accent obscured his words:

'Magik place trekker, tell ya vere's nowhere like et end thet's a fect. Vis ees me thed time een Endia, I alvays geet a tren stret here froem Deelhi.'

'Have you seen any other part of this country?'

'Nope min. Ven I geet tired of Bada Haveli arnd Udaipur I'll moeve on . . . but teel thet heppens I'll keep comin' 'ere min.'

Osman asked me about Bermuda shorts, 'Do people really wear those in the West?'

'Well, some people do,' I replied.

'In India the poorer people wear short trousers like that; no one would do it out of choice. Not even in Gwalior!'

From the roof of Bada Haveli we surveyed Udaipur with its many shrines and fine buildings. The largest sacred building, the Jagdish Temple, dates back to about 1640 AD. A pair of elephant statues stand guard at the foot of the steep steps which lead up to the shrine. The highest building is the City Palace, which gleams in white marble and granite, supreme over all below. Only the Lake Palace can rival it — floating below in the midst of Lake Pichola — it is surely one of the most spectacular monuments ever created by man.

The Lake Palace, like some vast Mississippi paddle-steamer fashioned from white marble, fills every inch of its island. Osman, Prideep and I looked about in awe. The South African was right: this was indeed a magical place.

We went down to the street where old men squatted, framed by doorways, shadows filling the folds in their crinkled skin. Sacred cows became traffic bollards at will in the narrow streets — around which large men in orange turbans swerved at great speed on their fragile scooters.

We wandered about the Bada Bazaar, where silver amulets

and bracelets are bought and sold. Dealers crouched on white cotton mattresses, perched above the gutter, squinting through thick spectacles at workmanship that is very fine indeed.

We walked out of the Suraj Pol, the Gate of the Sun, with its long iron spikes, ten feet above the ground, intended to stop the elephants of a hostile army from charging the doors. And we passed children who demanded 'one rupees' and little girls who giggled when they saw Osman. The sky — and the mountains which it touched — were reflected in the lake's green algae.

Five girls stood in the water washing their clothes. They were bare from the waist up. I averted my gaze and made Osman and Prideep do the same.

Suddenly the sound of hooves could be heard behind us. I turned, as my eyes crossed, trying to focus on the gigantic black mass of bones and flesh that was charging toward us. We stepped to one side and choked as dust swirled above the fresh hoof-prints. A buffalo had run amok and was making a beeline for the horizon. No one paid much attention. Haggard crones stopped talking to their friends for a moment, stepped aside as we had done, and continued chatting as before. Do buffaloes often carry on like that? Baffled, I put the problem to the back of my mind, and walked on, out of the town. Alone. Prideep and Osman preferred to hide in the shade of a tall acacia and spy on the girls who were now taking off the rest of their clothes.

Two hundred bicycles went by. Whole families balanced on the backs of the Calcutta-made frames, waving at all they passed. Where were they going? Were they following the buffalo, perhaps? What was the buffalo in pursuit of? These questions, and more, captivated me. So I decided to tag along too.

Thirty minutes later and there was no sign of the buffalo. A stall-keeper who sold Thums-Up cola pointed into the distance when I asked where the bicycles and the black brute had gone. Where were they going? The man waggled his head from behind a sea of cola bottles. I carried on along the earthen track, due east from Udaipur.

After another half hour, in pursuit of the bicycle tyre tracks and hoof prints, they stopped. The buffalo was lying under a tree, exhausted. About three hundred bicycles were sprawled around it in heaps of twisted metal. Their owners had formed a ring and were concentrated on a man in the centre.

The figure was dressed like a westerner in jungle green khaki shorts and a safari shirt. He held a black umbrella filled with large holes above his head. Silently, the front row of the audience stood up and paraded around the man in khaki shorts. They were all painted and dressed in bizarre costumes.

A man with a full black beard was dressed as a lady. One had a denim cone tied as a hat above his head; half his face was painted black, the other half white. Two men in dark glasses had swords, and another a club. The last capered about with two angelic wings attached to his arms. The audience stared. The buffalo panted. And I watched in wonderment as the characters began to dance.

The dance was choreographed with considerable precision, to the thud of a beating drum. The strokes grew closer together and the strange ritual continued. Three more men waved peacock feathers in the air, convulsing their bodies and heads from side to side as if they were possessed. Suddenly, and without warning, all the dancers turned to the man in khaki shorts and beat him up. The clubs and swords rained down until the khaki was ripped and the umbrella twisted.

The crowd cheered and clapped and leapt about with glee. I had a feeling that, having come from a place where men in khaki are respected, I might be unwelcome. I began to tiptoe away past the buffalo and bicycles, but a group of crouching men called me back. They made room between them for me to crouch, too. Dancers came and went; acrobats jumped in the air. Then, as suddenly as they arrived, everyone clambered back on the black bicycles and pedalled away at full speed.

I jogged back to find Osman and Prideep fast asleep. The girls had left. They had no interest in my adventure, which seemed more and more like a dream as I tried to relate it. They had both fallen in love but made me swear not to tell a soul.

CHAPTER 6

Abdul the Warrior

Nine years old became my Lingo,
When his soul began to wonder
Whether all alone his lot was
In that forest shade primeval.

In the stables of the City Palace, a Rolls Royce was rusting unused. Alongside it, together with a broken chair, a stuffed bear lay on its side — forced to snarl for eternity by a wicked taxidermist. Men with pink turbans sat under mulberry trees and the sun beat down. Relics of past glory had been left like toys abandoned by a spoilt child: a sedan chair and a set of scales made by Salter of London; paintings of hunting scenes and signed photographs of Queen Victoria.

We drifted about the palace rooms: from the mirrored suites of the last Maharaja, through the hidden gardens and durbar chambers inlaid with precious stones. Fruit bats, as large as eagles, with a wingspan a good three feet across, clung from the parapets. They alone seemed unimpressed by the grandeur of the surroundings.

* * *

Prideep was hungry. Lala assured us that the best place in town to eat dinner was the Naturaj Hotel outside Suraj Pol. It cost twelve rupees for as much *thali* as one could eat. We set off. Prideep's stomach had begun to growl uncannily loudly, and people gave him uneasy looks. Osman and I were so embarrassed that we made him walk ahead. We passed the soda water factory, the owner of which held out a signed photograph of Roger Moore when he saw me. Moore, he said, had filmed parts of the movie *Octopussy* in Udaipur a few years before. It was explained that James Bond himself had purchased one of the famous home-made sodas and chatted a while. Did I have a signed photograph of myself? I regretted that I had not, but would bring one when I came again.

The host at Naturaj beckoned us in with three fingers which were fused together. He stamped his feet and young boys filled the individual dishes in our metal trays with food. Buckets of pumpkin and potato were touted from one table to the next in case any one had been able to endure the first helping.

The people of Udaipur were very welcoming. Osman said that he would move here when we returned from the Great Thar Desert, and marry one of the local girls. Prideep agreed that it was a good idea and that he would live next door to Osman. They would wed sisters, identical twins, so they would not be able to fight over the prettier one. Osman and Prideep had become inseparable friends.

We washed our faces in the basin provided and wiped our mouths on the towel which was passed around. I felt as if I would never be able to eat again. Prideep was still hungry but I forced him to leave with us.

The streets were teeming with people. Hurricane lamps burned brightly, carried on turbanned heads.

We walked into the crowd and made our way past the clock tower and back to Lala. Three wedding processions were milling about, overlapping and exchanging guests. The bridegrooms, beautifully dressed, were swamped in bright brocades.

Tambourines jangled all around, but their sounds were smothered by the wailing of bagpipes, as each cortège tramped forward with hypnotic movements.

Each procession was led by a groom atop a fine white stallion. Some horses might have been unsettled by such a sea of people, but these had seen it all before. I turned and watched figures, concealed in white robes, stumbling forward. On their heads were turbans, and from the turbans sprouted neon strip-lights, four feet long. They pointed heavenward, lighting up the night.

Following the turbanned heads were mule carts. On each, petrol generators produced electricity and pollution amidst a grinding of cogs.

The processions passed Bada Haveli's keyhole doorway and left us behind to sleep. Our beds were so hard that Osman and Prideep came to me for 'insomnia medicine'. I handed out all I had — antibiotics, and they went away happy. The moon shone down and made shapes across the walls. The Milky Way burned brightly and the constellations shimmered above the little city of Udaipur. I thought of Lala's ancestors sitting on the rooftop and interpreting the patterns of the stars. The next day we would leave in search of treasure once more.

At five A.M. we emerged from Bada Haveli. Lala had been up for some time praying. He was from the Brahmin caste and was devout in his observances. The sun had not yet risen as we walked down to the Jagdish Temple to find a rickshaw.

The tickets for the Super Deluxe Luxury bus to Jodhpur were gold and red. Luxury was only in the name. Hens and squawking children were passed along the rows of seats. Their owners would claim them once the journey had come to an end. Now and again, the bus stopped. All the passengers would automatically unload themselves, together with all their belongings. They had just enough time to smoke a biri, or huddle briefly over a fire. Then the horn would sound and everyone and everything had trooped back aboard. Again the fowls and children had no identifiable owners and the wheels began to turn.

An aging public servant from Bihar pressed up against me. Not for comfort. Rather, the attraction was that an epic Hindi movie was to be shown.

Prideep had bought a bag of samosas and a small bar of dark chocolate which he passed round. The bureaucrat snuggled up to my shoulder and wriggled in anticipation of a film he had seen five times before. The saga lasted three hours, with the volume jammed on full. When the final song had finished and the titles appeared I cheered loudly with relief. But the solace was short-lived; for the driver stopped, rewound the tape, and pushed the 'play' button again. The only breaks to the monotony were the punctures, which were frequent.

An hour before we reached Jodhpur the bus made an emergency stop. The birds were thrown from the back, together with three children, and were hurled against the windscreen. The driver had steered wide to hit a wild boar which had been crossing the road. A great altercation began over who was to keep the dead animal. The driver, the on-board mechanic and a passing peasant all laid claim to the mutilated beast.

After an hour of shouting and heckling the bus driver won his case. The fare-paying passengers, pining for the film, had conducted an impromptu ballot. Delighted, the driver strapped the carcass onto the roof and accelerated. With blood pouring down the windscreen and the wipers toiling at full steam, we ploughed on towards our goal.

* * *

An hour later, having arrived in Jodhpur, I was unable to move. My backside felt as if it had fused to the seat. Osman dragged me from the bus. Thirty people had trampled over my camera and mashed the bag of samosas, which had fallen into the aisle. I was too weak to berate anyone.

At ground level, there was a grinding of wheels. A barrage of legless beggars headed for us at breakneck speed — propelled on their low red trolleys. Instinct told us to run. The wheels spun faster and faster. We took refuge in a dentist's shop. The surgeon held up a pair of pincers and beckoned me to sit.

Osman had decided to take Prideep to buy a watch. Prideep had been saving his wages and wanted to get the latest from the Hindustan Watch Company's range. They took a rickshaw to the Sadar Bazaar. Meanwhile, rumour had it that the most spectacular building in Jodhpur was the Umaid Bhawan Palace;

I would go there for afternoon tea.

The rickshaw drove to the palace of Umaid Bhawan from the city. The route wound up a steep incline, towards the gigantic pink sandstone structure at the apex of the hill. It reminded me of Sacré Coeur in Montmartre. A wide dome had been slapped down on top of the building — in an attempt to create a Mughal masterpiece.

Like many other palaces in Rajasthan, the Umaid Bhawan had been converted into a luxurious hotel. Built between 1929 and 1942 by the Maharaja Umaid Singh, the Palace was constructed at a time when unemployment was even worse than usual. The Maharaja had hired three thousand workers for thirteen years to complete the project. The fittings and ornaments, of a heavy art deco style, were a remarkable contrast to the light and delicate palaces of Udaipur. The hallways and even the lavatories, crammed with dead animals, resembled a taxidermist's workshop.

I strolled up to the reception desk. An immaculate clerk looked up.

'Would it be possible to take tea?'

'Yes, certainly; are you requiring a room also?'

'Are there any available?'

'Yes Sir, I am sure we can fit you in,' was the reply, as the clerk flicked through the empty register.

I would think it over. The underground swimming pool had just been cleaned. I was taken to inspect it. Reflections played about the walls and gave animation to the mythical sea monsters guarding the silent stone chamber.

A stuffed bear stood at the entrance of the grand dining-room. It was the only animal in the palace which was not in an offensive pose. It wore a pair of white gloves, upon which a silver tray had been placed. On the tray was a bottle of Pernod and two crystal glasses.

The doors, inlaid with deco lines, swung inwards as if by magic. Two hundred eyes stared at me: the walls were covered with the heads of stuffed animals. Tigers and rhinoceros, buffaloes and bears, an extensive range of big game, was represented.

Five hundred places had been laid with a spectacular arrangement of eating instruments. Yet I was the only guest to dine. A team of about twenty waiters ran to my assistance. I requested a table away from the animal heads. There was none secluded from the 'game park' theme, but perhaps in the far corner, with my seat pointed to the gardens, I would be pleased. I was.

The waiters began the type of routine that I had only seen on a film set. Two enormous fans were placed in front of my table to blow the flies away from the condiments. The butter, together with its silver dish, flew off the table. Servants in golden turbans dived about with jugs of water, plates of cakes and scones. The tablecloth was brushed whenever I dropped a single crumb. Like a famous movie star who had forgotten his lines, I yearned to be left alone.

After the jam blew from the table, I ordered the fans to be removed. Five giants wheeled the dominating structures to the other end of the dining room. Still, there was concern that my table should become infested with flies and hornets. Another team of waiters with cloths over their wrists danced about with fly swats. I turned away, trying to ignore the insect massacre going on among the silver spoons and forks. An ibex looked down at me with sad eyes as if he had seen it all before.

The door-wallahs had deserted their post. From their station came a creaking sound. The patterns of wavy and zigzag lines were pushed apart a few inches and two slight characters, with hand bags, slipped in. On seeing me they tramped over to my corner, cowering as if tormented by the wildlife stalking about the room. We became instant friends, almost as though we had met in a jungle.

'Bonjour Monsieur! I am Henri and this is Jean-Yves. We are French.'

'I am very pleased to meet you both. Have you been staying here long?' I asked.

'We 'ave come here two weeks ago. You are the first other person from Europe that we 'ave met.'

They chattered away. Henri's mouth twitched in a most alarming manner. Jean-Yves rolled his eyes about with disorientation. The palace was obviously playing on their nerves. The very fact that a Frenchman was prepared, after two minutes of conversation, to be so friendly towards anyone, especially one who had come from England, made me restless.

Jean-Yves asked if I was residing at the palace. His eyes blinked nervously, and Henri's mouth moved about unconsciously. Regretfully, I said that I could not stay. Indeed, it was almost time for me to leave. The Frenchmen seemed disappointed.

We began to talk of the severe design according to which the building had been constructed. I mentioned that they were very brave to stay so long. Jean-Yves tittered, raising his index finger in the air.

'Mais Monsieur, we 'ave protection from ze evil.'

I leant forward to hear what secret guarded them even in a place like the Palace of Umaid Bhawan. The Frenchmen glanced at each other and then at me. Henri whispered, 'Do you promise not to tell?' I swore a solemn oath.

They reached down the front of their shirts and pulled out identical talismans. Rust-coloured, about one inch square, both bore a sign like an asterisk within three concentric circles:

'We got zem from a secret place. From l'Assistant du Monsieur l'Alchimiste!'

My jaw dropped in stupefaction. They seemed heartened that I should be so suitably impressed.

* * *

Osman read the guide book of India aloud from cover to cover. No other passengers on the train from Jodhpur to

Jaisalmer understood a word of the English, but they cheered all the same. Prideep had rolled up his sleeves so that everyone could admire his new watch. It had a gold face and a brown leather strap. He was very pleased. The steam train had left Jodhpur, with its Palace of Umaid Bhawan and the two curse-protected Frenchmen, far behind. I was getting anxious to find the Dervish's contact and waste no more time travelling. The thought of rubies and emeralds drove me on like gold-fever. Prideep, who gave his bunk to a decrepit man whom he had befriended, slept on the floor.

I awoke in the middle of the night to see what looked like black beans crawling over Prideep's face. They were beetles. As usual it was impossible to turn the carriage lights out. The fans were working and guillotined all that went near them most efficiently. A swarm of dragonflies buzzed in through an open window as we stopped near a marsh. I tossed about, trying to sleep, as pieces of dragonfly wing and abdomen splattered across my face. Finally I fell asleep to images of chests filled with wondrous things.

★ ★ ★

Jaisalmer, founded by Maharaja Jaisal in 1156, had been the capital of the Bhati of the 'Lunar' dynasty.

It had not rained in Jaisalmer for as long as anyone could remember. Yet, in the first four hours that we spent there, rainwater caused floods three feet deep. Rickshaws lay marooned on high spots like beached boats at the seaside. A hunchback taking goats to sell on a buffalo-cart gave us a ride into town. The news on everyone's lips was that a camel had just drowned. It was very wet indeed.

As we set about looking for a hotel, I pondered the logistic procedure of a camel drowning. Small boys ran up with the business cards of hotels. Another pulled out three calculators and could thus exchange dollars, deutsche marks and yen.

Ignoring all, we pressed on into the yellow sandstone fortress to escape the importuning. I had heard that several hotels existed actually inside the fortress. Blocks of stone had been carved and placed one on top of the next; crenellations stretched as far as the eye could see, and the rain continued to fall. Enshrouded within concentric walls — high above the city — was a Jain temple. Next to it stood Hotel Paradise.

We took two rooms there for the night whilst arranging to get out to the isolated settlement of Mandha, where Abdul was said to reside.

Intricate designs had been chipped from the brittle yellow stone, forming spectacular patterns on its portals. The rain stopped and, for the first time, we looked upon the Great Thar Desert. From the fortress there was no romantic desert view of rolling dunes or distant tribal dwellings. The one significant feature between our vantage point and the horizon was an extensive rubbish heap.

The bleak scene — as if despised by nature and neglected by man — reminded me of Africa's Skeleton Coast. Weeks spent trudging up and down that barren Atlantic seaboard, while writing a book on Namibia, had been useful preparation for the Great Thar.

Several hundred birds circled the dump, swooping down in their search for food. It was very unromantic. Leaving our things at the Hotel Paradise, walked into the bazaar to find a man who could take us to Mandha.

A man with a Sikh turban and desert robes stepped from the shadows and proposed that he might be the one we were looking for. A pair of steely-blue eyes blinked from his badly sunburnt face. He told us that he had two camels and an unrivalled knowledge of the desert trails. No other could be a more faithful guide than he. Osman translated the peculiar dialect with some difficulty. He said that the man was suitable and that the camels would be fine for a couple of days' travel. We planned to set off before dawn the next morning.

The Paradise Hotel could not have been more wrongly

named. Osman and I killed one hundred and thirty-three flies in my room alone. Prideep had lured a pigeon into the other room, hoping that it would feast on the resident insect population. When he opened the window again five more pigeons flew in to roost. There was no electricity, the fan did not move, and candle wax dripped onto the floor. I dreamed of being far away from the Great Thar Desert.

Morale was very low, despite the reasonable prospect of finding a great cache of secret treasure. Time to rally the troops. As I spoke, I felt the confidence streaming back into me: a bracing sensation. After haranguing Prideep and Osman, I found myself enthused again. So I offered to take them to the best restaurant in town to celebrate our imminent success. The Trio was the best restaurant in town. It also was the only restaurant in Jaisalmer. We took a table on the first floor of the building. A wooden step-ladder led up. Constant power cuts meant that a blindingly bright hurricane lamp was supplied — placed behind my left ear — so that we could see the details of the dishes that were brought.

The waiter had managed to conquer the set of rungs whilst carrying four plates on his arms. What seemed like the whole insect population of Rajasthan slithered out of the desert night and flopped onto the starched white tablecloth. Prideep squinted in the lamplight, and rolled his eyes. He filled his glass with crawling black creatures and turned it upside down to trap them. Osman told him to behave. After a while I gave up picking each wriggling shape from my mutton stew. The food had become more substantial at no extra charge. Osman was delighted.

* * *

Igor Singh led his camels to Hotel Paradise long before the sun had broken across the horizon. Prideep tried to wash pigeon droppings from his face in the blackness.

The two she-camels were very old. Igor kept kicking them

to show their sturdiness. It was something which they did not appreciate at three A.M. We walked down through the town and out along a desert path. Igor Singh had no torch. When I gave him mine, he held it close to his chest, expecting it to become a gift. I held onto Igor's shirt-tail, Osman clutched onto mine, with Prideep stumbling somewhere behind him. It seemed as if we were casualties of some horrific war, blinded by gas.

By the time streams of yellow light appeared from the sky, we were quite far from the city walls. The yellow sandstone of Jaisalmer stood invisible within the rays. Our band stopped every so often to drink water from a goatskin. The camels would sit, their legs turned inwards, and their giant lashes fanning over golf ball eyes. Their names were *Unt* meaning camel, and *Qaisara*, which means empress.

Igor Singh was a disciplined man who would let neither his animals nor his guests relax for long. Covering our heads with shirts, we swaggered with exaggerated movements towards the horizon. Osman read bearings from the compass, pretending that we were tracking treasure with a map. But we had no map. It struck me that our guide could easily slit our throats, steal our money and belongings and still return to town before breakfast.

It was odd that a Sikh should, firstly, be in Jaisalmer and, secondly, have a Russian first name. Igor began to speak, Osman translated his words so that I might understand the life of this peculiar man.

'My father came to Rajasthan between the world wars. He was sick of Russia, the country of his birth, so he escaped communism and he decided to live in India. He married a Punjabi girl who was working in Jaipur. After Partition and all the slaughter accompanying the splitting of India and Pakistan in the mid-1940s, they wanted to get away from people and so they moved to Jaisalmer. I was brought up here.'

'Do you speak Russian?' I asked.

'I am a mixture, so have all the advantages of a crossbreed.

I taught myself about my mother's Sikh religion. And, as I am out here much of the time, it doesn't bother me to wear a turban.'

Osman and Prideep climbed on Unt's back and I was offered Qaisara. The she-camels groaned as we ascended. I was immediately gripped by motion sickness. Qaisara's gait made it like riding in the wispy shell of a boat through rough sea. Prideep was thrilled by the new experience. Enjoying his adventure away from Bombay, from time to time he reminisced to Osman, and speculated on the gossip which our trip must have provoked.

Qaisara sighed, I guessed in relief, as her parasite population seeped onto me. And, by early afternoon, there was nothing in front of us, and nothing behind, but sand. I had grown used to the idea of being in the Great Thar Desert: the novelty had quickly worn off.

We stumbled along all day under a sun which made our faces raw. My camel bags were at last in their native environment, much less of a burden to me, thrown over Qaisara's bony back. I wondered for a moment if my grandfather's expedition through the desert had been similar to mine. Perhaps one of his journeys had been across these very plains. Perhaps he, too, had gone in search of treasure in the Great Thar Desert.

There was no sign that it had rained in the desert. Thoughts of the camel drowning occupied me for at least an hour. Then, images of a chest brimming with rubies replaced those of floundering camels. My pace quickened and my mouth salivated with greed.

* * *

Osman began to shout. 'I see People! People!'

Rubbing the sand from my eyes, I turned round 360 degrees. Still I could see no movement. Prideep leapt about as if suddenly illuminated. He and Osman embraced like old comrades reuniting.

'What the hell are you talking about? There's nothing, you idiots!' I yelled, fearing that they had both finally cracked.

'There! Look over there!'

Osman placed his hand on mine and pointed. He was right. There, in the distance, was a tiny speck which looked like a flea, jumping about. Then others. My brain and all its contents seemed to have been erased. I could just about understand fleas and sand. The thought of a city or of driving a car seemed terrifying. Would I be able to live in western society again?

The specks grew bigger. They were not fleas, and dogs could be seen running about their feet. Was it Mandha, the place where Abdul lived? Yes, Igor assured us, it was.

Qaisara and Unt were given to a child to look after. Igor Singh led us to a group of desert folk. The men, each with a full beard and a face worn by the harsh conditions, sat in a circle around a smouldering camp-fire. The greetings were formal and drawn out. I prodded Igor to find out if Abdul was around.

'Tell mc! Is Abdul the Warrior here?' Igor paused and parted his chapped lips.

'Yes, the Warrior is in Mandha.'

'Has he the treasure?'

'Yes, he has it at his house.'

'Could we go straight there?'

Yes, indeed we could.

Abdul the Warrior had the physique of a bear. His face was hidden by a massive black beard: only his great hook of a nose seemed to escape the bristles. His back was rounded, and his immense hands shot forward as I drew near. The Warrior pulled me to his chest like a long-lost son being welcomed by his father. He did not mention the treasure. I knew that it would be impolite to ask of it before we ate.

Dates were brought and straw-coloured tea was poured into dainty cups. Abdul grinned ferociously, and sipped from the white china, which he held in his thumb and forefinger like an upturned thimble.

Three chickens had been roasted and buried in a bed of *pilau* rice. I fished for a leg. Abdul dug his hand into the mound of rice and threw a whole chicken across to me. He growled. I grasped at the bony feet and sunk my teeth into the breast. The Warrior seemed pleased and, rubbing his fingers into the thick mass of black bristle that sprouted from his face, he spoke. Everyone listened.

'You are friends of Yusuf Jahan?'

'Yes, Sir. He sent us to meet you. We travelled from the busy streets of Bombay, across Gujarat and Rajasthan in search of you. The Dervish said that perhaps you might help us on our quest.'

Abdul stopped me as I spoke: he obviously had some advance information.

'I understand that you seek the great treasures of the world.'

'Yes, Sir.' I shifted apprehensively. 'Do you have anything here that might be of interest?'

'You may see what I have, my humble possessions. I insist that you take any which are to your liking.'

Abdul signalled to one of his men who was weighted down by bandoliers and endless rounds of heavy-calibre ammunition. A tea-chest was carried in by two other men. My heart beat faster and faster. More dates were passed around. A pack of dogs began to bark outside.

Abdul reached for the chest. He lifted the lid off. I rubbed the vision of rubies from my eyes, peering into the darkness of the box. Osman and I gagged at its contents. Prideep pushed us aside so that he, too, might see the riches. Abdul was pleased with our speechlessness. He delved his great fingers into the tea-chest and pulled out the most grotesque coloured glass lampshade that I had ever seen.

A paraffin lamp was brought closer, and the Warrior ran his fingertips over an engraving.

'Can you read what it says?' he roared. I held the lampshade under the light and read out the legend:

'Made in Birmingham.'

Abdul the Warrior winced with delight and gasped, 'Do you know how far away that is?'

'Yes, Sir. It is many miles from the Great Thar Desert,' I said.

'Would you like it?'

Abdul was prepared to offer it as a gift. There was silence. Images of sand and fleas danced around in my mind as I tried to string a set of words together.

'*Aga-i Janab*, Respected Sir,' I began, 'you are a lucky man indeed to own such a valuable object. Fate favours us both, having extended great fortune to me also. For I already have an identical lampshade to this. It is destiny that has given us both such a wondrous thing.'

Abdul the Warrior had tears of empathy in his eyes. In the desert there is little beauty but there is a closeness and solidarity between all men. Abdul looked at Osman, Prideep and I, and said, very softly:

'My boys, stay here and live with me. It is my honour to be your host.'

CHAPTER 7

Leaving the Nest

To the Red Hills, Lahugada,
Holy Lingo joined the Brothers
To those seven nice young women,
To the daughters of the Giant.

Sizzling lumps of mutton were borne towards us on a silver tray. The waiter glided beneath the crystal chandeliers and cornices of Delhi's Gaylord Restaurant. His hair had turned white with years of servitude. Osman and Prideep howled like wolves, with uncontrollable joy, at the sight of food.

We had left Abdul the Warrior with his lampshade and desert life, and trekked back across the Great Thar to Jaisalmer once again. Then, after many hours spent jarring about at the back of packed local buses, we arrived in Delhi, the capital of India.

Osman had talked me into coming to Delhi, the city of his youth. He swore that, with his contacts and friends, there would be nothing to stop us finding antique treasures. Prideep agreed that we should have come straight to the capital in the first place. The two had bonded, become a gang and, although we were friends, they could never forgive me for dragging them to the single most unpleasant spot on earth.

In a moment of weakness I had promised to take them to Gaylord's before even getting a hotel room. They were allowed to have all they could eat.

The waiter had become so bewildered scribbling down the order, that Osman made him note down the dishes they would *not* require. There were only three of those . . . brains masala, fried brains and boiled brains masala. I had made them promise not to order brains. They had looked sad for a moment but then had agreed.

Osman held a truffle cake in one hand and a mutton steak in the other and took alternate bites of each. The dining room had gone quiet. Waiters and guests, security guards in tin hats, and the chefs, stood around and watched the spectacle. My face took on the colour of the crimson silk-covered walls and I pretended not to know my associates.

* * *

'Hey mister, change money? Something nice to smoke? Cute girl? Cheap flight? Want a room?'

'No, thank you. We have everything under control!'

The street corners of Delhi are packed with agents. Rumour has it that if one wanted to buy General Motors, the place to set the contract, or at least find out the market price, is on Connaught Place, New Delhi. The loitering youths act as fixers, and can easily sniff out liars and time-wasters.

When lunch was over, we lugged our bags with us, trying to look as though we often strolled the streets so encumbered.

My camel saddle-bags, which were never an easy item of luggage to haul about, were cutting into my shoulder more than ever. So we rested, bloatedly, in a heap outside an exclusive jeweller's shop. Prideep stared into the window and became hypnotised by a silver bowl, filled with glinting, gleaming gemstones. He prodded Osman and made him take a look. Mesmerised by riches, Prideep and Osman pressed their faces to the glass and panted heavily. When the window became clouded with the vapour, they slumped in silence on the ground beside me.

Just then, two Arab sheikhs, wearing the black-and-gold headbands of royalty, exited the air-conditioned jeweller's shop. Dressed in immaculate Bedouin robes, they walked over to a stretch Mercedes limousine. And, three paces behind, followed their entourage of advisers, bodyguards, secretaries, hangers-on and bearers of numerous just-purchased gifts.

As the sheikhs prepared to climb into their vehicle, they

glanced at the miserable heap in which Osman, Prideep and I were sitting. Our clothes were in tatters; our bodies were bathed in dirt and sand. The older of the two sheikhs said loudly to his friend,

'You know, India really is quite an amazing place! Look at that young man sitting over there.' The entire group turned to me and stared. 'He looks exactly like Sayed Tahir Shah!'

A few minutes later — still red with shame that my father's close friends should have observed me in such a state — I was squashed between Osman and Prideep in a rickshaw, searching for a place to stay. The driver pressed his thumb hard on the horn and swung into the gates of the inimitable Special Number One Hotel.

Special Number One rose uncounted floors into the sky like a reared-up, sprawling creature of the deep. Planned by idealists, the human element had overcome most of its utilitarian qualities. Its purposes now seemed to torment poor travellers with multiple forms and unnecessary paperwork.

I approached the reception desk, in the warehouse-sized foyer, already beset by a snaking line of dejected foreigners. They looked as if they were queuing for forgotten reasons, like people waiting in the bread-lines of Siberia. A cocky little man glared at me from the other side of the desk.

'Good afternoon. I would like to take two rooms please,' I said.

'Do you have a reservation?' The official straightened his tie, pulling his collar even further out of alignment with the rest of his garb.

'Yes, of course I have one. I made it by telephone several days ago. The name is *Shah.*'

A policy of lying often does the trick when faced by the clerk. And my last name is so common in India that there was a good chance of some Shah having reserved a room. Osman and Prideep seemed pleased with my boldness. The pockmarked face wagged violently from side to side,

'Sir, we don't make reservations over the telephone. We are full!' Having already lied, I decided to go further to capture the initiative.

'I also made a reservation for two rooms in writing.'

'Sir, we do not make advanced bookings of any kind. We have no vacancies. You will have to leave!'

The whip-hand calmness infuriated me. I pulled a note from my back pocket and slipped it to the official as covertly as the situation allowed. Again the head shook from side to side. This was officialdom of the worst kind — *no-hope bureaucracy* — which is its own reward: so pure as to be unbribable. I tried staring him out, while the people at the head of the queue gazed almost indifferently at me. After what seemed an age, the clerk's eyes crossed; he said that maybe after six hours we could get a room.

Six hours turned into eight hours and we were still waiting. The snaking line of demoralised travellers had sloughed layers of clothes. The humidity was almost unbearable. Osman went about shaking hands with servants and administrative staff, trying to press ten-rupee notes into their palms. No one took the bait.

After ten hours in the foyer, I was asked to pay large amounts of foreign currency in exchange for two room keys. I completed various multilingual forms in quadruplicate — it seemed more like a university entrance examination than registration at a hotel. All I could think of was taking a steaming hot shower.

We staggered with our possessions to the lifts, of which there were four. Only one worked. But as there was a power cut that was not functioning either.

Our rooms were on the top floor. Osman flew into a rage at having to climb the hundreds of stairs necessary to reach the accommodation. I was surprised that he did not adapt to the situation. I calmed him as best I could, saying that things had probably changed a good deal here while he had been in Bombay. Usually he never stopped talking of the benefits of Delhi. He was now consumed with embarrassment at the inaccuracy of his memory.

The receptionist had been away from three to nine P.M. Osman stormed over to the reception desk, where the man was torturing another hopeful. He stretched over the Formica and grabbed hold of the terrified bureaucrat.

'You bastard *Babu*, can come with us to the top!' he roared. 'You must teach these people respect,' he told me, over his shoulder, shaking the clerk to emphasise the point. I wondered if there would be repercussions: but, at least Osman was back on form.

Our party climbed the stairs. It felt like the ascent of K2. The receptionist stumbled in front, his left arm clamped in a half-nelson, followed by Osman, who was sniggering sadistically, with Prideep and me at the rear. Our shadows flickered on the slime-covered walls. It seemed that no human had visited the uppermost floor in a long time. An enormous raven sat perched at the top of the stairs, a sinister omen of things which were to come. The bird croaked at our intrusion.

Osman's captive lay slouched and panting on the top step. We moved over him like a column of soldier ants on the warpath. There was an eerie feeling to be so high above New Delhi. Probing about my room with uncertain footsteps, I was perplexed that such a haphazardly built structure could remain standing. For the first time in India, I was frightened. I put it down to the utter hostility of the accommodation, and its total lack of personality. Another raven marched back and forth on the window ledge. Its head moved at awkward angles, and for a moment I thought back to Blake and his vultures. Maybe he had sent this avian symbol of security to comfort me.

Osman had explained to Prideep that he would take him to all his old haunts. They would try to track down some girls he had once known. I was not invited to participate. Osman said that in the Old City he had a contact, more useful in my quest, who might be able to help. It was rumoured that the acquaintance had a warehouse full of Mughal jewels. Osman was not one to brag; his promises and contacts usually came through. Having put the negative experiences of the Great Thar to the back of my mind, I was determined to continue in pursuit of great riches.

The next morning Osman went out early to hang about on the street corners of Connaught Place. At lunchtime we met up and he announced that his old contact, Iqbal, was still in Old Delhi. We would take a rickshaw and go to meet him.

Osman suggested that we try to cross into the park at the centre of Connaught Place to hail a rickshaw. Motorbikes and Ambassador cars swerved in all directions to miss us. A white buffalo with wide-stretching horns was moving in slow straight lines across the park. Deliriously, it heaved at a Webb lawn-mower, a boy with a sharp stick prodding at its behind.

Osman jumped into the road and wrestled with a speeding blue rickshaw, bringing it to a hasty stop. We clambered aboard and ordered the driver to take us to the Red Fort. The driver stared into the air blankly and muttered,

'Airport . . . vich airport do you vant?'

'Red Fort! You idiot! In the Old City,' Osman yelled.

He and I had become very irritable in Delhi. I put it down to too many positive ions in the air, but did not dare begin to explain the concept of the electrical charging of ions. The possibilities for confusion were too substantial. Bombay's citizens, however, seemed much more easy-going than those in Delhi.

The Red Fort appeared on the right. I passed the driver two rupees. Osman had assured me that was the rate. But the driver chased after us, shouting how disgusted he was that we should be so miserly. Osman picked up the unfortunate man and threw him into a paan stall. Prideep fell down on the ground laughing as Osman dusted himself off and led the way into the Red Fort.

Inside the giant walls, package tours mingled with curio dealers. A brace of small shops had divided the forecourt territorially so that the owners could benefit equally from the visitors. The existence of such intrusions would have made the Mughal Emperor Shah Jahan, ('King of the World') the fort's founder, turn in his grave.

Osman hastened between the assorted curio sellers and pickpockets in an attempt to find where Iqbal might be. After scurrying about for twenty minutes, he announced that Iqbal was now in Chandni Chowk Bazaar. We would go to meet him at once.

Chandni Chowk sprawls behind the great Jami Masjid mosque — the biggest mosque in India. Rickshaws and bicycles dodged a group of sacred cows, languidly raiding an apple stall. Holy men blew magical smoke into the air, blinding both the cows and cyclists. Roasted peanut sellers ambled about with burners aiding the pollution and confusion. What made the holy men's smoke more divine than that of the peanut sellers? Osman thought it was a ridiculous question.

Each street was bordered by rows of stalls, crammed with odds and ends, dating back a thousand years. We pressed deeper into the labyrinth. Men would nod and point when Osman whispered Iqbal's name. The word seemed like a special key, capable of opening any lock.

Outside a modest silk shop a donkey stood in silence, as donkeys do, as if waiting for the world to end. We paused, as Osman sent the shop's junior to fetch his master. Silks in pink and red fluttered under the sluggish ceiling fans. Then Iqbal appeared.

Osman and he bear-hugged. Prideep and I were introduced, before taking places on a mound of white cotton cushions. Tea was brought.

'Peace be upon you, my friends,' said Iqbal. 'You are welcome to my humble house, anything that you wish I will have brought.'

Then Iqbal rubbed at his orange-hennaed beard, which glowed in the darkness of the shop. He was perhaps in his late sixties but somehow his age was irrelevant. There was an air of rectitude about this man. I had expected to meet another arms-dealing Dervish type. Iqbal seemed wizened by the experience of many years, but calm, at peace.

Pulling out a watch on a chain from his trouser pocket, he began to wind it up. I could make out Russian lettering on the dial. Iqbal noticed I was staring at the instrument and, to break the silence, I began to talk.

'You are most gracious, I hope that we did not disturb you. We have just returned from Jaisalmer; I am on a quest in search of treasures.' I spoke with a formality which somehow appeared appropriate. 'I have been residing in Bombay, Osman and Prideep have assisted me in my search to find hungry people who might be necessituous enough to help us secure such objects as jewelled daggers.'

'My friend,' said Iqbal, 'you must understand that a hungry person who has nothing is only interested in finding one crust of bread. If you give him that crust then his stomach is full and he is satisfied. You see, poverty is common in India; you can say that when a person finds one rupee in a gutter may be so happy that he feels rich. Hungry people are not the solution to your problem.'

'Then what is the solution?' I was interested by his observations.

'My boy,' Iqbal spoke each word with precision, 'this country is filled with very greedy men. You cannot blame them for being like that. They have crawled from the sewers and have climbed from the degradation which consumes much of this land. A man becomes very cynical here, the poor and ill die on the streets. The injustices of the caste system still haunt many unfortunate millions of people. Do you realise that if the very shadow of an *Achhoot* — an "untouchable" — falls on the food of a Brahmin, the Brahmin must throw that food away?

'I myself did have a remarkable collection of priceless objects until a few years ago. Then men with guns came one night and threatened to kill my wife and boys if I didn't hand the collection over. There is nothing left. You never know who will inform on you if you keep even one ring. At last I can sleep well at night, knowing that our lives are safe from the clutches of desperate men. The memory of such wondrous artifacts still brings me happiness. I am content that I could hold such things, if only to be their keeper for a while.

'Delhi has been robbed of countless wonderful treasures. They are now in the Arab Gulf or in the West. Go and see our new museum here near Janpath, they built it recently and filled it mostly with new or forged pieces! I will try to assist you because I don't want to see a friend of Osman's get hurt by vicious men. Will you come back to me in four days? I shall see what I can do.'

Before I left the shop I shook hands with Iqbal and sensed a curious energy from his touch. He seemed happy that I had gained something, although at the time I was not sure what.

* * *

Osman treated Prideep and me to ice cream at Nirula's Café on Connaught Place. There was an uneasy atmosphere. He and Prideep kept looking at each other and then at me. I asked them what the matter was. Osman stopped licking at the cone.

'There is nothing really the matter,' he said without looking at me. 'But we know that soon you will be leaving India, and it shall make us sad.'

I listened to his words and, instead of thumping him on the back and joking about or denying it, I said nothing. Time spent in India has a extraordinary effect on one. It acts as a barrier that makes the rest of the world seem unreal. I would read *Time* magazine each week, but India was strangely removed from the photographs and stories. At the same time I knew that my adventures there were close to an end. I was ready to move on. Characters flashed through my mind: Blake my guru, Himala my date, Prideep with his imp-like looks and, of course Osman, who had become my closest friend of all. Together, we had explored the darkest regions of Bombay and travelled across the Great Thar Desert.

India, with its nine hundred million people, is often referred to as the largest democracy in the world. The British once controlled the vast country but had little lasting effect on its people. I felt they never really came to grips with what they claimed to control. As they strove to dominate the subcontinent, it slipped from their grasp without them ever realising why.

The British failed to penetrate the culture and understand its dangerous capacity for absorption. This, at any rate, is the very widespread opinion of many Indians, scholars and others. I have heard it from Hindus, Muslims, Sikhs and Zoroastrians, as well as Christian converts.

In India, where all is possible, contradictory beliefs nestle together. An Indian friend, whilst talking of his nation, once looked at me squarely and said:

'How can you conquer a people with the self-confidence of the Hindus? India is a place where the cow is sacred: supposedly because once there was once nothing: no world, no people, not a thing . . . just a cow floating about in nothingness. One day — although there were no days — the cow let out an enormous belch and from that, all you see around you comes. The stars and sun, the planets and the grass beneath our feet, all came from the cow's gigantic eructation. How can you even begin to influence, to any depth, a people such as this?'

Four days after visiting Iqbal, we returned to his shop in Chandni Chowk. The doors were locked and none of the silk was displayed.

Osman rapped on the door, calling 'Iqbal Sahib! Iqbal Sahib!' A bolt on the inside rattled, and the door opened. Iqbal's son greeted us, his eyes red from crying. Osman bent down to his level and asked what the matter was.

'My father, Iqbal Jamal, died this morning in his sleep. He

has not been well for a long time. Before he went to bed last night he gave this to my mother and said that when you come back to give it to you. It is for the man from Englistan.'

The child held out his right hand, it was clasped around something. I could just make out a silvery gleam between his fingers. He placed his hand in mine and I felt the object. It was Iqbal's Russian pocket watch. Osman, Prideep and I were too moved to speak: we stood for a moment in silence.

The boy asked us if we would like some tea. Osman replied: 'No, thank you, we shall leave you now. When you have grown up and are in Bombay, go to the Colaba Tailor Shop on the Strand. I shall be waiting there for you.'

The child nodded and went back inside the shop.

We left Chandni Chowk and took a rickshaw back to New Delhi. Each of us was silent. The watch sat firm in my palm. It was still ticking. Although I had only met Iqbal once there had been a click of understanding between us. I sensed Iqbal's energy around me. The watch was almost like a gift in return for housing something of his spirit.

Osman looked at me quizzically. I knew what he was thinking, and I nodded as if to reply to his unspoken question. Yes, I did realise the honour and exceptional responsibility, and respect it.

A message had been slipped under my door at the hotel. It explained that, in accordance with the regulations of the establishment, where we had been resident for a week, we would have to pay double the normal rate from now on. I went down to the clerk and counted out some dollar bills. He consulted a calculator and stapled the money to an ornate multiple form. Exhausted with fighting the system, I almost admired the man's steadfast application of policy, irrespective of logic and without customary rewards. In some peculiar way, indeed, the rules were now beginning to seem quite logical. It was then I knew that I had been in India long enough.

At the Special Number One, I began the ascent to the umpteenth floor with the usual necessary dedication of a mountain climber. I stopped in at the laundry part-way up. There was no reply when I knocked, so I pushed the door open. Reflected in the flickering light of a black and white television screen I discerned about ten faces. The chefs and security guards scurried off back to their jobs, worried that I might report them. The laundry assistant was the only person left. I asked for my clothes. There was something strangely familiar about the man. It was not his face nor his build. Suddenly I realised what it was: he was wearing my best clothes, and had obviously dressed up ready to go out on the town.

Prideep and Osman were waiting for me outside my room. They were smiling. Prideep was whistling as if he was covering something up. Osman had spent weeks teaching him to whistle, and his broken set of teeth was very effective. They shuffled their feet and looked at the ground to hide their smiling cheeks. I muttered that I had been invited to the Japanese Embassy to dine. Osman sighed how unlucky I was. He, of course, had attended many such boring occasions whilst working at the American Embassy. I reminded him that he was only a janitor there. He pledged that while *nominally* only a concierge, he had had many special privileges. The way he put it, I was almost tempted to think that he had been the ambassador: undercover, of course.

The thought flashed through my mind that the Americans had perhaps appointed Osman Chief of Mission, rather in the manner of the old Soviet Unions, when the chauffeur or gardener was the real kingpin of their embassy. Anyway, Prideep and he were going out to find girls and enjoy a wild evening in Old Delhi's most amoral nightspots. Osman had put on his tie with spots and Prideep had donned his best shirt.

Osman and Prideep returned to the hotel at breakfast the next day. Their evening had been very different from my own. I had eaten *sushi* and was in bed by ten. Their story, I feared, could not have been more contrary.

Osman strode along the corridors like a soldier, and Prideep shuffled behind, chortling. They banged on my door to give me their report. It had been a night of debauched behaviour unrivalled in history. They recounted every detail. Osman decided to write the adventure down in English and give it to me for the book I was to write. The events of their evening, alas, were far too sordid. They went off to get some sleep, burbling like schoolboys after lights out, revelling in their impropriety.

At the telex office on Janpath there was a power cut. Indeed, I had the feeling that no electricity had been supplied to the premises for a very long time. Five ladies with large red *bindis*, red dots worn on the forehead by Hindu women, moved about behind the smoked-glass windows clutching candles.

One of the women, on seeing me, began frenziedly waving a sheet of paper above her head.

'It came! It came!' she screamed.

Her colleagues huddled round while I signed assorted receipts for a telex from my sister, who was living in Pakistan. The communication had been received weeks before, when electricity was briefly available. It had taken many days to get here, forwarded by land from Bombay. It read:

COME TO PESHAWAR STOP WILL MEET YOU AT GREENS HOTEL STOP HAVE GOT EXTRAORDINARY TREASURE COME AT ONCE STOP SAIRA

An audience had gathered, as there had been no other telecommunications for weeks. The crowd insisted on being told where Peshawar was, what my sister did and when I would be leaving.

'Leaving?' The idea of getting away from the chaos of India, and up to the North West Frontier Province — the Hindu Kush and the lands of my ancestors — was extremely appealing. What was this treasure of which she had written? I knew that telephoning to make enquiries about matters such as this would have been inappropriate. I would fly straight to Pakistan to see what the treasure was. Perhaps I had been looking in the wrong country, and some benign fate was luring me northwards to the Afghan borderland. Besides, I would still be in Gondwanaland . . .

The PIA office was nearby, so I booked myself on a flight to Islamabad leaving in two days. Then I set about making arrangements for my departure, and perhaps the saddest thing of all: preparing to leave Osman and Prideep.

I called Blake in Bombay, he was sitting on the rooftop,

'Hey Man, how is it up there? The vultures are taking chillies from my hand now, you've got to see this!'

'Blake, I have to go to Pakistan to see my sister for a while. I'll try and get back here sometime.'

'Man, I'd like to visit, but these vulture suckers are taking up all my time!'

The spindly line crackled and Blake faded away.

Osman and Prideep were eating breakfast. It was nearly five-thirty in the afternoon. I joined them, but said nothing. They knew it was time for me to leave them. I felt like a fledgling bird, about to jump from its nest for the first time. Osman looked across. I averted my eyes and he asked, 'When are you going?'

'In two days' time, I have to see my sister in Peshawar.'

'We must get back to Bombay anyway, our families will be waiting for us. It has been a long time since we walked down Marine Drive,' said Osman. He paused for a moment but began again when Prideep nudged him with his elbow. 'Tahir Sahib,' he said, 'will you come with us? We have something to show you.'

We took a rickshaw to Old Delhi, where it pulled to a stop

deep inside the maze of Chandni Chowk. A door opened and we ascended a staircase, then turned right into a huge studio.

On one wall hung a vast painting — the type that advertise Hindi movies — with powerful heros and heroines, gods and armies. The faces and acts were familiar, all too familiar. A group of men on camels were riding off into the desert. A steam train was rushing out of control. Gaylord's and the Chateau Windsor stared down, oozing with servants and tradition. In the centre there were three men, standing like cowboys, in lavish costumes. Prideep on the left, Osman on the right and me in the middle. Osman spoke jerkily, almost choking:

'Our words of thanks will dissolve,' he said, 'but maybe this will help you to remember the good times. They were the best times we have ever had.'

CHAPTER 8

Here Comes the King

Wrathful then was holy Lingo,
At those wanton Giant's daughters
Rose the flame of indignation
From his boots up to his top-knot.

War correspondents sat about eating chicken shashlik and making up the news. They swapped tall stories in the darkness of Lala's Grill at Green's Hotel. Mercenaries and missionaries ambled about, stranded in the border town after the end of the Soviet-Afghan war.

A Danish prosthesis expert had befriended me. He said that as long as I ate chicken I would probably be all right. I thanked him for this first tip on survival in Peshawar and he wandered off to fit an artificial limb.

Peshawar had been a crucial base during the Soviet-Afghan war. Mujahed commanders, international aid organisations, drugs dealers, Russian spies and a bevy of journalists, transformed the ancient border town into a thriving metropolis.

Four million Afghan refugees fled to the North West Frontier Province of Pakistan. With the end of the war against the communist forces, the refugee populace had begun to go back to Afghanistan. Yet their return was hampered by an abundance of mines, and total lack of food in rural areas resulting from the devastation of Brezhnev's war.

Peshawar, still a cocktail of people — thrown together because of the war — ran on its own lines.

My sister, Saira, had come to Pakistan initially to report on the conflict for several western newspapers. Now she concentrated on the refugee repatriation question and the feuding of Afghan parties. A veteran reporter for newspapers and television of various wars, she had made her name from her front-page eye-witness accounts of the allied air strike on Baghdad in 1991.

A blue and yellow rickshaw had taken me to Green's Hotel where I hoped to meet my sister. Having flown from Delhi to Islamabad, the capital of Pakistan, I had travelled northwards to Peshawar.

At Green's I climbed to the reception desk over parcels and packages, which looked suspiciously like containers of explosive devices. Men with walkie-talkies crouched behind potted plants, chain-smoking American cigarettes. They watched each other through orange-tinted glasses, eyeing the bundles nervously.

My sister had left no message, the receptionist had never heard of her. I took a room on the second floor and prepared to wait. The sound of the evening call to prayer radiated out over Peshawar.

There was a knock at the door of room. I opened it to find a young boy holding a tray with a Coca-Cola already poured into a glass over ice. It made me remember the Chateau Windsor and the friendly army of obsequious servants. I took the drink and sipped, for the first time in many months, real Coca-Cola.

Ten minutes later a harder thudding sound made the door bend inwards. I pulled it open, expecting to find the boy returning for the glass. But a huge Afghan filled the frame, a black bushy beard obscured his face. Bandoliers stretched from shoulder to shoulder, and what I made out to be a Russian Makarov handgun was thrust into his belt.

'I am Akram,' he said.

The voice roared from somewhere amongst the bristles. I was unsure what my reaction was supposed to be, I played along, hoping for some more information.

'Peace upon you! Welcome, Akram Khan. I am Tahir Shah.'

'I have been sent by your sister to look after you.' Akram boomed.

'Excellent, come inside, out of the corridor.'

Akram sat squarely on a chair, having drunk copiously from the cold water tap in the adjoining bathroom. He preferred to keep the bandoliers strapped tightly across his chest.

'Tell me Akram Khan, where is Saira Jan?'

'She said that she would be back in seven days from now. She has gone to Kabul to cover the feud between two warring clans.'

Akram saw worry contort my face and he tried to comfort me. For Kabul was an extremely dangerous place to be.

'She is with a very brave band of *Mujahedin*, Afghan Freedom Fighters, who have gone into the battle to try to bring peace to the factions. There is little danger.' He stroked at a clump of hairs growing from his beak-like nostrils, adding, 'Until her return I am responsible for all your desires. We can go tomorrow morning to collect Saira's jeep which has just been repaired.'

'Very well, what time shall we leave?'

'I'll be here at nine.'

He stood and strode from the door, his giant feet pounding out into the corridor. I sat on my bed, forcing myself not to worry. The next day would teach me more of the situation, and perhaps it would bring a clue to the great treasure which Saira had mentioned in her telex.

The Danish relief worker, Adam, joined me for breakfast. A doctor at a relief clinic, his work in prosthesis was well known in Peshawar. A copy of *The Muslim* was stuffed under one arm together with an artificial hand which he fondled lovingly during the meal.

'I've been making alterations to this hand for days,' said Adam enthusiastically. 'It's for an old Afghan woman whose left hand was amputated after a bullet wound became very infected.'

'How is she coping with the loss?' I asked.

'It's astounding, people learn to adapt and survive if they have to: human beings fear potential disasters, but if a catastrophe occurs they learn to live with the consequences.'

Peshawar's bright morning sunshine broke through the tinted windows and Lala's Grill lost its funereal air for a moment.

Adam went off to fit the prosthesis and Akram and I took a rickshaw past the Qissa-Khwani Bazaar to find the jeep.

Afghans strode about, chatting on street corners and embracing old friends. There was an air of confidence and sophistication amongst these men, a nobility which I had rarely seen before. A woman crouched outside the Post office, a *burqa*, a garment like an upsidedown shuttlecock, covering her body. Two little children were playing together at her feet. Coins were sewn into their clothes and *kohl* was painted around their green eyes.

The bazaar smelt of melons and leather. Rays of crisp white light streamed through holes in the canvas roofs. I bought a *shalwar kameez* — a baggy suit like pyjamas — and a pair of leather *chappals*. The shoe seller soaked my chappals in water before I put them on, to soften the leather.

The bazaar snaked on for miles. Melons as large as medicine balls were carried about by muscular stallholders. Dogs barked and chased black and white cats and we turned left into a scrap-yard. Akram pointed to a once-red heap of nuts and bolts.

'This is Saira's jeep,' he said. 'Isn't it wonderful?'

His eyes shone as if he were witnessing a miracle. I muttered and *urr-ed* indistinct praise at what I saw. The wheels and engine had been removed and stacks of bricks were holding up the chassis. On the front right side a spent shellcase was propping up the wheel arch. Akram pulled the canvas back to reveal a nest of life. Two boys were curled up asleep, their bodies intertwined with a litter of yellow puppies, around a large boiling pot.

The third child was covered from head to toe in oil and grease: he was stirring a huge pot of soup with a spanner. He looked up and smiled so broadly that my resentment at the situation disappeared. The other boys woke and the soup was served from a set of grubby Ford hub caps.

'These are Afghan boys; they are too proud to beg,' said Akram. 'I managed to get them this place to work from. They will accept no money. Their father and mother were killed in Panjshir valley. An old uncle who is blind came with them; they look after him too.'

In a few minutes a boy of about thirteen had fitted the engine back in place. As he wielded a spanner, as long as his forearm, his younger brother started her up. The yard was filled with a dense blue smoke that seemed almost too thick to enter one's lungs. Cheers mixed with the smoke. The cauldron was lifted to the ground and a piece of broken glass was handed to Akram — a home-made key.

An assortment of wheels were produced and fitted with some difficulty; I suspected that they were not those which had been removed from the vehicle when the work had begun. Akram handed a large bar of milk chocolate to the youngest of the boys.

The elder brothers stared down at the infant, and nudged him. The boy stretched out both hands which were folded around the bar of chocolate, he tried to give it back to Akram. The eldest child spoke with shrill words in good English.

'Baba, you have been kind already to my brothers and I, we cannot accept.'

A set of miniature fingers caressed the shiny foil wrapper as Akram insisted that they take it. The smallest child put the chocolate down and held out a squirming ball of yellow fur: his gift in exchange.

Akram took the puppy and held it tightly in his folded arms. We left the oily yard as the fumes filtered upwards. The dogs and family of brothers climbed up into another jeep, and the cauldron was filled with water again.

* * *

Green's Hotel ran wild with rumours. Journalists slouched in Lala's Grill nonchalantly, then ran off to file the bogus tales to editors around the world. Akram and I decided to play a practical joke: Afghans love jokes.

When the foyer was at its busiest, we lounged about talking loudly.

'Tahir, did you hear that the King of Saudi Arabia is coming on a secret visit tonight, to hand out funds to refugees?' shouted Akram as loudly as he could.

'That's amazing news, but where will he be staying?'

'I heard from my cousin who is the receptionist at Dean's Hotel that he will be resting there, but under a false name.'

'What time is he expected?'

'Oh, at about seven this evening.'

'Where did you say he was staying?'

'At *Dean's* Hotel.'

There was a rustle of palm leaves and men in white suits with gold bracelets stopped talking into their walkie-talkies and rushed for the door. One by one, the journalists caught the gossip and dashed out to hail rickshaws. Akram and I went into Lala's Grill for tea.

Akram slurped his tea, almost choking with enthusiasm at the immediate response. Then Adam surfaced, his face glowing with excitement.

'Adam, what're you all shaken up about?' asked Akram.

'You'll never guess who's coming to Peshawar tonight!' Akram kicked me under the table and we gasped together: 'Who? Tell us who!'

'Fahad ibn Abdul-Aziz, the King of Saudi Arabia! He's bringing his entourage on a secret mission to deliver Stinger missiles to the Mujahedin. It's a great secret, and I don't know if I should tell, but he'll be staying at Dean's Hotel, incognito of course.'

'Oh, of course,' muttered Akram. There was no detail which Adam could not supply. People capered about, telephones rang and distraught journalists yelled down landline connections, to their editors. We decided to go down to Dean's to see what chaos we had created.

A camera crew were setting up high wattage lamps in front of Dean's Hotel. In the reception area, the poor manager had given in to the bevy of journalists. Running nicotine-stained fingers down the list of guests, they searched for an Arab name.

'Ahmed Hussain! It has to be him, room 302!' an American voice shouted and was trampled underfoot as the seething mass of pencils, hand-held tape-recorders and flashguns swarmed up to room 302.

Akram and I had seen enough. We drove back to Green's, both delighted. Akram moved his eyes from the road to the dozing yellow puppy on my lap, and said:

'Beware little one, human beings are funny things.'

* * *

Waiting for my sister, and the treasure that she had promised, was almost too much to bear. I could not leave Peshawar in case she returned in my absence; and I could not sleep for the glorious images of a hidden hoard. So I forced Akram to take me to Saira's house to see if there had been any news.

We drove out from Green's towards University Town, a suburb of Peshawar. The jeep hummed along, swerving to miss cattle and painted Afghan lorries.

After some miles of ploughing through the frenzy of petrol tankers, cars, auto-rickshaws and buffalo carts laden high with rice, the road came to a sudden end. A single man, armed with a shiny silver whistle and a road worker's helmet, held the frantic mob of fast-paced chaos back as if by a magic spell. Taking a lump of white chalk, he scratched a line at right angles across the road.

A dozen petrol tankers with flashing lights and blaring horns revved their engines. A row of suicide bus drivers jolted their gargantuan wheels right up to the line. A thousand rickshaws, buffalo carts and cyclists, readied for motion. But still the worker, the whistle in his teeth, held his ground. Then, thrusting a solitary round-edged spade into the dirt, he began to dig.

The raging mass of transport, animal and mechanic, looked on at fever pitch as the construction works began. But, just as the horde was about to explode across the official boundary, a cyclist veered from the paved track, cross country, to by-pass the line, the official and the shiny silver whistle.

Without a moment's hesitation, the swarm of vehicles and buffalo followed, releasing their brakes and careering off the tarmac road, and on through a graveyard. Akram pulled over to the side of the road. Instead of surging at breakneck speed through the dusty field of graves with the rest of the mob, he climbed out of the jeep consumed with fury.

He marched down into the middle of the flow of vehicles heaving off the beaten track. Then, forcing the greatest of the petrol tankers into an emergency stop, he opened its door, and dragged out the driver by the throat. Showing no mercy, Akram threw punches at the poor wretch of a man, who was soon unable to stand.

Rather surprised at Akram's spontaneous rage, I asked him whether such a random display of force had indeed been necessary. Akram, who was still pulsating with anger, caught me in a cold stare and said,

'That driver, whose blood now covers my hands, dared to drive over the grave of my own ancestor. He shall not do it again!'

When we had overcome the area of road works, I asked Akram how he knew where to go, as the shops and stalls seemed very alike.

'It's very easy, Tahir Jan. You turn right at the ruined fort and left at the sheep-pens.'

Opposite the sheeps' billets, in a very rundown area, we came upon a huge mansion. Gates swung open and we were ushered inside. A servant informed us that nobody was in residence.

After some argument, he gave me a local telephone number to try.

I dialled the number from the foyer at Green's. An Afghan voice at the other end of the line seemed to be very shaken. He said that they had heard nothing and, in any case, it was better if I came to his house the next day at two P.M. There was cause for concern, especially as reports from Kabul had announced that battles between warring Afghan factions had led to substantial casualties.

We took an early lunch before the meeting at the Peshawar Club as Adam's guest. The club was set deep in the military cantonment — an area which the British had developed for themselves. Everything was whitewashed, and box hedges were tended by doting gardeners.

One of Adam's young patients, Habib, came too. The son of a blacksmith, his father had died near the northern Afghan city of Mazar-i-Sharif. It had been there that Habib had learnt to speak good English. His right leg had been completely blown off in a midnight bombing raid; and his little sister had lost an eye. The parents had died shielding the children as the roof caved in.

Habib's prosthesis had been very complicated, mainly hampered by the size and shape of the replacement limb. It reached up to the bowels and was jointed in several places. Adam was pleased with the work and was thrilled to speak about the surgery.

Habib ate slice after slice of chocolate cake which Akram ordered for him. Sug, the yellow ball of fur, sat under the table, his tiny black eyes shining from the fluff. He barked at the waiter who came on tiptoe to take our orders, hoping that the dog had fallen asleep. Habib petted Sug and let him chew his fingers.

The waiter reappeared and walked across the gardens to our table. He staggered under the weight of an enormous tray of pilau rice and slices of beef. There was a gnashing of fangs and suddenly a yellow ball of fluff was charging at the man's legs. With a rip of woollen cloth, the waiter cried out and ran up a tree. We sat staring in astonishment as he managed to scale the tree without spilling the contents of the tray. Sug sat beneath the boughs and revelled in victory.

The Dane introduced me to Camilla, an elderly English lady with a strong Yorkshire accent.

'You must come and see my class of little Afghans,' she said. 'They're usually as good as gold. But today they behaved very naughtily. I was telling them that in England we call our dogs names like Fido and Rover, just like in Afghanistan where they call their dogs Mohammed and Ali. You know what they did?' I shook my head in silence. 'They all stood up together and walked out!'

I explained to Camilla that in Afghanistan people never give the names of the Prophet or his family to animals or objects.

'Oh,' she replied, 'that must be why my driver hit a tree when I nicknamed my station-wagon the "Allah-car".'

Akram stayed in the jeep and I pressed the buzzer on the wall precisely at two P.M. Two wrought-iron gates swung open and armed men escorted me inside a vast compound. Toyota Landcruisers were being loaded up with rocket-propelled grenades and cases of ammunition. Rows of Kalashnikov AK-47's stood lined up to be counted. All the Mujahedin were dressed in baggy trousers and American army jackets. Men crawled on their stomachs, others were climbing ropes or firing off heavy-calibre rounds into the air. I had never seen anything like it.

Three guards — armed to the teeth — led me into a sitting room. I sat on a straight-backed chair for twenty minutes. My heart was pounding. Not only was I anxious for my sister, but for my own safety. No one had seen me enter except for Akram. There is no detail that I can remember of that room. I just recall my hands running with sweat and the pulse in my temples.

It was then that a balding man with a few short strands of grey hair appeared. I waited for the words that my sister had been injured or killed. The old man looked deeply upset. He put out a hand and clenched my fingers in his.

'Good afternoon. Please sit down.'

He spoke with an English accent which surprised me, rather like a soldier from Sandhurst. Just as he was about to sit, a stout Afghan with a bear's curved back and coal-black beard strode through the room. Mumbling a few words to the balding one in Pashtu, he left us alone.

The old man, whom I later realised was a formidable hero of the resistance and a former brigadier of the Afghan army, seemed to be a little more confident. I broke the silence.

'Sir, I am the brother of Saira Shah. I have come from India where I was living. My sister told to meet me her in Peshawar, but I understand that she is still away. Do you have any recent information about the expedition?'

The Brigadier drew a very deep breath and nodded slowly. Then he spoke, 'Come with me, we will go to talk somewhere a little more secure.'

He stood up and walked to the door. The fortress which we were in seemed to be very secure indeed, but I decided to comply. Perspiration poured from my face; the heat outside was no help.

We climbed into a Landcruiser and four heavily armed men jumped into the back. No words were uttered. Akram and the dog were asleep outside the gates, I did not call out, but sensed that the situation was getting very serious.

The Brigadier turned from the front seat and spoke slowly:

'Do you realise that it is not my responsibility for your sister, and that I have nothing to do with this?'

I was determined to keep very calm.

He continued:

'Do you love your sister?'

'Yes, Brigadier, I do. What exactly are you getting at?

What is the need to move about like this?'

'Saira has been in great danger. I have no idea where she is or if she is still alive. I cannot help you.'

The Brigadier could see that I was very shaken by his words. He stopped talking, and the Landcruiser halted about ten miles from the fortress, in the countryside. I recall nothing of the hut where we were taken, just that there were small purple flowers growing in front of the door.

The Brigadier pushed me forward. A Mujahed commander stood guard, picking his teeth with a bayonet. There was a smell of burning wood and the sound of logs being chopped. We entered the house. A fierce-looking figure in battledress — festooned with fragmentation grenades — saluted as we crossed the threshold.

In the sitting room, the same bear-like man with the black beard sat. Beside him was a girl with a *chadar* veil covering her face. I averted my gaze, in accordance with Islamic courtesy. She turned and spoke my name. It was Saira.

The Brigadier had been playing an Afghan joke. Only when we met initially and the man with the black beard, Akbar Shah, had passed through like a shadow, had he heard that Saira had made it back. Before then he admitted that he, too, was nervous and had not been able to think of words with which to console me.

Back in the compound, Akbar Shah filled his green tea with heaped spoonfuls of salt and bellowed with laughter. We went back to Saira's red jeep, Akram woke up and started it with the piece of broken glass. Saira, tired out, had gone home to sleep.

The next morning I went to Saira's house and found her writing about the foray into Afghanistan. I had taken a rickshaw there, managing to avoid Akram. For, if the hoard was as wonderful as I suspected it to be, I would have to be careful as to whom I entrusted with the secret.

The bathroom had been turned into a makeshift darkroom, and several reels of Ilford film were hanging up to dry. The thought of the treasure was driving me crazy. At four A.M. I had switched on the bedside lamp and scanned the crumpled telex that Saira had sent to me in India. I read again and again the four words: *HAVE GOT EXTRAORDINARY TREASURE.*

Saira stopped typing and made me some tea. I sipped the drink and, trying to subdue my elation, I mumbled,

'In your telex you mentioned something you'd located . . . treasure wasn't it?'

My sister topped her cup up with milk and said quizzically:

'Treasure?'

'I thought that's what you said; of course it might have been mistyped by the telex operator.'

My mind raced as I thought of all the possible mistakes an Indian clerk could have made, resulting in error with the word *treasure*. Saira gulped half a cup of the milky tea and exclaimed,

'Ah, the treasure.'

'Yes, yes,' I stammered, 'I knew that's what you had written.'

'I hope it's still okay. It's been left in the cellar for weeks,' she said.

'Can I see it?' I gasped, 'Can we go and have a look right away?'

'Well, I suppose so,' Saira said, leading me through the house. We arrived at the cellar door. 'It's in the basement, or was when I left. I do hope that no one took it while I was in Afghanistan.'

'That would be terrible!' I said, surprised that she could be so nonchalant, so carefree, about such an important matter.

We descended the stairs and Saira fumbled for the light-switch at the bottom. She flicked the switch and led the way through three illuminated chambers. Behind the door of the third there was a large cardboard box which had been wrapped in newspapers.

'I hope you appreciate how special this is,' Saira said. 'It was brought out of Afghanistan by the Mujahed leader Zahir Khan.'

I had heard stories of the great commander Zahir Khan. Some said he was a madman, others that he was esteemed by God and given special protection. He rode a snow-white horse, that he was said to have captured from a Russian General: who had brought it from the Ukraine. He had trained the animal to crouch down on its knees when Soviet helicopter-gunships swooped by.

'He risked his life to bring us this box; to bring to us what is naturally ours,' said Saira.

Naturally ours? I was desperate to find out what it was, but was baffled by what she had said.

Saira tore away the newspapers and revealed the contents of the box. My confusion increased when I saw what was inside. For it was a box of very ripe apples.

'They are from our ancestral orchards in Paghman,' said my sister. 'Zahir Khan picked them himself. They're more precious than any gemstones. They are the fruit grown on Afghan soil: in the garden of our ancestors.'

* * *

The Brigadier had accepted our invitation to dine. He had said that he would be pleased to come; but, in accordance with Afghan tradition, he gave no date or time. And of course it would have been rude for us to press him. For two days we supervised the cooking of a feast at the mansion. Afghan meals have to match the esteem in which the guest is held. The Brigadier was expected at any moment. Another two days passed and we were still sitting around waiting for the guests. There was no word.

Then, just as we were giving up hope, Akram rushed in and announced that a convoy of about twenty jeeps was turning off the main road in our direction, and would arrive any minute. The Brigadier and his chief commanders, a dozen men, entered the house. About one hundred of his fighters sat in the garden, brandishing every kind of weapon, from Kalashnikovs to blunderbusses, waiting to be fed.

The presence, the aura, that surrounded the Brigadier was most unusual. He sat crossed-legged on an Afghan rug in the durbar room. A *pakol* cap was propped on his balding head and an army jacket covered his square shoulders. He sat silent for a moment. A mysterious power seemed to radiate from the man, an air of absolute confidence. He spoke with precise deliberation, in almost a whisper. Everyone leant forward to hear his words.

'Your sister is very brave. You must be proud of her,' he said. 'The party was shelled four times, but they escaped the danger. I selected my best men to escort her and they would all have been willing to give their lives for her protection.' The corners of his mouth turned upwards and he smiled like a cheeky schoolboy, 'I hope I didn't scare you with my little joke!'

'I am grateful for the help which you have given my sister,' I said.

The Brigadier produced a tin insulated with polystyrene and removed the lid. Inside there was what looked like a large lump of yellow marzipan. He Brigadier motioned me to smell it. It smelt of marzipan too. Then he said, 'This is so hard to get, I like to keep a supply with me.' I looked in query at Saira and she whispered,

'C5 . . . plastic explosive!'

The men in the garden chatted and smoked cigarettes until the food was brought. Several lambs, chickens buried in trays of rice, huge flaps of naan bread, bowls of beans in yoghurt, and many great melons, were devoured in a few minutes. Almost every scrap of food had disappeared.

The men rubbed the grease into their beards, stretching out and waiting for their leader to speak, while green tea was served. The Brigadier eventually put down a leg of lamb and started to talk again.

'The war in Afghanistan weaned children who have known

nothing but hostilities. Now that the Russian forces have pulled out, the struggle continues between numerous factions vying for power. For the refugees the road ahead will not improve. Their lands have been destroyed by chemicals and mined beyond all reason. The international aid organisations come, their people prance about, but often, sadly, are manacled in their corruption.

'Go to the bazaars and you will be able to buy any aid, from jackets and grain to pills and even grenade launchers. The Afghan factions shell, rocket and ambush each other and end more lives, as if the war did not claim enough. The fighting continues, exterminating the ordinary people.

'The future of the warring in Afghanistan, which dictates the future of Peshawar to a great extent, still seems very bleak despite the Soviet withdrawal. The one unifying element to all Afghans is Islam. It bound them together, inspired their heroism during the conflict with the Russians, but is now becoming too fundamentalist in its more fanatical believers. Remember, for ten years, foreign interests have been supplying fanatics with arms. Further, the Cold War and other factors have been behind the rise of fundamentalism. There is no doubt that some powers have actually backed both sides, for reasons of their own. Islam, as a result, has been hijacked, in some places by men who commit blasphemy in its name.'

The Brigadier's words became clearer when, the next day, I visited a clinic for children with my sister. A line of long beds bathed in bright sunshine ran along one wall of a room. Children with burns more horrible than I can describe were wriggling about like deformed animals. Indeed, I would hardly have known them to be children if I had not been told.

Little girls, of perhaps five or six had had their faces wiped off: the disgusting effects of Russian napalm, used in what the Soviet Airforce called its "International Duty". Only the remains of a mouth were left, and a hole where the nose had once been. Akram said it was good that those children were now blind,

'They shall not see how ugly they are on the outside. Tahir, they are beautiful inside.'

Legs had been fused together and fingers melted off. A boy called Ibrahim smiled, his bright blue eyes shining inside a scarred face. He was like any other child, perhaps like I once had been. But Ibrahim had both legs missing. They had been so badly embedded with shrapnel that amputation had been necessary. We spoke for a few minutes, he told of his escape from the *Rouss* shortly before the Russian withdrawal.

'The helicopters came and the sky went black. Bombs fell all night, and there was the sound of bullets. I looked outside and I could see tracer bullets flashing through the air. My father went outside to shoot. He was killed that night.'

'What will you do when you get better?' I asked.

'I will go back to Panjshir and make sure the *Rouss* do not return. I still have hands and my eyes are good!'

I raised my camera to a little girl who had a gaping hole in her lower abdomen. I remembered how in the West people seem to give more money to charity when there are pictures of suffering. I would document the results of unmitigated evil. The child screamed and screamed in a fit of terror. A nurse came to comfort her and we left the room. As I was leaving, I asked the nurse why the little girl had been so afraid of a camera.

'Sofia thought your camera was a gun. Her parents were shot dead in front of her; she was hit in the stomach and left for dead. She is a very brave little girl. We are very proud of her.'

As I left I noticed a poem written by a child pinned next to the door. It read:

When I see fields of wheat I remember
My own village with green fields and high trees,
When I see a river I remember the rivers
Of my own province, Paghman.
When I see the mountains I remember the range
Of the Hindu Kush. I will never forget

My friends, nor how I went with them to the nearby hills,
Covered by green grass,
With hundreds of cattle grazing there;
And then we were forced to leave.

PART TWO: CENTRAL GONDWANALAND

West and East Africa

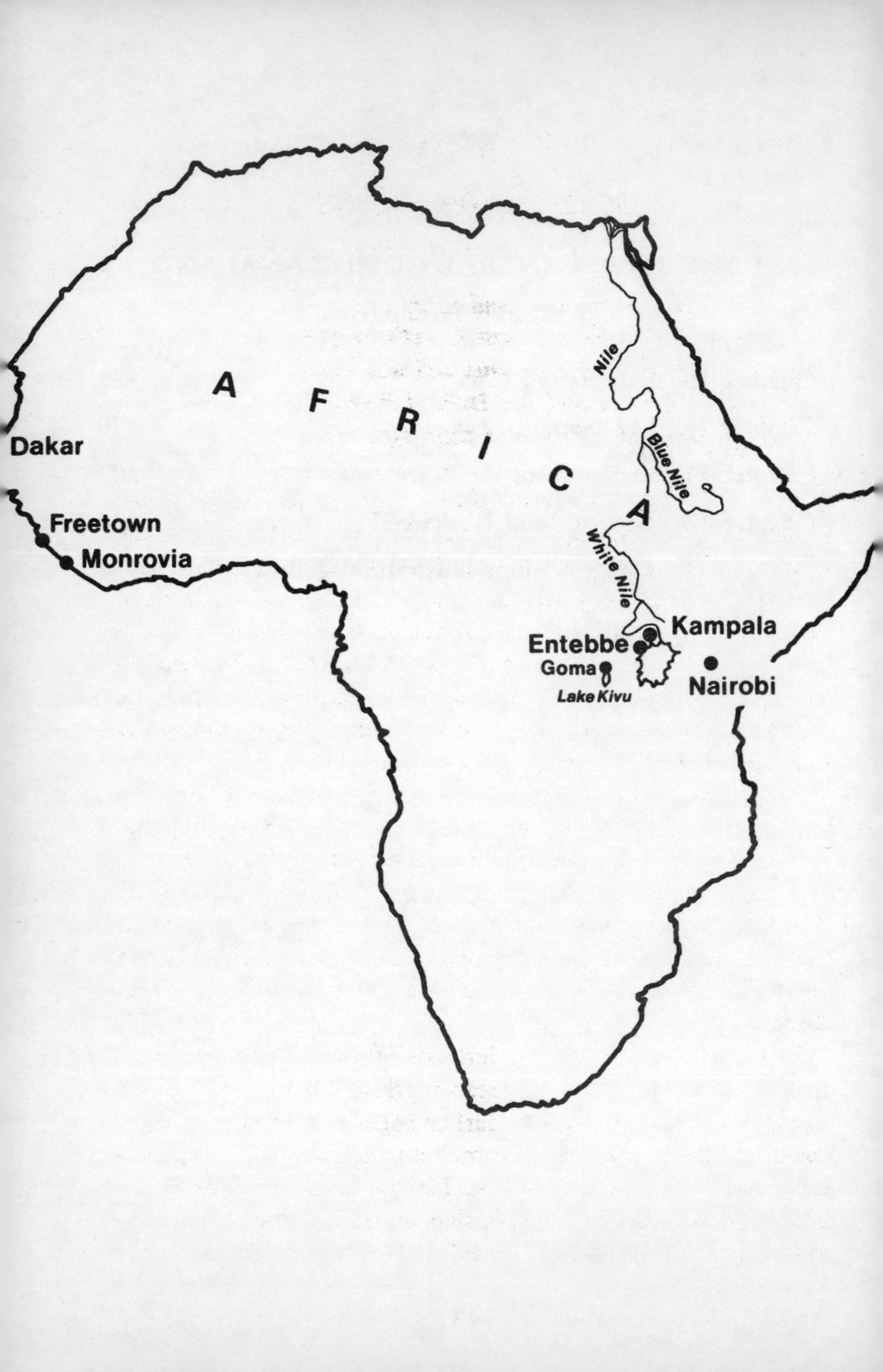

AFRICA
Nile
Blue Nile
White Nile
Dakar
Freetown
Monrovia
Kampala
Entebbe
Goma
Lake Kivu
Nairobi

CHAPTER 9

Rats Eating Cats

Saw a pestle hard and heavy . . .
With it thrashed those Giant's daughters;
Thrashed them till they bellowed loudly,
Fled and roared like Bulls of Bashan,
Fled and hid them in their wigwams.

A pair of pregnant ladies sat either side of me on a bench. They looked at each other and giggled. The one on the right made a joke in Wolof and they both rolled about in laughter.

I had come to the Clinique Troy in Castor — a suburb of Dakar — in Senegal, to get a visa for Sierra Leone. During the journey from Asia to West Africa I had tried to bury all memories of greed. The apples from Afghanistan and the mutilated bodies of the innocent had helped me to understand that treasure was more than a chest of jewels.

Blake's mention of *Macumba*, a magical science thought to be more comprehensive than any other, occupied my reasoning. There was one man whom I knew could assist this pursuit. His name was Max, and he lived in Freetown, the capital of the West African country of Sierra Leone. If Macumba had, as some claimed, derived from the most ancient lore in Africa, it had at least — by association — some resonance with the Gond theme.

The journey from the borderlands of Pakistan's north-west frontier, to West Africa, had been anything but simple. A travel agent in one of Peshawar's darker backstreets had sold me a cut-price ticket. Although somehow the fare was extremely convenient, the route was not. Having diced with death by taking the 'Flying Bus' from Peshawar to Islamabad, I first flew to Damascus. From there, I jetted on to Aden in Yemen, before taking an evening cargo flight to Moscow — then I was hustled on board an indirect flight to Paris. And, it was from there — as my internal clock was spinning out of control — that I ventured on by air to Dakar.

⋆ ⋆ ⋆

When I was told that the maternity clinic issued visas I had hardly flinched. My travels in India had made such practices seem normal. Assuring myself that the experience of Bombay, Rajasthan and the Afghan frontier would hold me in good stead for what was to come, I was determined to press on across Gondwanaland.

My passport was examined thoroughly. A hundred irrelevant questions were asked and it was hinted darkly that maybe I just wanted to get close to expectant women, rather than to obtain a visa. I pleaded with the director — a middle-aged lady dressed in a blood-drenched surgical gown — who had just delivered twins. Finally, agreeing that a visa could be granted, she led me into the operating theatre and offered me a cigarette. The mother was recovering from the trauma of childbirth with her twin daughters.

'It will take forty-eight hours,' said the director, blowing smoke into my face.

'I was hoping to leave Dakar as soon as possible . . .,' I said.

'All right, come back at five this afternoon.'

At five P.M. the director's assistant — who was a nurse — took my money and handed the passport back to me. I checked the visa. It filled a whole page and was striped in several colours. Just as I was leaving, I noticed that the wrong dates had been entered. Plucking up courage, I informed the assistant. Without batting an eyelid, she ripped out the page and stamped a new visa in another part of the passport.

'Will there be anything else?' she growled.

I went back to my hotel feeling as if a piece of my anatomy had been amputated.

⋆ ⋆ ⋆

The Hotel Monlogie had been recommended by a burly Parisien at the airport. He had been unloading crates of gear for the Paris-to-Dakar rally. The famous desert race was just ending, the first drivers having made it across the wasteland of Mali to Dakar. The tension was electrifying. People were rushing about, everyone shouting in French. It seemed that the whole of Paris was in Dakar. I had no visa for Senegal, and was very surprised to be waved through without any bureaucratic contretemps.

Hotel Monlogie was on Rue Lamine Gueye. A faint line of blood could be made out about three feet up the wall: a sign, my guidebook assured, that bedbugs shared the premises.

Men in wide Mauritanian robes flapped about the dusty streets of Dakar. Their fingers were concealed, tucked into a flap of cloth around the stomach. As I stared at the fine gold embroidery, two small boys came up and started to rub my knees. The sensation was not displeasing and I allowed them to continue for a moment, before my western thought-patterns forced me to question the reason for their activity. They looked rather disappointed. Just as I was going to ask the cause of their dissatisfaction, they ran off. The smaller one tossed back a black piece of curved metal. It was the key to my hotel room.

A doddery old man staggered over to where I stood and took charge. He spoke French with a thick accent that I could barely understand. I had soon become his property and, when a younger man came up and offered to take me around the city, he protested vehemently. After a while the man, his face wrinkled with blue-black lines, gave up, and insisted I go on, even if with the other man.

The newcomer, after telling me that his name was Joseph, pulled out a lump of gold — the size of a golf-ball — and offered it to me as a gift. His legs were bulging in black denim jeans and he wore the colours of a Rastafarian. I refused the nugget, suspecting that an obligation would ensue, and asked him for a good place to eat. 'Chez Lourcha on Rue Blenchot,' he said.

Joseph accompanied me there. A French woman slid a plate of spaghetti in front of me and threw a spoon at Joseph, screaming for him to leave. He shuffled his feet in the doorway, asking for a commission for bringing a customer. The woman slammed the door in his face — and turned my chair to the far wall — where a poster of the Eiffel Tower seemed to be all that was holding up the ceiling.

The next morning I went to the bus stop early and caught a coach to Barra Point. My intention was to get to Banjul, the capital of Gambia, from where the flight to Freetown would leave.

Rally cars and relay runners were bounding towards Dakar. The stripes of sponsorship and names of multinationals enveloped all. They became a blur as the vehicles pulled away, as we drove to the south of Dakar, and entered a forest of baobab trees. Grey trunks twenty feet thick stretched from horizon to horizon. They were spread out from each other, unlike a normal forest; and somehow looked more like a herd of grazing elephants than anything else. Baobabs are among Africa's most bizarre trees: they can live for over a thousand years. Their enormous trunks store water and in a drought they actually shrink, as the water is used up. The giant pods have seeds containing concentrated vitamin C.

Sitting next to me on the bus was a Frenchman who introduced himself as Auguste Lecomte. He fingered an immaculate copy of that very morning's *Le Monde* — Francophone Africa is splendid at distributing the papers — and read a line at a time through pince-nez. A few minutes later he looked up and spoke.

'We are nearly at the ferry point, and should get to Banjul by about six,' he said.

'Are you here on holiday?' I asked.

'My boy, my profession is to travel around the world buying excellent rare banknotes to sell to dealers. Did you know that Gambia's *dalasi* are quite sought after?'

I replied that I did not. Opening his case, he displayed perhaps a hundred currencies, each in mint condition. Tugrik from Mongolia, metical from Mozambique, Icelandic krona, dollars from the Solomon Islands, and many others, lay jumbled about.

I sensed a heavy breathing down my neck. Monsieur Lecomte obviously felt the draught as well. We hunched up our collars, but the cinnamon-scented breath continued. I turned around and focused on an emerald pair of eyes — which dilated with curiosity and envy. A mouth on the same face yelled:

'Khey meng, how ya dawing? I'ng Oswaldo, Oswaldo Rodriguez Oswaldo.'

His vice-like hand was thrust into mine and pulled me towards the seat behind. He addressed the Frenchman,

'Khey meester, ya wanna buy dis stuff?'

His fingers fumbled in a pouch around his waist and he fished out two handfuls of grubby Argentine banknotes. Monsieur Lecomte grimaced, appalled by the abruptness of the heavily-breathing Argentine. Declaring that the notes were worthless, he turned away to finish reading the editorial in *Le Monde*.

Oswaldo Rodriguez Oswaldo leant back, pushed a dark brown trilby onto his forehead, and sat in silence. Short, almost stunted in appearance, with well-proportioned features and an immaculate moustache, he smelt of lavender.

Outside, the baobabs stood motionless. There was no wind and the sky was free from clouds. The bus moved closer to Barra Point; it felt almost that we were driving through an oil painting.

On the ferry to Banjul a man, who said he was a hundred years old, changed my Senegalese C.F.A. currency into dalasi. He studied each note through thick lenses, reading the numbers aloud in Wolof. Oswaldo followed in my footsteps. I had the feeling that I would rather be alone, but Oswaldo craved company. The money-changers, who had refused to accept his pesos, had asked where Argentina was. We sat on a blue iron bench and watched Gambia draw closer.

'Where ya gooing meng?'

'I'm on my way to Freetown, to visit a friend. What about you?' I asked.

'I'ng gooing to eest.'

'How far east?'

'All de way meng. I caming from Buenos Aires in sheep to Dakar. Long tyng meng.'

'Where are you from, exactly?'

'Patagonia.'

I recalled geography lessons and the teacher rolling the word *Patagonia* around his mouth with an educated satisfaction. Oswaldo was short, perhaps five foot three. He swung his stubby legs in the air and clicked a pair of decomposing cowboy boots together. He never stopped moving. Before speaking, he would rub his pencil-line moustache with his thumb nail; and would laugh loudly three times, as if to clear his throat.

A boy selling wooden pots made from the branches of the baobabs offered them around. Oswaldo was delighted. He grabbed the boy and screamed, 'Ha Ha ha! Khey meng I lika wota ya gote dare. Give us looks!'

Four assorted-sized bowls were brought out and the Patagonian passed a bundle of Argentine pesos to the child.

'Ya taka dem to za benk, Okhey?'

The boy shuffled away, wondering what to do with the large collection of multicoloured bills. Oswaldo opened the mouth of his voluminous rucksack. He fished out a shirt and a pair of red jeans and put the baobab bowls at the bottom. I asked why he had such a large rucksack and only two other pieces of clothing.

'Che, dee reeson's cos I buying lots souveneers, I lika dis stuff meng.'

I hoped we could get away to Banjul before the boy's father saw the pesos.

Having stepped off the ferry onto the shore, a child of about nine took Oswaldo by one hand and me by the other and led us to the Hotel Apollo. The wooden bowls clicked about as we took our first look at Banjul — capital city of the former British dependency.

Hotel Apollo was run down. But without being discourteous, one could say that the whole of Banjul had lost any air of elegance that it might once have commanded. There were two main streets: Buckle Street and Wellington Street. Hotel Apollo had once been painted white.

The owner was named Haji, and he greeted us warmly, his long Mauritanian-type robes dragging in the dust beneath his feet. Oswaldo asked if the hotel accepted Argentine pesos. It did not. But, as an act of diplomacy, Haji offered to reduce our board by a third if we would pay in a European currency and stay two nights.

Having agreed, our bags were carried ceremoniously up to a rather dilapidated room. A peculiar contraption filled one corner. The bag boy flicked the switch to turn it on. Before it started up, I heard the sound of his bare feet pounding as fast as they could away from the room. Cogs within the machine began to grind. This was followed by the noise and vibrations, as of a pneumatic drill. As we stood there, plugging our ears with our thumbs, water was sprayed across us and the walls. Oswaldo grappled with the apparatus, which was very like one of those machines film crews use to create wind and rain. A small plaque on the side, inscribed in Gothic script, read *Desert Cooler*.

Oswaldo combed back his short brown hair and applied a thick layer of green brilliantine. The room now reeked of lavender. The Patagonian pulled on his red jeans, opened his shirt to the waist and, after cackling three times, yelled,

'To those deesco meng!'

He dragged me out of the hotel, hauling me up and down the two main streets, requesting that I ask for the best dance-hall in town. One man pointed left, another right, and a third looked very worried. There was a shimmering red glow coming from a bar off Buckle Street.

'Khey Brit, we gooing dere!' He pointed a stubby arm towards the bar and pulled his shirt front further apart, revealing a hairless white chest.

A thunderous rhythm was being beaten out on two drums. Some torn sacks had been tacked together and hung in front of the doorway, almost as if they were keeping some kind of poison gas inside. Oswaldo clicked his heels to the drum-beats, then we entered the red glare.

A room, which seemed little bigger than an aeroplane's lavatory, was packed with all kinds of life. Oswaldo ordered himself two bottles of *Jewel* lager, I asked for a pomegranate juice.

'Khey, dis nice stuff!'

Oswaldo seemed overjoyed and, in his enthusiasm for the situation, he slapped the man next to him very hard on the back. I prepared for a bar fight. But the Gambian man was too drunk to co-ordinate hostile movements. Oswaldo handed him a bottle of Jewel lager and the two men began to dance.

When the boys had stopped drumming, we each pulled up a packing crate and sat. Oswaldo's dancing partner was a Gambian called Robertson. In his early sixties with a fat, chubby face, he began to tell his life story. A career as a sailor had shown him the world. He spoke twelve languages, one of which was Spanish. Oswaldo was ecstatic when he discovered his new friend had been to Argentina. He puckered his lips and kissed Robertson squarely on the forehead. The two men began to sing Spanish sailing songs, acting out the sordid parts in full detail.

The manager's baby son was sucking at an empty lager bottle and making gurgling sounds from between the crates on which we sat. Robertson patted the infant on the head affectionately as he continued with his tale. Then Oswaldo broke in, swigging from the dark green bottle in his left hand as he spoke. Suddenly, while he was talking, the Patagonian calmly reached inside his right boot and, in one motion, pulled out a stiletto. Springing the blade open, he threw it between the fingers of the baby boy. The drummers and the proprietor looked up. A chicken which had been roosting in one corner flapped to the door. Robertson stopped talking and stared in horror. Oswaldo took a sip of his lager. Then he pulled at the knife, which was deeply embedded in the floor. A scorpion was skewered halfway up the blade.

'Khey meng, eets beeg one,' he muttered, as he scraped it off with his foot onto the floor. Robertson cheered. The landlord, who was shaken, grasped his son in his arms. Then the drummers beat out a special rhythm to compliment Oswaldo, the unusual Patagonian. He lounged back on the crate.

The manager — who had been deeply moved by the stranger's bravado — came over. In his hands was an old biscuit tin which had lost most of its paint. He pulled open the lid. Inside was a dusty bottle of Heineken lager. Wiping a tear from his left eye, the landlord murmured gently:

'I have been keeping this for a special man and a particular night. That man and that night have now come.'

We ate breakfast the next morning at Café Express on Buckle Street. I had decided to take the evening flight to Freetown. Oswaldo said that he would like to come too, as he had never flown before. Having seen his display the previous night with a stiletto, I thought it might be to my advantage to have him along. After the meal we would go and buy tickets from the travel office.

A schoolboy came and sat at the third chair. He said nothing, just sat motionless. His and Oswaldo's legs dangled above the ground. Oswaldo hummed what he said was the Argentine National Anthem. One hotdog was brought and we divided it into three. Each of us chewed at the sausage as long as was possible. The child jumped up, shouted '*Jirijef*, Hello,' and ran off with his satchel swinging behind him.

A reduction was given for students on all flights to Freetown. I had no student identity card. But, in the interminable ticket queue, I used some Letraset to turn an international driving licence into a student identification. The letters were rather crooked, but it did the job. Oswaldo flashed an Argentine identity card. The lady nodded approvingly and the tickets were written out. Oswaldo was very happy.

'Macanudo! Lets gooing sunshining!' he said.

'What's that?'

'In that beach.'

An hour or so later I found myself supine on the beach front of the Atlantic Hotel. Fleshy British package tourists waddled about, clutching towels, suntan oil, brown sauce, and plates of fish and chips all at once. I told Oswaldo not to point. He explained that to get a *tang*, you must lie in the sun for four hours.

The rays burnt deep into my back and chest until I was sure that something was wrong. Gambia is near the equator and so the heat is very intense. At three P.M. I tried to stand. My skin had shrunk, and I felt like the inside of a cooked frankfurter trying to burst out.

Oswaldo looked worried for a moment. Then he said that we had better get to the airport. A woman from Blackpool had given him a ballpen with a scaled-down replica of a tower trapped inside. When he tilted the pen, the tower moved. Delighted with his new possession he showed it to everyone he met. But I was not interested. Instead, I staggered towards the Hotel Apollo, feeling like a boiled lobster.

The Air Ghana flight was delayed three hours. The plane sat on the runway for half that time, waiting for some repairs to be done to the fuselage. Engineers with troubled expressions hurried up and down the cabin shouting, and hurling spanners like boomerangs back and forth. The lack of security checks before boarding had been rather disconcerting. Oswaldo took the stiletto from his boot and ran it across his fingers. I told him to put it away before we were both arrested. The stewardess clambered about, handing out rock-cakes and glasses of fluorescent orange squash. An aging Ghanaian lady insisted on sharing my seat, as the plane was now full.

As we munched on our rock-cakes, the pilot suddenly hauled back the throttle and the craft swooped out of Banjul airport into the African sky. Orange juice and rock-cakes flew about as if there were no gravity. Oswaldo screamed at the top of his lungs and swung his red jeans about his head. Pulling a sick bag over my face, I pretended not to know him. The woman sharing my seat writhed about, increasing her territory. There was a tap on my shoulder. I turned round and was handed Oswaldo's trousers which had been propelled into the row behind us.

At Freetown's immigration, our passports were taken away. They were put in a black box. Two guards patrolled back and forth for about ten minutes and then opened the box. The documents were returned, dripping with stamp-pad ink. Rumour had it that, on entry to Sierra Leone, a large amount of foreign currency had to be declared and immediately changed into leones at the official rate. The routine searching of luggage often resulted, a source had assured me, in the confiscation of one's belongings. Oswaldo handed me a piece of chalk.

'What's this for?'

'Cross da bags, amigo.'

He had noticed that all checked luggage was efficiently crossed in white chalk. But what about the currency regulations? Oswaldo leapt into the lair of officials and they forced him to hand over a wad of Argentine pesos. The soldiers looked as if they believed that the unknown notes might be even more valuable than dollars.

As I walked through, a very strange thing happened. I concentrated deeply on the end of the line of salivating officials. Some were handing out forms, others brandished white chalk.

I moved straight ahead without turning. There was no sound behind me. No one called back or grabbed me. For some reason I managed to get by without changing any money at the official rate. It was as if I had willed them not to see me.

Max was studying philosophy at Freetown University. He had written in his last letter that I should to take a room at the City Hotel, as it would be more comfortable than his floor. We had not met before. When I was about twelve I had placed an advertisement to be circulated world-wide asking for interesting and unusual pen-friends. Max's letters had always been unusual. Many had been covered in blood, while others spoke of fantastic experiments and ceremonies in which he had taken part.

With one letter he had once enclosed the dried intestines of a small fly-eating lizard, together with some dogs' claws, which he said that I was to boil up into a kind of tea. He had come to West Africa to learn more of the rituals of *ju-ju* and the secret societies of Freetown.

A Frenchman from Marseilles with an aristocratic air let us share his taxi into town. He loaded four Purdey shotguns into the back of the Renault and rolled up the corners of a handlebar moustache as we jerked along. Thick jungle undergrowth abounded on either side of the road. Monkeys swung from tree to tree and the sounds of a seething insect population hummed around us. Oswaldo began to tell the man from Marseilles all about his homeland. Removing the stiletto from his boot, he showed it to the Frenchman, who admired the Patagonian quality.

Freetown was dark and depressing. We crossed a stretch of water in a launch and walked up the slope to the City Hotel.

It was in a state between dilapidation and total dereliction. The crumbling façade was subsumed in moss and creepers. Yet it must once have been almost palatial. Corinthian colonnades held up the remains of the roof, and the lintel of the main doorway had been replaced with an iron bar. A symmetrical pair of flights of winding steps led to the door. The wrought-iron gates were rusted from neglect.

A white man sat on the veranda under the light of a paraffin lamp. He was the proprietor, and said he could provide Oswaldo and me with a room. The Frenchman from Marseilles sniffed haughtily and carried his shotguns off into the night to find a more salubrious place to rest.

The owner was an Italian from Switzerland. He had not returned to Europe in over four decades. His skin was pallid, as if it had not been exposed to light in years. The building was bathed in an aura of decrepitude. A giant, standing at least six foot nine, moved into the lamplight and picked up our bags. The owner spoke in French, mumbling, 'This is my son, he will take you to your room.'

The creature, whose resemblance to Frankenstein's monster was more than uncanny, trod his way up three flights of stairs, whilst demonstrating his unusual talent of holding a lit candle in his teeth. The candle flickered as we progressed from one draught to the next towards the attic. The banisters, and indeed, all removable pieces of wood, so the giant said, had been incinerated to heat the house.

On the second floor, a naked man was washing a shirt in a basin. His broad smile revealed three gold teeth. The stairs creaked beneath our feet and, as we stumbled upward, Oswaldo edged closer to my side.

Two beds filled most of the attic room. Neither had mattresses, only tattered sheets on bare springs. A swarm of mosquitos fought above the sink and flitted around the peeling pink walls. The giant strode to the sink and relieved himself in it. I asked for the room key. There was no need for a key, I was assured, as there were no locks. Instead, we were invited to come down for a drink and to get anti-mosquito incense coils. Oswaldo went down immediately, while I took a shower on the second floor.

A slow stream of water fell onto my head. It was cold and

pleasing. I washed my sunburnt body with enormous care; it could just endure the pressure of the cold water. When the drops became less frequent, I glanced upwards at the nozzle to see if it was clogged. I noticed a gap of about two inches between the boards above my head: they were the floorboards of my room. In the candlelight, the white of a single eye rotated and blinked above me. Shrieking, I ran from the shower. The sound of footsteps pressed across the ceiling, as I made for the stairs to get to the putative privacy of the attic room. Half-way up I met the naked man with gold teeth. We paused for a moment. I might have asked him the reason for his voyeurism, but the fact that he was naked and that my badly blistered body was protected only by a face-cloth, gagged my questions.

Oswaldo had become instantly chummy with an assortment of villainous-looking men on the veranda. They lounged about on broken chairs smoking home-made cigars. The old Swiss man had passed out and was lying on a mattress on the ground, an empty bottle of whisky at his side. A man called Olivier introduced himself to me. He was a French Senegalese priest who, he said, was an expert in both yoga and karate.

An infant boy weaved between the clouds of cigar smoke and mosquitos, selling bubble gum and matches. It was easy to imagine Graham Greene lounging back on a broken wicker chair on the veranda of the City Hotel.

I tried to reach Max on an antique telephone. The dial had lost its spring and only the digit '1' worked properly. I banged the disc with my palm, but it still did not work. At that moment Oswaldo burst in and grabbed me by the shoulder.

'What's the matter?'

'Caramba! Dere's dieemonds and goold . . . we gooing now!'

We charged out onto the veranda. Oswaldo whispered that I was not to show much interest, as the men suspected we were there to gain from their secret wealth. The giant held up a flaming torch. He, the gold-toothed man, Olivier, Oswaldo and I climbed into the back of a jeep.

We drove out of the town into the night. I looked upwards into the night sky and saw the Big Dipper beginning to turn silently above us. The sound of bats and the chirping of crickets echoed all around as the bald tyres of the jeep spun along a muddy track. Oswaldo glanced at me nervously. Putting a fist on his left boot, he felt the stiletto, and nodded at me. We were both prepared to be robbed and left: but the opportunity to go on a midnight gold and diamond run was too great to miss.

The jeep pulled onto a side track about ten miles from Freetown. The glinting lights of the city were no longer visible; just two flares burning on the jeep. The dense undergrowth seethed with life of all types. Mosquitos and all manner of insects buzzed around the flares and headlights. In the distance I could make out a wooden hut. The jeep pulled up at the front door and we descended. A man inside began yelling in Creole when he saw Oswaldo and me. The giant calmed him and we were all ushered into the shack.

A bottle of locally-brewed alcohol was passed around. It burnt into the Patagonian's throat, making his eyes bulge as he choked aloud. Three pouches were fetched by the old inhabitant of the hut, who brought a torch closer to illuminate their contents. The pouches were upturned on a packing crate.

What looked like small pieces of ground glass sparkled in a pile. They were of irregular shapes and only some of the surfaces shone. In another heap, gold — perhaps eight to ten ounces — was admired by all. Oswaldo's and my eyes widened with avarice. The shadows of greedy men danced about the dark walls. Oswaldo pulled at Olivier's arm and asked where the diamonds and gold were from. The priest narrowed his eyes and whispered:

'They come from the mountains. Diamonds and gold are in the village paths and when it rains they are washed up. People come out and dig them from the ground with knives.'

A session of animated negotiating followed, lubricated with a seemingly endless supply of firewater. Some money changed hands in the untrusting candlelight and we left for Freetown with the smugglers.

As the jeep fish-tailed towards the City Hotel I thought of treasure. It was deserved far more by this sort of men. I myself no longer had a grasping fascination for such instant wealth. It was as if the appeal had been treasure for the sake of treasure: as if I had been driven by its romance, its mystique, and by its awe alone. India, Pakistan and now Africa seemed to have exorcised the lust: though not the quest.

Early the next morning I managed to contact Max. He arranged to come to the City Hotel and take us to lunch. Oswaldo and I sat in the bar waiting for him. The night had been very uncomfortable.

Oswaldo had put a little beer in one of the baobab bowls, and left it on the floor. In the morning the bowl was full of cockroaches. Some survivors were crawling over the dead, their tiny antlers poking around the corpses. He gave the black insect carcasses to the boy who had been selling bubble gum the night before. The child was thrilled and plodded off to dissect the remains.

A procession of school children paraded past the hotel as we waited for Max. Dressed in neat green and yellow uniforms, some played instruments, others clapped their hands, as banners were waved from side to side.

The old owner made one of the smugglers get down from the bar where he was sleeping. There was no more beer, he informed me gravely: but appearances had to be maintained.

Max arrived. It was odd to meet the man to whom I had been writing for so many years.

Oswaldo and Max glanced at each other like different species of animal. Oswaldo, whose hair was smoothed with brilliantine, wore his brown trilby and well polished cowboy boots. Max's appearance integrated him neatly with the City Hotel. His hair was long, greasy and very black, and his face — which was

The author. (*Photograph courtesy of Karan Kapoor*)

A group of Mujahedin relax after lunch, North West Frontier, Pakistan.

A truck of bananas destined for a market in Liberia.

A group of women heading for the market at Ruhengeri.

acking on sugar cane in
e Kivu region of Zaire.

Cakes of brown soap for sale in Rwanda.

Rwandan children pose with baskets of pungent fish.

Michael Jackson on a wall i
Kampala, Uganda.

. crowd gathers to watch our boat pushing out in search of the Nile's source.

. baboon in Kenya.

An elephant en route to Maralal, Kenya.

Wilfred Thesiger in his garden at Maralal, Kenya.

dark with dirt — was peppered with infected sores. A pair of tattered sneakers were rotting about his ankles and a cluster of leather pouches hung around his neck.

We, all three, snaked our way about the silent town. Almost nothing moved. A sense of utter despondency prevailed as if Freetown was not advancing or even attempting to progress. Max pointed out the giant cotton tree which is a landmark in the centre of town. Nearby, at the American Embassy, we were given glasses of sterilised water and allowed to see newsreels two months old. Max had adapted here as I had done in Bombay. Freetown had become his life, his very existence.

Outside the embassy came the sound of sirens. Flashing red and blue lights blinked from a motorcade and five jeeps with outriding motorbikes sped past. The few people about stood still and lowered their heads. Oswaldo gasped,

'Khey meng, what's dat?'

'That's the President going to work!' said Max.

Like many African nations, Sierra Leone's leadership had gained power by coup d'état. Indeed, as soon as one group gets control, another is scheming secretly how they may take over. But Captain Valentine Strasser's coup of Spring 1992 was exceptional, even for Africa: for Captain Strasser was just twenty-seven, and his deputy — Solomon Musa — was a mere twenty-four years of age.

We were each presented with a bowl of boiled seaweed. It had been partially fermented and then covered in a watery meat sauce. I suspected that the meat was cow's brains. Max had ordered this delicacy for us all at his favourite restaurant. He picked up lumps of the green sludge in his nicotine-stained fingers, tossed his head back, and dropped the morsels down his throat one handful at a time. Oswaldo and I stared at each other blankly.

'Don't you like it?' huffed Max in surprise.

'Slightly too much salt for me,' I grunted.

Max grabbed my plate.

'I'ng plenty eat Okhey!' squeaked Oswaldo sadly at his full plate. Max finished the three portions. Then he sucked the ends of his fingers, which had become splayed from extensive nail-biting.

The café was behind an abattoir on the second floor, somewhere on the outskirts of the town, past the Cuban Embassy. There were no windows, but on one wall was a faded photograph of the Prince and Princess of Wales on their wedding day.

When Max had finished the seaweed he rubbed his hands in his hair to clean them off. Then he lit a cigarette and removed the filter. We had written about many things in our letters, such as music, our friends, and places in which we had lived. Max was an avid fan of the Grateful Dead, an American rock band. But his extreme fascination for *ju-ju* was of most interest to me.

Sinister ceremonies take place at night around the darkest corners of Freetown. A number of societies, most secret in their operations, participate in ominous rituals. Max spoke of his involvement with these groups.

He had become the pupil of a *Babalawo* — a medicine-man — one who practices *ju-ju*. Although, technically-speaking, *ju-ju* refers to a fetish or image used in a magical rite, today its use is much wider. *Ju-ju* can be something that causes a change in the natural and supernatural worlds. It may be a potion, an ointment, a talisman, a sign, or even a magical word or phrase.

'It wasn't easy gaining the trust of my teacher,' said Max. 'He knows that I appreciate the honour. I have immersed myself in this science: I must become one with it.'

Max paused, and I frowned, wondering exactly what he meant. Staring deeply into my eyes, he pushed up the right sleeve of his shirt. A series of dots and lines had been tattooed into his copper-coloured skin.

'What is it for?' I asked.

'This is ju-ju to protect. There is evil here.'

'Vat evils?' Oswaldo asked.

'*Alé*,' said Max. 'That is ju-ju, or medicine, that puts harm on someone else.'

'You mean *black* magic?' I said.

'Yes, black magic,' said Max. 'Alé is my real interest but my teacher won't let me even think about that for years to come.'

What of the secret societies? Max had studied their history but was very unwilling to share what he knew.

'Many things,' he said, 'are better ignoring. These matters are taken very serious around here.'

Having read about the Alligator Societies and the Leopard Societies in Sierra Leone, I asked Max if such accounts could have been true.

'The Human-Alligators, as they are known,' he said, 'were at first thought to be people who were turned into reptiles by magic. They would kill someone — often eating the victim's corpse — before reappearing as humans again. Later it was found that people were just dressing up in alligator and leopard skins to kill people. That stuff has been forced deep underground following persecution by the authorities.'

'But does it really still go on?' I asked.

Max nodded slowly,

'The various societies have become more crossbred and have taken influences from new sources recently; each sect affects the practices of the next, even my Babalawo uses a Borfima,' he said.

'*Borfima*, what's that?'

It's a symbol, a source of power, and a centre for magical activity,' replied Max.

'What *is* it?' I persisted, trying to find out more.

'I've just told you,' said Max.

'No, I mean what is it made from?'

The cook came to collect our plastic dishes; he seemed suspicious of our conversation. When he had left, Max continued in a low voice:

'I have made Borfimas my special study,' he began. 'The most likely origin for many of the societies' cannibalistic activity seems to have started in order to feed the Borfima.'

'*Feed*?' I asked.

'Feed,' replied Max. 'To keep the Borfima bag as an effective medicinal tool, it must be supplied with newly killed or extracted human fat or blood. It will gain the strengths of all that is fed to it.'

I was still rather confused by what Max was saying; he saw my uncertainty and continued:

'I was just reading of a mysterious society in Angola, the *Butwa* sect who keep a Borfima.' He pulled a worn sheet of yellowing paper from his back pocket, and said:

'This is what the Englishman Butt-Thompson wrote of the Butwa Society's Borfima:

> *'The duiker horn is said to contain human flesh, hair, nails, bone and sinew. In the larger horn are animal claws, bits of lion and leopard heart, of feet of elephants, hide of hippopotamus, shell of tortoise, bird bills, eye of osprey, eyebrow of vulture, head of the "ngweshi" snake, heart of python, head of puff-adder, nose of crocodile, brow of hyena, head of dogfish, and human and lizard gall, a tooth of a field rat, a scorpion, a burned honey bee, a baby's head, a human caul, some soldier ants, some powdered meteorites, some sand from the footprint of the founder of the Society, a head from a dead chief, a piece of tree upon which an official of the Society committed suicide.'*

When Max had finished reading, he closed his eyes and grasped one of the leather pouches which was strung around his unshaven neck. There was a tense silence. Oswaldo shifted nervously in his broken chair, then he gave me a tortured look as I addressed Max:

'Can we meet your teacher? I think that it is important,' I said in a wheedling tone.

'That'd be quite impossible,' he replied. 'Getting him to

have anything to do with *me* was accomplishing the impossible.'

'Then Max,' I said, 'can't you make the impossible happen again?'

* * *

At two the next morning we crept from the City Hotel. A cat was stalking a giant toad on the veranda next to the sleeping Swiss owner.

Enticing his master with a bottle of local whisky, Max had managed to persuade the Babalawo to meet us. As we stumbled behind him into the darkness towards the rendezvous, Max kept on repeating how difficult it had been to arrange. Understanding the gravity of the meeting, I thanked him.

Freetown seemed more alive in the hours of darkness than during the day. We left the city, walking past the abattoir and the restaurant to which Max had taken us.

A few of the shacks housed shadowy figures who could be heard talking and laughing. Insects buzzed in the undergrowth into which we walked.

Max explained that traditionally secret societies were located deep in the bush, and only the initiated had known of their whereabouts. A revival of the societies in Freetown had taken place, and men such as his Babalawo now practiced very close to the city, or at times actually in it.

Initiation, Max said, was fundamental in gaining membership of a sect. The Societies native to West Africa are often formed from the people of several tribes, even of different nations. Boys would traditionally be taken into the bush to be initiated, a process that was known to last for weeks, even months. They would be instructed in hunting, defence, and in the secret qualities of the jungle's plants. But of the greatest importance to them were their studies in the magical and occult arts.

Max explained that, as such initiates respected the force of the Babalawo's incantations, we must also do so. We agreed that we would abide by the ways of the cult.

Oswaldo was very quiet and trudged along less than enthusiastically. I sensed that he was trembling. Reluctant to have anything to do with such dark matters, he had had conventional Catholic beliefs instilled in him as a child. Max led us into the forest as if he knew each step of the path.

After half an hour of walking I smelt burning meat. This was followed by the sound of someone whistling. Flames could be seen through the trees and, as Oswaldo and I trod softly behind Max, he also began to whistle. He led us into a clearing, illuminated by three burning torches. Between them sat a figure who poked at the embers of a dying fire. Max greeted the man in Creole. It was his Babalawo.

The mentor ignored Oswaldo and me, and continued to poke rhythmically, almost as if he were in a trance. Max told us to remove our shoes and socks, as he did the same. The ground was warm and damp underfoot, and covered in dead leaves.

I tried to make out the contours of the Babalawo's face. It was hard to tell his age, perhaps forty, perhaps sixty. His head had lost much of its hair. A striped tee-shirt covered his chest: the lines of it ran from his neck to his navel. He poked away at the fire as we sat and watched. I peered up at the sky, the stars looked down and I felt a little more secure.

Max had closed his eyes and sat cross-legged in silence. The Babalawo dropped a handful of herbs onto the embers. An asphyxiating, sweet-smelling cloud ascended from the fire as the leaves ignited and were consumed in flame.

The master began to chant in Creole. I nudged Max, hoping that we could learn of the significance of the words, but he did not translate. Instead, taking some bluish-grey dust from the fire's edge, he rubbed it across his face and over the backs of his hands. Oswaldo and I did the same. The ash smelt aromatic and soothing as I pressed it over the bridge of my nose and onto my cheeks. Was this the sort of ceremony that Blake had mentioned? I wondered how my mentor might have reacted if he were in my position. Such a rite as this must have influenced the Brazilian Macumba of which Blake, my own teacher, had told me. Of that magical system, which took its roots from many lands, I longed to know more.

The Babalawo began to squeal like a tortured pig. Then, panting, he thrust his arms high above his head, shouting out what must have been the names of spirits.

Max seemed to know precisely what was going on. He stood up and made his way over to a very low-roofed hut. After a few moments he returned with something in his hands. The master took the object and, in return, passed Max some more leaves. Max motioned to us what to do.

Copying him, Oswaldo and I each pressed a broad leaf onto the roof of our mouths. My mouth was numbed by a bitter taste. And, on trying to move my tongue, I realised that it was paralysed. I glanced in horror at the Patagonian, who winced miserably as if he, too, had fallen prey to the Babalawo's magic.

Max handed Oswaldo, and then me, an egg. As before, we did exactly what Max did. He broke the shell and gulped down its contents. We did the same, despite the handicap of our oral anaesthetic. Then, Max put the actual shell in his mouth, crunched it up, and swallowed it. Oswaldo looked very miserable, but we both copied Max in silence. My stomach seemed to twist as it was presented with the raw egg, followed by the shell. Oswaldo's stomach also gurgled in surprise at what it had just ingested. Max looked pleased with us.

The Babalawo stood up, clasping the object that Max had brought from the shack. The size and colour of a haggis, it smelt, as it passed by me, of something which had died quite some time before. A rusty razor blade was produced by the Babalawo. He held it between his thumb and forefinger with dexterity, leading me to believe that he had handled it on many such occasions. At that moment it became apparent that the razor was not just intended for show. It was no mere symbol, for the Babalawo wiped it, and readied it for use.

Oswaldo and I glared at Max through the orange torchlight

with expressions that called for an explanation. The egg had not been pleasant, but we had swallowed it, together with shell, in the interests of magical science. But what was the blade's purpose? Max seemed a little concerned and he spoke for the first time. His words struck Oswaldo and me with horror. He said simply:

'The Borfima is ready to be fed.'

The witchdoctor's dark shadow fell over the Patagonian, who sat cross-legged, rigid with terror, as the Borfima, blade, and Babalawo, approached him. He was too petrified to move, as the Babalawo took his arm and prepared for the operation of drawing blood from it. Just as the blade's edge was about to press down on Oswaldo's skin, he leapt up screaming. The doctor fell back, clutching his beloved Borfima to his chest. Max was not sure what to do. He cried apologies to his master who called for us to leave.

Oswaldo was silent as we stumbled back to Freetown, he was clearly upset and mumbled a prayer in Spanish. Max had left his Babalawo, to accompany us back through the woods. I regretted bringing the Patagonian along. But his outcry had done nothing to curb my interest in ju-ju. Indeed, this interest had only just begun.

Long before dawn we walked to the bus station. It was deserted. Oswaldo had made it clear that he would not spend another night, in fact another hour, in Freetown. We might have parted company then and there, but I sensed that a journey south — to Liberia — might reveal important new material. In any case, Max was reluctant to help any more, in spite of our long postal friendship. Besides, he said that the spirit of the Babalawo would be searching for us: and if he were to find us, he would certainly feed us all to his adored Borfima.

One could never be sure when the next vehicle bound for Liberia would leave, but we stood a good chance of getting one as it was still early.

Oswaldo and I crouched in one corner of the terminal, which resembled some gigantic aircraft hangar. Still there was no light, just the sound of rats as they scuffled about. A very young girl slept against one wall; in her arms was a newborn baby. There was no sign of the mother. The two clung together to keep warm.

After about an hour, a brand new Land Rover stopped for a moment outside the terminus. Oswaldo went to ask for a ride, at least part of the way to the Liberian capital, Monrovia. We were in luck, for the driver — who was going to Kenema which was on the way — would take us there for free.

The road was excellent by African standards, and for four hours we bumped along, only stopping from time to time to get out at checkpoints. The jungle was thick and lush on both sides of the road. And, as the warm rays of dawn turned the cobalt sky pink, we could see smoke rising intermittently from a clearing, or a crook-backed woman walking to fetch water.

The Land Rover dropped us at the vegetable market of Kenema. Oswaldo bought a cucumber, cut it into slices, and squeezed the juice of a lime onto the pieces. It was a refreshing breakfast. The market was still being set up. A selection of unusual roots and berries were displayed in round wicker baskets. Each basket was minded by a woman with a head scarf — who chattered in friendly competition about the day's business. Oswaldo led me to the bus stand as if he had been there before. He had a very good sense of direction but, when I complimented him, he just laughed his usual three times.

A yellow Peugeot 504 was filling up with passengers. In fact, it already seemed full. Ten people, a nanny goat, a large quantity of baggage, and a baby girl in the arms of her mother, were already aboard. The driver assured us that his vehicle was bound for Monrovia and there was plenty of room for two more. We clambered onto the back seat. The goat was passed onto Oswaldo's lap. The baby was handed to me by its mother, who was sitting on my right.

We set off. The communal taxi stalled four times because it was too heavy to move. The driver pumped the accelerator until the engine sounded like a dragon roaring. Only then did the wheels begin to move. The driver hooted with joy and the 504 slunk its way along the craggy dust track towards Monrovia.

Oswaldo squeezed hold of the goat as the front right wheel plunged into a deep hole. Screams of panic followed, and the goat, which was bleating in terror, passed water profusely over Oswaldo's red jeans. The liquid soaked down onto the plastic seat and seeped under my thighs. Looks of silent misery passed between us.

A dust storm filled the car. Someone made the mistake of opening windows to release the grit. I chewed on the particles. When the animal began to choke violently, Oswaldo handed it firmly to the woman beside me. She was more willing to hold the brown goat than her own tiny infant.

The baby had begun to sweat tremendously. I pointed this out to the mother but she just shrugged her shoulders. Drawing in a monstrous breath, the infant promptly spewed the contents of its stomach over my chest and lap. It mixed with the piddle and an offensive odour penetrated the innermost reaches of the cabin. The mother caught me in an angry stare and, in the confined space, managed to turn away in disgust. All the other passengers refused to hold the child.

Four hours passed and all the initial feelings of embarking on an adventure had drained away. Arms and even toes poked about in the cab, hoping for another millimetre of space. The only breaks in routine were the strip-searches which took place at every checkpoint at least twice an hour. Twisted limbs unfurled themselves on the ground, like butterflies breaking from their cocoons.

Each passenger was led into a bamboo stall, where they removed their clothes. Anything which the soldiers thought to be contraband was confiscated. In one of the earlier searches I found a Kalashnikov AK-47 pointing at my chest. Its owner was a boy of about sixteen. He calmly removed my watch and put it on his own wrist. It did not seem to be a subversive item to me. So I asked politely for it back. Pushing the barrel of the AK-47 closer to my heart, the boy in fatigues replied:

'It is *my* watch now.'

The saliva in my mouth was thick, like spaghetti. Before even trying to spit, I had to cut what felt like strands of it with the edges of my incisors. Oswaldo's trilby had gone, through pollution, dust and dirt, from dark brown to a shade of light tan. He looked very miserable. We jolted along on a track whose undulations were surely too extensive to be natural. Oswaldo suddenly gave out an unnatural, throaty laugh. Wriggling my left hand free, I manoeuvred it to pat him reassuringly on the shoulder. He was clearly beginning to crack.

At that moment the Peugeot 504 came to an abrupt stop. A soldier was waving in the road. We all trooped out. The goat and baby were passed from hand to hand and laid down on the grass. A very stern-looking major strutted up and gave orders that all belongings were to be vigorously searched. Parcels were unwrapped for the hundredth time and even shoes were removed. The major pointed to the car, and two young soldiers ripped out the back seats. We heard shouts as one of the lads ran to the officer with something wrapped in a cloth. All the passengers froze. The major ripped the cloth away to reveal a wad of US dollars and a large nugget of gold. The driver was seized and put in a makeshift bamboo cell.

Another man confessed that the money and gold belonged to him.

Oswaldo and I sat quietly awaiting the verdict. The officer announced that the smuggler and the driver had been arrested and the vehicle detained. Neither vehicle nor driver could be released as they had been abetting the smuggler. The major began to interrogate the two guilty men. It was then that an albino who spoke excellent English sidled up to us. He was the teacher of the local school.

Word had spread fast that two foreigners were visiting. We agreed that we were foreigners who were, in a broad manner of speaking, *visiting* the village. The albino bowed deeply and asked with ornate courtesy if we would come and talk to his pupils. Before I knew it, Oswaldo and I had jumped across a ditch and were in front of a class of maybe twenty young children.

A mouse was scuttling about in a cage in one corner of the classroom. The teacher introduced us to his students and said that we had come especially from far away to teach them. Oswaldo began a very long and serious lecture about Patagonia, the politics and tribulations of its culture and people. The children stared up blankly in silence. Oswaldo was thrilled at the opportunity of having a captive audience. It was a perfect therapy for him after the horrors of the drive.

The albino teacher told his pupils to sing the school song. They stood up and a chorus of shrill voices ran around the room.

'We have a problem here,' began the master as the children sang. 'You see we can't get the books and pens that schools in the cities can. At the moment we only have three pens for the whole class. I spend much time getting the children to learn the lessons by heart because they shall not forget them that way.'

He was a very polite and dedicated man.

Oswaldo dug deeply into the back pocket of his jeans. He pulled out the piece of white chalk and the ballpoint pen from Blackpool that the English woman had given him. I rummaged in my saddle-bags and found a couple of notepads. Oswaldo handed them to the albino.

'Dees are for yoo meester,' he said.

The teacher looked at the ground and said that he could not take them, especially as they had come from so far away. We insisted, and Oswaldo gave him his address in Patagonia. The educator exclaimed that we would always be welcome in his school, and that he would never forget the day we came.

Oswaldo and I returned to the taxi which still had not moved. By a great stroke of luck, it transpired that the major had once been to Banjul, where he had met Haji, the owner of the Hotel Apollo. Pleased that we shared a mutual acquaintance, he agreed to allow the driver to take us to Monrovia. Two soldiers would accompany us and afterwards would make sure that the driver returned to his bamboo cell. One of the soldiers managed to squeeze between the mother and me. The other clambered onto the roof and banged hard when he was secure.

Just before we set off, the twenty schoolchildren appeared, led by their teacher. The eldest of the pupils tapped on the window against which Oswaldo's face was lodged. The Patagonian wound down the glass and the boy passed him a brown mouse.

'We thank you, Sirs, for helping us . . . have this,' he said. 'We will not forget you in our village.'

The wheels turned again and the students waved as the yellow Peugeot 504 left a cloud of dust in its wake.

Twenty minutes before it was due to close for the night, we arrived at the Liberian border. Two piles of forms were counted out; one for Oswaldo and one for me. We scribbled answers to what seemed like unending sides of photocopied questions. With only five minutes left, we were less than halfway through: all the gaps had to be filled in full before we could leave Sierra Leone. It was clear that we would have to spend the night. But Oswaldo and I had no more leones left, and it was far too dangerous to risk exchanging foreign currency at the border on the black market. There was no official bureau-de-change.

A young Liberian man from Monrovia staggered about, clutching a bottle of whisky in one hand, and balancing a battered straw hat on his head. Oswaldo sidled up to him and began a short dissertation of the merits of Patagonian life and cuisine. The Monrovian winced and led us to his rented room which was in no-man's land.

A line of kiosks stretched out across the no-man's land. Liberia was about half a mile away. We were permitted to walk freely about the area, as all the soldiers and bureaucrats had gone to bed.

The Monrovian stumbled away into the moonless night with his bottle and straw hat, insisting that we take his bed. We explained that we had no leones with which to pay. But he was planning to spend the night drinking at a bar. Taking the lantern, he left us in the darkness.

Oswaldo always slept with his boots on. The left one was like a scabbard for the stiletto, which he would whip out at the first hint of trouble. We stretched out over the large bed.

A colony of insects lived in the bed. I could feel what seemed to be beetles crawling over my hands and face, searching for food, I supposed. It was almost comforting not being able to see anything in the blackness: I imagined that I was back with Osman and Prideep strolling up and down Marine Drive in Bombay. Then Blake's form appeared and I watched him sipping vodka and feeding chapaties to a line of greedy vultures.

Oswaldo began to snore.

Just as I was falling into a deep slumber, a thudding noise hurtled across the corrugated iron roof. Instinctively, Oswaldo and I clutched each other like children terrified of a ghost. When the sound stopped we let go, both trying to conceal our fear.

Then again came the sound of feet charging at speed across the metal roof. A cat seemed to be screaming — almost a human screech — as if it were being torn limb from limb. Oswaldo and I were paralysed with consternation. Our imaginations ran wild.

We huddled together, all the muscles in my back and my limbs were rigid as we waited for the morning to come.

The young Monrovian was sitting outside our room, eating breakfast. A pineapple and the pelt of some small mammal lay next to where he sat. Oswaldo asked what kind of skin it was. The youth replied:

'It's from a cat. A couple of rats killed it last night and ate it. I'm going to make a pouch from the skin.'

Oswaldo and I decided to risk entering Liberia without exit stamps from Sierra Leone: an offence said to be punishable by imprisonment. The mouse jostled about in Oswaldo's shirt pocket as we walked to Liberia. A boy on a bicycle pedalled up and said that the border guard wanted us to return to Sierra Leone. We strode on, in defiance of regulations.

At the Liberian border post we each handed five passport photographs to an officer's clerk. These were then stapled neatly into a large leatherbound tome. More forms were produced and we were led to a cell with smooth cement walls and floor.

I began to remove my clothes and empty out the contents of my saddle-bags. My toothpaste was squeezed from its tube. It was inspected for diamonds. The back of my camera was prised off with a coin and the film exposed to light. All potentially subversive pictures were thereby destroyed. Following this encounter I went to ridiculous lengths always to mail my films — and my notebooks — back to England after the last frame had been shot. Oswaldo thought my obsession was insane.

I stood motionless, no longer caring to what lengths the conscripts went to make me angry. Then one, the youngest, picked up my stick of anti-perspirant. He removed the lid and slowly began to wind up the deodorant. Several hundred American dollars were concealed under the stick of deodorant. The scent of sandalwood wafted about, and sweat began to drip into my eyes. The consequences of having undeclared money were very serious indeed. Unable to resist any longer, I grabbed the stick from the boy and rubbed it under my arms. The room was filled with broad smiles and laughter. Oswaldo and I were allowed to enter the Republic of Liberia.

Still there was no sign of the yellow Peugeot 504. We had

not got round to paying for the ride, which was to be expensive. Oswaldo suggested that we could hitch with one of the trucks going to the capital, thus escaping the misery of the yellow cab. We asked around for a ride. Four lorries were going to Monrovia but still had to clear their paperwork; so we sat about waiting for the first to negotiate the red tape.

A Chevrolet station-wagon pulled up. Clouds of exhaust fumes surrounded battered bodywork. In most other countries the vehicle would have been scrapped as a moving safety violation. I went up and asked if we could have a lift. A middle-aged man in a moth-eaten orange three piece suit said that it would be a pleasure for him to take us. We were to be his guests. His name was Daniel, but we were to call him 'Danny.'

Oswaldo and I lounged in the back seat. Danny's ten-year-old son and sister were also in the car. They had just come from Conakry, the capital of Guinea. The exhaust pipe of the vehicle led directly, curiously, into the car. Oswaldo and I covered our eyes and mouths with our shirt sleeves.

As soon as the windows were opened billows of black dust swept in and mixed with the carbon monoxide. For six miles the crumbling Chevy rumbled on. Then the fan-belt broke. An assortment of worn replacements were fetched from the boot. Danny fitted one in the extreme equatorial heat. Oswaldo and I were both parched and reeling.

Another half hour passed and there was a puncture. The heat was so tremendous that it was unbearable to leave the shade of the cabin to change the wheel. A bald spare was brought out by Danny's son and we secured it with a single wheel nut. I choked as my lungs filled with dust and exhaust gases. Then we began to move.

Oswaldo's once brilliantine-soaked hair was stiff with dust and sweat, standing straight up like a sheet of cardboard. He looked at me and tried to manage a smile. Time and again he and I scrabbled under the bonnet, fumbling with the engine, scraping our knuckles as we struggled to fit yet another fraying fan-belt. Neither of us had any knowledge of mechanics, but we were propelled by the desperation of survival.

Twenty miles from Monrovia, a line of metal spikes on a bar had been dragged into the road. Danny pulled over and we were made to enter an office where a man in civilian dress sat with his feet resting on the desk. He toyed with a hand-gun, caressing the trigger of what seemed to be a Colt .38.

Our belongings were brought and dropped on the desk. The figure shouted at me with arrogance.

'What's your purpose here?!'

'Sir, we are tourists in your country, we are travelling to Monrovia.'

'No tourists ever come here,' he exclaimed. 'You are obviously lying!'

Oswaldo and I drooped silently, too weak to argue. We would have pleaded anything, said anything, just to be allowed to go on our way.

Oswaldo's shirt pocket twitched. The man pointed to be shown what was hidden inside. A miniature nose probed for air. The Patagonian reached up and gently removed the brown mouse. The man behind the desk motioned to hold it. Oswaldo stretched out his hand. The official clasped the animal by the tail. Then, in one abrupt motion, he clubbed its head against the desk with the end of his revolver. A little blood spurted from the head, before he flung the body against the far wall, dead. Then he snickered sadistically. Oswaldo was close to tears. The rodent had been a symbol of the kindness of a simple people, amidst the barbarism of a totalitarian regime.

Just then, during the interrogation, came shouts from one of the soldiers outside. Danny was brought into the office, together with a box of medicines from his car. Oswaldo and I were ordered to leave. In the shade of a cement wall, Danny's son brought us each a plastic bag of water. The liquid was cool and tasted like nectar.

An hour passed and Danny came out of the office weeping.

A conscript announced that he was to be put in prison, as he did not have the correct paperwork for his medicines. He would be taken to Monrovia under escort to face trial. My friend and I would also be arrested if we interfered. We were to leave in the next vehicle that crossed the checkpoint. I pleaded with the official in charge, but he was ready to reinforce his tyrannical orders with force. Danny was taken away.

Oswaldo went back into the office. He stooped down on the smooth cement floor and picked up the carcass of his mouse. Then, behind the building, he dug a modest grave. The Patagonian crossed two twigs and placed them on the upturned top-soil.

As we stood in silent prayer I heard a car approaching. Oswaldo turned and pointed with the words, 'Khey meng look dare, man on yelloo roove!'

The Peugeot 504 taxi with the dust-covered conscript still clinging dutifully on top — brandishing a Kalashnikov — moved uneasily towards us. The car stopped and the goat leapt over the reluctant mother. I gawked at the sight of the group. All the passengers were now bedecked in gold, ivory and fine clothes. The transformation was unbelievable. It seemed incredible that the travellers could have concealed such items during the strip-searches and random checks. The driver was watched suspiciously as he went into a bush to relieve himself. Oswaldo asked if we could have our old places back, as the Chevy's owner had been imprisoned. It was agreed. Then, the soldier banged on the roof once more with the palm of his hand and we sped off towards Monrovia. Oswaldo and I were distraught at leaving Danny and his family stranded with the tyrant in civilian dress. We sat, brooding in silence, counting the minutes until we reached the war-ravaged capital.

The contents of the yellow Peugeot 504 piled out at the Disco Hotel, in a rather rough district of Monrovia. Oswaldo took the twelve-inch stiletto from his boot and stuffed it up his sleeve. He led me away from the yellow Peugeot and its soldier, sick baby, goat — which had gone into labour — and a quantity of luggage which could have sunk a ship.

Although weak and exhausted, we had been hardened by the experience of the last two days. Oswaldo's stride was longer than usual, he chewed at the inside of his cheek and scowled at all he saw in a bitter and twisted manner. I had not seen this side of the Patagonian before. No longer did he laugh or fool about. The murder of his mouse and the imprisonment of an innocent man had affected the South American deeply.

Through a series of complicated international banking transactions, Oswaldo had managed to have western hard currency sent from his village in Patagonia to a bank in Monrovia. The financial situation in Liberia was quite bizarre. United States dollar bills were the legal tender of the country. Instead of incinerating them, the United States sent worn-out dollar bills to Liberia. A shortage of notes prompted the Liberian government to mint its own dollar tender, with the same theoretical value as the American originals. But the black market value for the genuine American notes was much higher.

Liberia's civil war devastated the capital city and much of the countryside. The signs of combat were all around. It often happens in Africa that an unpopular president is butchered or forced to flee as his regime is toppled and replaced by another. Samuel Doe, the previous president, who had lost the battle to keep his position, had allegedly had his ears chopped off by the forces which overthrew him.

Two men were wrestling on the stairs of Maxim's Hotel. They seemed to have no intention of moving until one had fallen to the bottom. We clambered over them and found the manager holding out a key to the best room. Oswaldo snatched it as if it had been stolen from him in the first place. My clothes had been bonded to my skin with layers of black dirt. I peeled the filthy socks from my feet.

Oswaldo leapt into the shower, and cackled so long and loudly with zest when hot water hit his back, that the landlord came to see what the fuss was about. I asked him to bring a couple of towels, as none had been provided. He went away. An hour passed. Oswaldo had sung many a Patagonian ballad; I was getting impatient to get clean, too. Another hour passed. I hammered at the bathroom door. Oswaldo had begun to belt out his favourite Argentine saga — 'The Life of Martin Fierro.'

Still there was no sign of the towels, so I shouted down the corridor. A faint cry radiated from some back room from which there came a distinct smell of burning.

A fist pounded at the door: I walked over and opened it, expecting to be handed two clean towels. The manager's head was servilely bent at right angles to my stomach. There was no sign of the towels. Instead, a plate was pushed at me: on it were the charred embers of something which had caught fire. The manager gasped,

'Here's your toast, Sir.'

At last, I forced the Patagonian from the bathroom and I took a shower.

Oswaldo turned his red jeans inside out and put them on. We went out into the town to eat. Our stomachs had almost forgotten the concept of digestion. The thought of mountains of food had kept us going since Freetown. Oswaldo pulled the collar of his shirt closer to his neck and we entered an elegant Lebanese restaurant. Monrovia has been dominated economically for many years by the Lebanese community.

A menu was produced and Oswaldo waved it aside. The waiter looked displeased. I, too, was surprised.

'Sir, are you here to eat something?'

'Meng . . .'

'Yes Sir?'

'Breeng one of evryting!'

The mad Patagonian looked at me for approval and I nodded.

He laughed three times and I knew that everything was back to normal.

Kebabs, pizza, sirloin steaks and strawberry milkshakes were shuttled to our table by a troop of waiters. The Patagonian took alternate bites of each succulent dish. Osman would have approved.

At the next table sat a tall man with a thick black beard and Mediterranean looks, dressed in a cream gaberdine suit. He was laughing at our extravagance. Oswaldo invited him over to join us. The figure stood up and walked over. His fingers, neck and wrists were enveloped in pieces of gold jewellery. The clasps and bracelets jingled as he sat. He spoke through a New York accent.

'I'm Jacques,' he said.

'It's nice to meet you; are you just passing through like us?' I asked.

'No, I've been living here a few years. If I can stand the place I'll stay a while longer.'

'Are you in business?' I inquired; he looked as if he was a successful man.

'Yeah, you might say that,' he murmured, 'I'm in metals.'

'Any in particular?'

'Yes,' said Jacques as he paused to sip a drink, 'Gold.'

He picked a Kent cigarette from a soft packet and lit it with a gold lighter which I admired:

'It's a Bic fifty-cent lighter. I made a cover in 18 carat gold. Passes the time, but I'm really getting fed up with it here.'

'Where do you get the gold from?' I asked.

'I go into the bush, three or four days' trip. Buy it there. Then I bring it back to Monrovia and melt it into ingots. Why don't you guys come around tomorrow? I'm melting in the morning.'

Placing a cream business card on the table, he sauntered off.

My stomach had surely shrunk. It felt as if food was stacked up my oesophagus, waiting to be digested. Oswaldo ploughed on. Sweat was dripping into his eyes and mixing with the tears which were pouring down his face. His greed had transcended the pain barrier. His fork was raised from the plate, his eyes spun, and he moaned, 'Just one udder mouf meng!'

Oswaldo was unable to sleep all night. His indigestion was very bad: he ran hunched to the bathroom time and again and groaned with self-pity.

Next morning we went to meet Jacques. His office was on the third floor of a modern apartment block. Security cameras moved about like eyes on stalks when I pressed the bell-push.

Jacques was berating a young African who stood in front of his desk, staring blankly. The young man left.

'What's dat probleng?' Oswaldo asked.

'This city is driving me crazy!' yelled Jacques. 'I went back to the States for one week. Just one damn week, that's all. When I came back not only had my car been stolen, but my safe had knife marks in it and my partner had withdrawn a hundred thousand dollars from my account and fled. It's really beginning to get on my nerves.'

We went into a sealed-off room. Inside was a workbench and a small furnace. Jacques rotated dials and turned off the gas. What looked like a cake tin was carefully slid from the fire. When it had cooled, he tapped out a shiny brick of metal. It was solid gold. My eyes met Oswaldo's. There was no need to speak, the dilation of our pupils must have said more than words.

Jacques seemed to be the sort of man to whom one could talk at ease. He would listen and give encouragement if he thought it necessary. Oswaldo crouched over the gold ingot in the work room: he had evidently fallen in love with the substance. I sat with Jacques in his office and told him about the ceremony with Max's Babalawo. Then I began to explain to him about my interest in the Gonds and Gondwanaland.

He, too, had read about Gondwanaland and had been enthralled. He spoke of a tribe, believed to exist in Central Africa, said to be related to the Gond people of India.

'They are thought,' began Jacques, 'to live in Zaire, on the east side of the country: in the very heart of what was once Gondwanaland.'

'Where do they live, exactly?'

'At the summit of the Nyiragongo volcano.'

The idea of venturing to the very centre of Gondwanaland suddenly seemed important, as if the quest might provide information until now unknown.

A people related to the Gonds, could that really be true? It seemed severely implausible, especially as man had not appeared until millions of years after the continents had separated, about 45 million years ago.

But Blake had spoken of Macumba: whose magical arts had been influenced by the peoples of Africa and India . . . perhaps there had been an ancient affinity — impalpable and not time-bound — between all Gondwanaland's people. Perhaps a sister tribe to the Gonds did exist: the Nyiragongo seemed a good place to look.

Wresting the block of gold from Oswaldo's clenched fingers, I began to lead him away. As we were leaving, I turned to thank Jacques. He lit a Kent cigarette and inhaled.

'Fellas,' he said 'go to Zaire, climb the Nyiragongo and breathe deeply, for you will be standing at the core of Gondwanaland.'

Oswaldo agreed to accompany me to Zaire as long as I would promise him it lay to the east. Geography was not his strong point, Patagonia's confines were the extent of his knowledge: the rest of the world was to be discovered on his great adventure. He also made me swear a solemn oath that I would avoid all contact with the dark arts of local magic. I gave my word. Then I went back to the hotel to take a nap, while Oswaldo went off to tell the travel agent all about the tourist trade in his native Patagonia. One of his cousins there had requested that he drum up business wherever possible. I had suggested that there might be a lack of Liberians with the will and finances to patronise his cousin's tourist lodgings. He had looked me sternly in the eye and had said,

'Are yoo crazee?! Peeple loove Patagonia!'

As I lay on my bed dreaming of lost tribes and volcanoes, Oswaldo burst in and said with zest:

'Khey chappy! I ordered us tomorroow to Zaire. Flighting ees at six afternoons.'

Oswaldo's first trip in an aeroplane had filled him with a new kind of excitement: one that he wanted to relive. He had developed a passion for flight, and insisted that all journeys that could be done by air, were done by air.

CHAPTER 10

My Name is Zakaria

Called their wives, and lit some torches,
Blazing torches made of flax-stalks;
Played their horrid game of marbles
With the bored-out eyes of Lingo.

Two soldiers had taken off their jackets and were smashing at a man's body and skull with the butts of their rifles. The sound of bone meeting wood mixed with the gasps of the victim. He did not cry out, but took the blows passively.

I wondered if such sights would be commonplace in Zaire.

Oswaldo and I were standing outside the airport at Goma, waiting for a taxi. Air Zaire was relaxed about scheduling. Timetables had not existed and we were bundled aboard the first plane leaving Kinshasa, the capital, having flown there direct from Monrovia. Oswaldo wanted nothing more of cities; we were both inspired to get out into the jungles of Zaire. I longed to walk at the heart of Gondwanaland.

The ticket agent had seemed to think that everywhere was the same away from Kinshasa, for he handed us each blank tickets and ordered us to stand in a line.

So we found ourselves on the eastern edge of Zaire, in Goma, a city on the border with Rwanda. It had been an enormous stroke of luck. For Goma was the nearest major town to our destination: the fabled Nyiragongo volcano.

After an hour of hanging about a soldier moved us on. He said that in Goma there were no taxis, and if we loitered we would be arrested. Noting his unhealthy interest in my camera, I grabbed my saddle-bags and we started to walk into the town.

We passed some children who were sitting on engine blocks,

their faces devoid of all youthful animation. And, as the infants lingered glumly, the adults stared at us with tortured, transfixed expressions — as if there was nothing to look forward to. No one smiled. No one laughed — for both, like comfort, are luxuries.

A stretch Mercedes passed us at high speed — gliding through the slums from the airport — towards the town. The vehicle seemed alien: almost like a spaceship, from some development of the future, and a world away. Gaping as if it had been a vision, we continued on the long walk into Goma.

Oswaldo perked up when he saw the discotheque, optimistically called *La Planète*. Above it there were rooms for hire. Before I had a chance to object, I found that I was sharing a room with Oswaldo, and several hundred assorted beetles. Directly below the room was a throbbing box filled with sinister sounds, and with dense red revolving lights.

We went down from our room into the red glare. There, in the vibrating disco, sat two western girls, their faces pocked with mini-craters from chafed mosquito bites. They were aid workers from Finland. Oswaldo danced with the thinner of the two. He pulled her close to his chest and she twitched with pleasure. Her friend was called Roxanne. All she was interested in, I soon learned, was fantasising about food and drink.

After two years in the Kivu region she had almost forgotten her native diet. She edged closer to me and put her hand on my thigh. I went to the drinks' counter and brought her a large brown bottle of *Primus* lager. She knocked back the beer in a couple of giant gulps. Then she remembered the conversation and began to speak enthusiastically of the taste of caterpillars and locusts.

'What do they really taste like?' I asked.

'Caterpillars are a bit like eating dust, but with a few wild herbs they're not bad at all.'

After some time, having managed to escape the clutches of

Roxanne, I clambered back to the room. A woman was lying naked on the bed, her hair twisted in numerous individual short spiky plaits, which radiated from her scalp like antennae. A man was stretched out on top of her. Employing basic sign language, I tried to make it clear that my friend Oswaldo and I had hired the room for the night: and that I was now ready to go to bed. The man cursed in Lingala, as the couple stumbled downstairs towards the throbbing redness of the disco.

Doors slammed all night and still there was no sign of Oswaldo. Franco's music — he was the most famous Zairean musician — made the walls vibrate until half-past three. Next morning the room shook with banging. Oswaldo was taking off his jeans, but was so drunk that he had forgotten to remove his boots first.

When the morning sun streamed into the room, the first thing I focused on was six legs. One pair were much smaller than the rest. My eyes moved up the bodies which ran in the same direction: each was topped with a groaning, moaning, very unhappy head.

Getting to my feet, I kicked Oswaldo, scolding him like a mother whose daughter had been out all night:

'What the hell time did you come back, and who the hell are your new friends?'

Oswaldo did not move. He was doubtless hoping that I would think he was dead and leave him alone.

A huge chicken was pecking at crumbs on the floor: a long cotton string dangled from its leg. The body in the middle turned, a mop of blond beard covered its face like a Balaclava. With a pained expression, he put out a hand, and croaked:

'Hey man, my name is Zakaria, but you can call me Zak.' With that he collapsed into a stupor once again.

Opposite La Planète there was a Belgian delicatessen, where a deliciously fresh croissant and a cup of aromatic coffee were the breakfast placed in front of me. A photograph of Zaire's ruler stared down from the wall. I had read about this man.

He had made the news in the West when he had removed crucifixes from churches and replaced them with portraits of himself. His palaces were said to be spread throughout the country. It all seemed quite astonishing, particularly as he had once been an ordinary soldier, named Joseph Desiré. That was before he changed his name to Mobutu Sese Seko Kuku Ngbeandu Wa Za Banga. He had assumed control by coup d'état in 1965.

The delicatessen's owner was one of the last colonials to have braved the uprisings following independence and the authoritarian regime of Mobutu. He changed some dollars for me, unofficially. The local notes, all bearing Mobutu's grin with leopardskin cap, were of several different sizes. Even bills of the same value varied in size. The Belgian said it was because of the shortage of paper recently.

At La Planète, the huddle of legs began to untangle themselves and their owners attempted uneasily to stand. Zak pulled up the boy — who was about nine and had a terrible hangover. His name was Marcus.

'Well guys,' began Zak in a drawl, 'thanks for the floor space, that was a rad night. D'you have plans today?'

'Yes,' I said, 'we're off to climb the Nyiragongo volcano. It's a very special, international scientific expedition.'

Oswaldo had been leaping about since he had heard about the Nyiragongo and its significance: he loved volcanoes.

'Che!' he cried out, 'Can Zake came claymeng vocannow? Pleeese che.'

I muttered that Zak and Marcus could tag along if they would aid the expedition in every way possible. They promised to do so.

Marcus grabbed up the chicken. We left La Planète and started out of Goma, hoping for a truck to pick us up. Oswaldo and I were laden with our belongings. I would always keep my saddle-bags nearby, even though at times they could be inconvenient. Various hardened travellers had cautioned me never to leave my possessions alone for a moment in Africa. I noticed that they generally travelled by car. Some had porters to carry the baggage. None had ancient saddle-bags.

A massive sculpted hand — clutching a burning torch — sprang forth from a triangle of white cement like Excalibur: the symbol of Mobutu's tyranny. We tiptoed past.

The Nyiragongo volcano had apparently last erupted in 1977, sending a three metre high wall of lava towards Goma and forcing the townspeople to flee into Rwanda. Oswaldo spluttered all he knew about erupting volcanoes: he had once done a school project on *Parangaricutiro*, a village covered by the erupting lava of the Paricutin volcano in Mexico.

Marcus was a peculiar boy: he chain-smoked lumps of black tobacco which he rolled in broad green leaves. He never said anything, just ambled along behind the rest of us, pulling at the string to make his chicken hurry. I asked Zak if Marcus spoke English. He replied:

'Man, he don't speak nothin. He was hexed as a baby . . . best dude I ever knew.'

I wondered how Zak had found out that Marcus had been bewitched, if they were unable to communicate in speech: indeed, how did any one know to call him Marcus? But it would have been rude, somehow, to have asked.

Zak, who came from Seattle, had played ice-hockey for Washington State. His body was muscular and stocky, and his feet were size thirteen: perfect for the world of professional ice-hockey. Zak had a set of crude false teeth — many of his own teeth had been knocked out in hockey matches. He would remove the dentures from time to time and put them in his jeans pocket. 'They're a bit too big,' he mumbled, as he carried on chatting. His stories of players having fingers sliced off with skates and limbs gashed, made Oswaldo and me reel in abhorrence.

'Zak, what exactly brought you to Zaire?' I asked, for it seemed curious that an ice-hockey star should be attracted to Central Africa.

'Well,' he said slowly, 'there is a reason.'

'What is it?' I probed inquisitively.

'*Mokele-Mbembe*,' he said.

'What on earth is that?'

'It's supposed to exist in the most remote parts of the jungle, where it lives in caves and on the banks of rivers.'

'But *what* exactly is it like?'

'Its body is said to be as large as an elephant's; some say it has a giant horn mounted on its nose; its neck is long and muscular, and the tail is like that of an alligator. It can live on the land or in water, and its a kinda greyish-brown colour and about thirty feet long.'

'Deenosaw!' said Oswaldo firmly, wiggling about.

'Yeah man, it's a kinda dinosaur. I came here to track it. No one from the West has ever positively seen one. I figured if I hung out here long enough I'd eventually bump into a specimen.'

'Searching for Mokele has not been easy,' said Zak pensively.

'Why soo hard, amigo?' asked the Patagonian.

'Well,' said Zak candidly, 'there's an old pygmy myth which makes things a bit tricky.'

'What do the pygmies say?' I inquired.

'They say that if you see Mokele-Mbembe and tell of it, you will die a horrible and agonising death . . . so getting witnesses to step forward has been hindered.'

'Is this the precise area it's supposed to be living?' I asked.

'Not exactly,' began Zak, 'it's thought to exist mainly around the Mainyu river over in Cameroon.'

'Did you go and look over there already?'

'Yup.'

'How long did you stick it out?'

'Eighteen months,' said Zak, 'I guess we just never bumped into each other over there . . . so I came to this part of the jungle. I like it here.'

Maybe, I mused, Zak had seen the legendary creature already, but was gagged by the peril of the pygmy myth.

After we had walked for an hour, a petrol tanker rolled along. Zak jumped into the road and the driver slammed on the brakes.

'Yo man, we need to go to the Nyiragongo! You dig?'

The African driver, who was recovering from the whiplash of the emergency stop, threw up his arms and said, 'Quoi?'

'Hey man I don't speak ya language, you speak American?'

The driver spat. Oswaldo blushed and asked in his own brand of French if the vehicle was going towards the Nyiragongo. It was. Although Zak had spent such a long time searching for the mysterious Mokele-Mbembe, he had not mastered any Central African dialects, let alone French. The driver motioned us to climb aboard. We jumped up onto the slippery tanker and clung on as it squirmed between deep pot-holes towards our goal. Near to Kibati, on the Rutshuru Road, we descended.

Out of the jungle undergrowth rose the steep slopes of the Nyiragongo. A sense of primeval desertion surrounded the remote peak: this was the very centre of Gondwanaland.

As we stood in awe and breathed in deeply, I could taste the sulphur and vapours on my tongue. A silence, the like of which I had never before known, surrounded us. Everything was still, almost as if in respect for this quintessential form. Torrential rain began to pour from the sky. Yet, instead of taking cover, we all stood in wonder and felt strangely affected.

A boy wearing purple plastic shoes appeared from nowhere, a banana leaf shading his head. He could take us to the top for a few zaires. Oswaldo handed him a note and he led the way. As we climbed higher up the thin mud path, the terrain changed in density to a lighter mixture of ferns and shrubs. Marcus choked now and then and exhaled black smoke in time with his steps. Steam sprang from fissures on either side of the track. And the stench of sulphur was all around.

After about five hours of climbing we reached the cloud level. It was like walking into a wet white sheet. Zak sang hockey songs, with Oswaldo improvising, as the child in purple plastic slippers leapt from crag to crag ahead of the group. He turned to Marcus and asked him a question in Lingala. Marcus said nothing, as usual, but looked at the sky and put his left hand on the back of his neck. The other boy nodded. Whenever anyone asked Marcus a question, whether in Lingala or French, he did this. It seemed to make perfect sense to all Zairean people.

The enormous chicken squawked and stopped to peck at the mud. I wondered if it was the first domestic fowl ever to have ascended the Nyiragongo.

By the time we reached the layer of solidified larva, Zak was staggering along with Oswaldo stretched across his arms. There was still no sign of the Gonds' sister tribe. Oswaldo moaned in Spanish the words from *La Cucaracha* that there was no way he could walk another step. The boy in purple plastic shoes looked round, surprise on his face that we could have been afflicted so easily with such exhaustion.

Suddenly, a bushy red beard pushed out of the apparently virgin undergrowth. It was attached to the face of a massive Australian. He had ferns tied to his feet and was carrying a banana leaf on his head. His name, he informed us, was Howard.

'G'day sport! What's new from the old country?' he asked me.

I replied that as far as I knew everything was fine. Pulling a bottle of Primus lager from his belt, he bit off the top, and indicated that it should be passed around. Marcus' eyes lit up. He snatched the brown glass bottle and gulped down the contents in five seconds flat. Howard looked sad that a minor should have already taken such a liking to drink. I asked Howard what he was doing in Zaire.

'Well, things in Brisbane were down, really down. Felt it was time to chuck in the job and go walkabout.'

'What did you do in Australia?' I asked.

'I was a computer systems analyst.' He chuckled.

There was something I had to know. Plucking up courage, I put the question bluntly,

'Howard, please tell me why you're wearing ferns on your feet and a banana leaf on your head.'

He looked at me as if I was absolutely insane: as if I were enquiring why birds fly. He shook his head slowly and said,

'Don't you know?'

Then he walked off into the undergrowth again.

Zaire had a strange quality which, however unpleasant the conditions, made it assuredly one of the most enchanted places. Completely unexpected things would happen. I had been guilty of thinking like a westerner when challenging the reasons for Howard's appearance. The Australian had striven to cast away these obstacles of thought — leaving behind the life and mentality of a systems analyst — to attain salvation in the Zairean rain forest.

The longer I stayed in Zaire, the more outlandish seemed the events which took place, and the more I began to understand the limitations of my knowledge of people. Real people.

The boy in purple plastic shoes shouted out. We had reached the crater. There was no one about. Perhaps Jacques had been mistakenly informed about the Gonds' sister tribe; but what faced me now drove all thoughts of lost peoples from my mind.

I had expected the crater to be a few feet wide: nothing serious, just a gap. Rain plunged down as we sat on the rim, and stared in stupefaction at its enormousness. The Nyiragongo's diameter seemed to be several hundred metres across. Black cloud was mixed with the steam that bathed us. Oswaldo yelled louder than I had heard him yell before. No echo followed his roar and, in a remarkable way, his cries hardly dented the silence.

As he held my legs, I bent over the precipice. Exhilaration and a sense of absolute elation grasped me, as I peered down through an abyss of vapour. The Nyiragongo was alive — I was sure of it — and I could almost sense it breathing. Was this not Gondwanaland's core pulsing beneath me?

Our guide was growing nervous. It would soon be night and we should descend the volcano before darkness fell. Noises of the twilight had begun in the rain forest, as wild animals caught their evening prey and birds sang out in warning of our presence.

Oswaldo, Zak, Marcus, the chicken and I reached the road and started to walk towards Goma. An hour later there was still no sign of a car. At ten P.M., the whine of an engine was heard, then headlights appeared, and a small white Renault came to a halt just in front of us. The driver was Belgian. A doctor — going to a patient in a village halfway to Goma — he was willing to take us to the crossroads where he had to turn off.

The old settler chatted away in excellent English about the days before African rule.

'I remember when there was a dying man at the top of the Nyiragongo,' he said. 'I had to climb up at night to save him. There was so much snow that we built an igloo on the summit to take shelter, as we couldn't move the patient for three days until more painkillers came.'

The doctor had been unable to readjust to his native country after living in Central Africa for so many years. I was beginning to understand the curious addictive force of Africa. The longer one stayed, the more dependent upon it one became.

At the crossroads we clambered out of the car. It hooted twice and drove away, leaving us in the middle of nowhere. Oswaldo switched on the penlite torch he always carried in case of an emergency. We walked for hours. Morale plummeted. Zak's ice-hockey jokes had been told and told again, and a steady stream of rain fell from the night sky. After a few miles we saw a side road that seemed as if it might lead off to a village.

By group decision we agreed to take a chance and venture down the track. Several miles later the road suddenly ran out, and a wall of jungle sprang from the ground in front. Maybe the track had been reclaimed by the jungle, or perhaps never finished. The rain fell harder and we assembled in a huddle. Marcus grasped the bedraggled chicken close to his chest for warmth and we each moaned in turn.

But in Zaire, when things were at their lowest ebb, something unusual always happened.

A pretty, teenage girl stepped out of the jungle ahead of us. I wondered for a moment if she was from the Gonds' sister tribe, but she did not resemble the Indian Gonds. Her hair was twined in hundreds of short antennae and her cheeks had dimples. We followed her into the undergrowth. It seemed as if we were entering an enchanted forest: each of us stepped cautiously with expectation.

The trees sprouted taller and thicker and the stars were hidden by their foliage. After an hour or so of trudging I began to fear a trap. Something or other, at any rate, was going to befall us.

Suddenly, Oswaldo stopped whining and stood motionless. Then Zak and Marcus froze, transfixed. I stared up at one of the most phenomenal sights I had ever seen: a chateau of typical European design stood squarely in front of us. Its reflection was visible, lit by the moon, in lake Kivu.

The girl shuffled towards it and we followed, each of us thunderstruck.

A figure, bent-over with age, moved towards us in the darkness. He looked even more shocked than we to meet like this. Addressing me in French, in an almost poetic tone, he said:

'You have returned! We have waited all these years. I knew that this night would come.'

Moving over to Zak, he hugged him with all the strength left in his frail arms. His wife — who was much younger — walked over, her eyes peering to focus on us. She put out her fingers to touch mine. The door of the chateau was unlocked with a great iron key and pushed open. As I tried to come to terms with the paradoxical circumstances of the night, we entered the building, guided by Oswaldo's penlight.

A hall led into a expansive living room: where original paintings hung on the walls and, enormous pieces of mahogany furniture stood about. A chandelier three feet across hung from the ceiling. Two tall glass doors led to the lake.

The man and his family, the remnant of its former staff, had been guardians of the property for many years. They had lived in the stables all this time. It was obvious that the colonials had left in a tremendous hurry. Many of their belongings and personal effects were spread randomly around the house. We lit candles and paraded about the rooms.

The main door swung open again; the girl brought in a bucket full of *songo*, boiled cassava, and *medeso*, black beans, as well as a jar of clean water. As we chewed on the cassava roots we heard a tapping noise. Oswaldo went to open the door.

The decrepit man shuffled in, bowed under the weight of a child who lay outstretched in his arms. The infant boy was placed carefully on the sofa. His forehead dripped with sweat . . . I suspected that he had malaria. Oswaldo fished some quinine tablets from his pack, crushed one, added water in the palm of his hand, and fed it to the child.

The guardian of the estate looked pleased with our attention and stuck his fingers down his trousers, pulling out a creased piece of paper. He handed it to Zak who unfolded the purple corners. It was so worn that it seemed more like cloth. Mobutu's face looked up from amongst the creases; it was a one-zaire note. Zak pressed it firmly back into the palm of the old gentleman, who stooped a little lower in respect.

Oswaldo carried the boy back out to the stables where the family insisted on huddling. They uttered blessings in Lingala and French and pulled socks over their hands, to keep warm.

Oswaldo made up the bed. Generations of moths had munched their way through the starched white sheets, the remains of which covered the great expanse of the black mahogany bed.

As the wind ripped across lake Kivu, eerie shadows played on the walls of the bedroom. Oswaldo, Zak, Marcus and I made excuses that for our safety we should all sleep in the same room. We lay in a line, with the hen at our feet.

Beams of yellow sunshine broke over the surface of the lake and lit up each of our faces in turn. The chicken scratched about, pecking for moths amongst the line of forty toes.

Rising before the others, I wandered out into the garden where newly-born gnats cavorted in the bright sunlight. It was only then that I understood the extent and grandeur of our lodgings.

Vines and untamed creepers concealed much of the stonework, their stems woven about the complicated architectural features. At one end of the chateau a tall lancet window looked out onto the jungle-fringed garden. Mossy tiles covered the roofs and a fine balustrade balcony was hidden beneath a carpet of green. A wrought-iron garden chair lay upturned and entombed in brambles. Pulling it out, I sat upon it in the middle of what must once have been a manicured lawn. My mind reeled at the vision, labour and expense of erecting a building like this in such a place — and having to flee it, perhaps at only a few minutes' notice.

As I sat there I suddenly felt ashamed at our intrusion. I tried to convince myself that we had had good enough reason to spend the night uninvited in someone else's home. It was easy to imagine a Belgian family taking tea on the lakeside lawn: nothing less than dangerous political developments could have caused them to decamp from such a paradise.

Back inside the house, my three companions were still fast asleep. I wandered into the drawing-room whose tall french windows looked out onto lake Kivu.

Sunlight streamed in as I perched on a faded beige chaise-longue. An object was poking out from under one of the cushions. Without thinking I reached to see what it was. My fingers sensed something and pulled out a small pink cloth doll, with a lopsided smile and long woollen brunette hair. Holding her on my palm, I suddenly felt despondent, for there was a sense of something tragic around me.

For a moment I had contemplated staying forever, but this was not *my* home: we had been privileged to be guests, and now we should leave.

The caretaker and his wife brought some *matoke*, cooked bananas, for our breakfast. Their child was feeling much better after the medicine. His fever had vanished. Saying how pleased I was, I explained that we would have to leave almost immediately. The man looked at his wife and she stared back at him and then at me.

'It is not possible: leaving? You have just arrived.'

His temples frowned with absolute disbelief, before continuing with the same dignity and respect,

'Are you going back to *l'autre coté*, the other side?'

I explained that we would indeed have to return there for a while.

'When will you come back from the other side?' asked the old woman.

'As soon as we can,' I replied.

The woman whispered close to her husband in Lingala. Her words were strung together like a rope of pearls, formed from the back of her mouth. When she had left, the man asked Marcus something in Lingala. As usual, he craned his neck back and put a hand behind it. The man nodded in agreement and his wife returned. She was clutching a baby, just a few months old.

Zak and Oswaldo went over and began to play with it. They were, in a flash, very paternally orientated.

The guardian of the estate took me aside from the baby and its admirers. As before, he addressed me in French:

'Monsieur, we are poor,' he said. 'Our youngest child, who lies there, is destined to have a simple life like ours. We want him to be educated and see wondrous things. Monsieur . . . will you take him to the *other side* and see that he is educated?'

I asked him to repeat his words three times to make sure that I understood the question. Each time he spoke, asking the favour, it hurt him more. It was as if I were torturing him, making him admit a mistake, a foul deed.

We stood together: he waited for my reply. I gazed out

through the long panes of glass to lake Kivu, which sprawled away from the bottom of the once-landscaped gardens. Such beauty enveloped the place that it seemed enchanted, as if by a spell. I thought back to the pollution of the West, the problems of its societies, and the misdeeds of educated men.

The guardian looked expectantly, his eyebrows knotted together and I addressed him.

'Where we come from there are bad men. They lie, they steal, they are discourteous; these are the values which they teach each other: even the educated, on the Other Side. Monsieur . . . we have come to *Zaire* to increase our own education. We shall return soon to our own countries, but we must return alone.'

We collected our belongings and walked into the hallway. Oswaldo first, then Zak, me, and lastly Marcus and his chicken. The old man and his wife embraced each of us in turn and seemed genuinely miserable about our leaving. Their teenage daughter appeared, with a clump of pink and white flowers. She handed them to Zak and he blushed. Oswaldo and I grunted disapprovingly and we moved out into the daylight.

It felt more as though we were leaving after a weekend with friends, perhaps in Sussex, than exiting a Belgian chateau somewhere in Zaire's jungle, on the banks of lake Kivu. Oswaldo turned to the old couple and told them in French that they were to live in the chateau from now on and not in the stables. Then he gave them his malaria tablets. The old concierge's black eyes twinkled with a childish delight; he thanked us all.

Zak looked sternly at Marcus and prodded him in the back. Marcus stepped forward, his arms outstretched towards the Zairean. His palms cupped his pet chicken with a string dangling from one ankle. The old man took the bird and thanked Marcus with feeling. We all knew that there was a severe lack of protein in the Kivu region and that the bird was destined for the pot. Marcus stuffed his right hand into one pocket and dug out a handful of wild seeds. He placed them in the guardian's palm and we began to walk up the steep bank to the road and let our more usual adventures begin once again.

* * *

Zak wanted to see gorillas. He carried on at length about how he was preparing to relinquish soon his long and tedious pursuit for the Mokele-Mbembe, and take up a more important and arduous quest. For the hex of the pygmies was impeding his progress. Zak intended to head for the Tarra river in Venezuela to stalk the *Ameranthropoides loysii*: the 'missing link'. The creature was named, so Zak recounted, after François de Loys, who — in 1920 — tracked then killed the only example known to exist. Zak wanted to begin his study with mountain gorillas which themselves had been thought to be fictitious until 1901. He said that it would be of great importance to gain an understanding into how Loys' man lived. Only when armed with such knowledge would his new quest be successful.

He took Oswaldo aside and got him fervid with the prospect of hacking through a jungle in search of primates. Then Oswaldo and he ambled over to convert me to the idea. They worked together like a pair of collies trying to trap a stray sheep. Finally I agreed that we would all go in search of gorillas. Where were they easiest to find? Zak, who knew all the answers, cleared his throat, swept the mop of yellow hair away from his eyes, and then began:

'National Volcano Park in Rwanda is where Dian Fossey studied groups of gorillas in their natural rain forest. There are seven extinct volcanoes in a line.'

'Vocannows!' screamed Oswaldo, enchanted at the idea of scaling another peak or two.

Zak continued, 'We can go to Bukavu, get visas and then cross into Rwanda. But it means we should go straight past Goma and on southwards. I know it's a hassle going right down to Bukavu, but it's the only place to get a Rwandan visa around here.'

It was agreed. Shortly afterwards we caught a lift in a blue and white pick-up truck that was heading all the way to Bukavu, a town situated almost squarely on the three borders of Zaire, Rwanda and Burundi. Getting the ride had been a considerable bonus. As we rattled along I mused that it must be fate's hand at work.

Eight enormous straw baskets filled with *tilapia*, a fish not unlike perch, were placed precariously upon our laps. A group of women with bright headscarves cackled in surprise at our discomfort. In Africa there is a total acceptance of circumstance. Comfort, and the very concept of it, is only appreciated when it has been experienced.

Marcus was sulking and pining deeply for his beloved chicken. The two had been inseparable. Visions of the bird being lowered head first into a cauldron — with a little water and seasoning — haunted us. I wondered for a moment if the little family realised that the chicken had climbed the Nyiragongo.

The haul of tilapia had been caught on lake Kivu and was now being taken southwards towards Burundi. The driver had heard that there was a shortage of food on the Zaire-Burundi border. Trouble with the engine of the pick-up had caused delay, and had led the fish to rot. For three days the tilapia had lain covered in the baskets whilst a mechanic tinkered under the bonnet of the vehicle. The stench of decomposing fish was nauseating. But the women, who chattered away in Lingala, seemed not to notice the pungent odour. Instead, they stopped gossiping every now and then to stare at us and cackle with toothless laughter.

It rained for much of the afternoon and the drops of water blinded us as the driver accelerated. By the time we reached Bukavu night had fallen. And the fish — which had been washed clean if not fresh by the rain — were ready to be sold. We stumbled away to find the cheapest part of town.

Zaire can be extremely expensive for foreigners. All the hotels were completely full; all, that is, except for the Hotel Joli Logi. As soon as I stepped inside the door I realised why it had been the last to attract guests.

Oswaldo and I shared one room, Marcus and Zak took another. Our room had no windows. Having signed the register, we were each handed a bucket for our natural functions.

Oswaldo and I would blink for a second and the wallpaper would appear to move. It was Bombay wallpaper all over again, or claustrophobia. The patterns slithered into each other and would occasionally, I could swear, spring up and flit about the bare light bulb. Forcing Oswaldo out of bed, we went out to explore.

Across from Hotel Joli Logi a single drum was beating. It managed to grasp a harmony of notes and complement a voice: the shrill voice of a male child who sang in perfect pitch.

Oswaldo had taken the stiletto from his boot, expecting trouble. Yet when we heard the voice he murmured that its purity would protect us. We stumbled over to the bar with its inevitable red light, from where the sounds radiated. Oswaldo pulled back a shawl at the entrance and we went in.

Bottles of Primus, with the large white insignium of Zaire painted across them, were held by all. Everyone was happy; women constantly burst out laughing and rocked about clutching at the brown bottles. Three tall men were dancing alone in the middle of the floor. They shook about with great dexterity in time with the drumbeats. Oswaldo and I fell back together, in surprise: for the three men were dancing on crutches. They had not a leg between them.

A woman the size of a walrus sidled across waiting to dance, her hands clenched around a bottle of Primus. Pulling me tightly to her chest, she jerked me about the room until, that is, she spotted Oswaldo. He was evidently more her type. Her eyes crossed with glee as she bounded over to pilot the Patagonian around the floor.

For the first time in Zaire I had seen people truly happy. There was still hope, still sincerity, amongst the people. The core was intact, only the government was rotten.

* * *

A visa more elaborate than any I had seen before was stamped into my passport. It bore out the theory that, in Africa, the smaller the country the bigger the visa. We rested for a day in Bukavu, a city that had been developed by the colonial-era Belgians and had begun to disintegrate since independence.

The city is not an African entity. Colonial settlements developed in sub-Saharan Africa, and in those all the drawbacks of western society were encased. In African tribal communities, many such problems do not occur. Bukavu had been left with a skeleton of paper-pushing systems and a token of administrative symmetry. But other than the physical infrastructure there was very little else. Abject poverty forced the majority of the inhabitants to occupy the city's sprawling slums.

Zak, Oswaldo, Marcus and I gathered our belongings and walked out of Bukavu towards Rwanda. The frontier was only a few miles distant. As we walked, a thousand people seethed forward in silence beside us. What seemed to be the whole population of Bukavu was moving out of town. They had been ordered to attend a political harangue. Each face was expressionless, each person stared blankly ahead as if hypnotised by a sinister force.

'Eets just lika Patagonia,' said Oswaldo, 'lika de festeeval vee doo in weenter.'

'You're from Patagonia?!' cried Zak, overjoyed to have met a native of the area.

'Yep!' replied Oswaldo.

'Man, you ever seen a *Megatherium*?' said Zak.

'Nope,' was the reply.

'What about a *Toxodont* or a *Glyptodon*? Man, you must have seen a Glyptodon!'

'Nope,' said Oswaldo blankly.

'What are all those things?' I asked.

'They're just the most incredible animals that a few select crypto-zoologists working in seclusion have reason to believe still exist . . . in Patagonia!'

'But *what* are they?' It seemed that I had asked this question before.

'A Megatherium was a kinda giant sloth, that walked about on its back legs, was about fifteen feet tall and had immense hooked claws; some say it was as big as an elephant and had the tail of a komodo dragon. The skeleton of one was found in the eighteenth century near Buenos Aires. There's no reason why it ever became extinct,' said Zak.

'Vat's *Tooxoodoont*?' murmured Oswaldo.

'Toxodonts were like huge rhinoceroses covered in coarse hair, they — and giant armadillos called Glyptodons — have been said to still thrive in the mountains of Patagonia.'

Oswaldo looked pleased that his homeland was famous for something of which he had not known. He turned to Zak and said,

'Zake, came to Patagonia and vee goo looking dem!'

Just before reaching Rwanda, we passed a stadium. The population of Bukavu had filled the rows of seats and were preparing for an address. A compulsory political rally was being held by one of Mobutu's men. We slipped away and entered a valley. Spanning the two hillsides was a great rusting iron bridge which had once been covered with ornate metalwork. Crossing from one side of the valley to the other, we stared back at Zaire. Marcus shook his head in ridicule at our visa stamps; as he was indigenous to the area he could walk straight across the border with no papers.

At the border post there was only one soldier. He had been deserted by his companions, who had left to drink beer. We chatted for a while as he toyed with the trigger of an

American-made assault rifle. The trigger finger's nail was chipped and broken, yet the others were neatly coated in a thick red nail varnish.

A rumbling of wheels upon the bridge made us turn: a black Mercedes with diplomatic markings pulled up. The soldier saluted. We stood and watched like a line of crows on a fence. The driver said that he was going to Kigali, the capital of Rwanda. Oswaldo stepped out of our line-up and asked politely if he could take our party to the capital: for a small consideration of course. The driver agreed, so long as we bought him beers along the way. His name was Ben. The soldier with the red nails waved his rifle in the air to bid us a safe trip and we began on the road to Kigali.

Our relief at leaving Zaire was like a force that united us all. It seemed almost as if a long, sustained war had suddenly been declared over. Travelling in uncertain circumstances has a way of binding one with another, forming lifelong friendships in a short time.

The road to Kigali was perfectly paved. There was not a single bump or pot-hole, and we glided along at great speed. Ben, who was an ambassador's chauffeur, got very drunk. He requested that we stop every few miles so that he might imbibe another bottle of beer. The purpose of his trip to Kigali was to gather items on the ambassadorial shopping list. Simple things like stationery, toiletries, processed cheese and chocolate, which were hard to get in the Kivu region of Zaire.

Rwanda is one of the smallest countries in mainland Africa. Its geography is hilly and it is covered in lush fields and woodland. The road wound through some of the most exquisite areas of Africa that I had seen.

Oswaldo and Marcus were thrilled to be riding in the luxury of a limousine. In Africa the concepts of comfort and travel are rarely synonymous. Travel usually implies being squashed up for hours or days on end, seeing more of the ear of the person next to you than the landscape outside.

Old ladies drew in smoke from wooden pipes and children waved as our vehicle passed. The scenes had the gentle contentment of a paradise: I was certain that the future of Rwanda would be one of harmonious prosperity. Yet, a short time after I left the small central African state, everything changed. An age-old tribal rift between the Hutu and the Tutsi tribes flared up once again, leaving many hundreds of thousands dead. The cattle herding Tutsi have been at odds with the Hutus — an agricultural people — for centuries. Although the carnage of the early 1990s might have ended, the rift itself has not.

* * *

Rick and Gracie Schmetman were standing in the middle of the road. Both had designer hairstyles, solid gold wrist-watches, and wore identical Vuarnet reflective sunglasses. I recognised them instantly as Californians, having spent time in their country.

Oswaldo was in an irascible mood. Our changed circumstances were not to his taste. He had developed, remarkably quickly, delusions of grandeur at having been transported in a Mercedes limousine. Ben dropped us on the road to Ruhengeri to await a ride to the Parc National des Volcans, where gorillas are native to the rain forest.

The couple from California saw us and waved. Unlike other Americans, West Coast folk are a breed of their own. Zak and I looked the other way, hoping that they were trying to attract a passing relative or long-lost friend. Oswaldo, however, stumbled over and introduced himself. Then the three came up to where Zak, Marcus and I were slouching.

'Oh my lord, isn't this wonderful? It's just so great,' announced Gracie, massaging her hand in mine.

Rick and she wore identical golden raincoats with transparent buttons. Oswaldo started to tell his new friends of his native land.

Rick suddenly froze, yelling:

'Gad, stop, stop, I must get this down!' He clicked his fingers and, in a trice, Gracie had brought out a stereo reel-to-reel recording machine. It had a microphone with an extra long lead.

'Testing, testing . . . Okay, now when I put my hand up like this you can start talking.'

Oswaldo nodded approvingly and Rick raised his hand.

The Patagonian had filled two long-playing tapes with such vital data as the sound of snow falling in his home village and his impersonations of a rough-riding gaucho, before a tractor and trailer appeared. It stopped, allowing us all to clamber aboard. Oswaldo's prattle continued; the more he was encouraged, the longer he could talk of his childhood and relatives back home.

Rick reloaded his pair of long-lens Nikons more than once with black and white film, clicking away at the new-born star.

Then the recording machine ran out of tape. It was returned to its case and I took the opportunity to ask what all this activity was for. Rick leant back on the side of the trailer and explained, 'Hey man, ya see my wife and I, that's Gracie over there . . .'

Gracie heard her name spoken and lifted her golden sleeve to wave with a clenched-face smile. 'We just flew in from Los Angeles to write a travel book.'

'Wow, that's really interesting. What's the central theme of the piece?' I asked.

'Well man . . .,' began Rick again, sweeping his head from left to right, as if to look around for lurking plagiarists, 'the book's going to be a conceptual dialogue if ya like about the world and inner empowerment. The theme will be space and its effect on society and social understanding of philosophical values as we know them.'

I nodded, with false studious attention.

'What makes my companion, Oswaldo, such a prized source of information?' I asked.

Rick thought hard for a moment. Then, with great deliberation, he said:

'You guys are special.'

'Thanks.'

'No,' continued the Californian, 'you guys are *really* special.' I could tell by the simplicity of his language that something had moved him deeply.

'Why's that?'

The socio-babble reasserted itself, with the effort to communicate: 'Because you represent the first perceived signs of a truly multi-racial societal state in Africa at this point in time! Boy, is this gonna rock them at the Department of Hinterland Studies!'

For some reason, Rick had decided that Oswaldo, Zak and I were indigenous to Rwanda. He was passionate about his task, and thrilled with the material he had collected so far: describing Oswaldo's incomprehensible monologues as 'pure gold dust!'

I hadn't been to California for nothing. 'Right on: I hear you — are you going to transcribe the tapes, Rick?' I asked.

'Yuh, you got it, you got it!' he yelled, working himself into a frenzy. 'We're gonna geta real African linguist back at UCLA to translate the little fella's words.'

I glanced at Oswaldo, who was ecstatic at finding himself the centre of a major anthropological study.

But something was obviously troubling Rick.

'There's one thing I have to know . . .' he blurted out all of a sudden. 'I can take the truth, I'm prepared!'

'Rick, what do you want to know?'

'Give it to me straight . . . I can take it straight!'

'Sure, I'll tell it to you straight,' I said.

'Is your friend there . . .' he said pointing to the Patagonian, 'really a pygmy?'

Confused at what to answer, I closed my eyes and nodded slowly.

Zak, who had noticed that I was at a loss for words, came to my rescue.

'Vertically challenged genetically,' he corrected. 'What're

you going to call the work, Rick?'

Rick and Gracie stiffened. They turned to each other with raised cheeks, each seeking approval from the other to divulge the secret name. Rick funnelled his hands round his mouth, and whispered:

'We're gonna call it . . . "WIDE"!'

* * *

We checked into a hostel at Ruhengeri which had six beds in one room. A large spider was embalming its prey above our heads. Rick took pictures with a powerful flash that he had attached to the body of his camera. I empathised with the spider for this intrusion of privacy; for wherever I went Rick and Gracie followed, taking copious notes on all I said and did. To my annoyance, they had found one last spool of recording tape. Marcus liked to watch the sprockets of the recorder turn round and round. He kept on signalling to Rick to turn the machine on, again and again. Rick was worried that the batteries would soon be exhausted; he fumbled in his shoulder bag and pulled out a round disc. It was a luminescent red yo-yo. He handed it to Marcus.

Plates of heavy black beans and carrots, served in a bright green sauce, were brought to the room by the proprietor's wife. Rick, who had made her stand against a white wall, blinded her, using his high-powered flash unit. She ran away blinking, making wailing noises, to her husband.

There was a fierce knocking at the door of the room. I opened it and the owner of the hostel barged in and grabbed Rick by the throat. Then he yelled in French that the Schmetmans were to leave immediately, and they were to hand over the film they had taken of his wife. Rick dropped the canister of film onto the paw-like palm, and he and Gracie gathered up their belongings. Euphoria replaced by despondency, they walked out into the night to find a new place to stay.

The spider, which had finished digesting all four legs of its dinner, seemed to peer down to see what had happened below. Silence surrounded us. In one corner Oswaldo was scratching away with a blunt pencil. He looked up.

'What are you writing, man?' asked Zak.

'Meng, dis mee travelling boooks.'

'Do you have a title?' I asked. Oswaldo covered the twisted pencil lines with his fingers and nodded.

'I calling eet "LOONG"!'

We walked out of Ruhengeri towards Africa's first national park, accompanied by the buzzing sound of Marcus' yo-yo running up and down its string.

Women were working in the fields, bending down and scything grass. One would sing, a scarf tied tightly about her head, as the others joined in with the chorus. A track led through meadows filled with chalky-white and yellow flowers.

The seven volcanoes of the national park suddenly came into view, protruding from the jungle like a line of camels' humps. Each was covered in a forest of trees and banana plants, which shrouded luxuriant vegetation of all kinds. One plant blended into the next. Many were bowed down under the weight of gigantic green and red fruit. We pressed on, high up into the groves of tall bamboo where the canopy was thick and became denser with each step.

A barefoot child appeared with a machete competently gripped in his hand. The machete was his stock-in-trade: he hacked through the stems, having offered to take us to where the gorillas were.

It began to rain. Some plants collected the water and stored it in their bowl-like leaves. Troops of monkeys swung from branch to branch, and birds called out warning of our arrival across the jungle.

Mountain gorillas are known for moving about one area in small groups, usually guarded by the dominant male, the

Silverback, who is said to have strength enough to tear a grown man limb from limb. As no one is ever quite sure where the gorillas are on any one day, it can take hours to locate them.

The boy with the machete cleaved a path just wide enough for us to ease our way through. A rhythm guided his blows, as he wielded the blade skilfully, chopping only what was necessary. We followed in single file; and behind the party the jungle closed in again, healing its wound.

The vegetation was denser than any I had seen before. One plant overlapped with another, creating an abundance of nature that seemed all but impossible for man to dominate.

Everything but ourselves was hidden as if in camouflage and blended perfectly into the green mixture. Dressed in the colours of bright synthetic dyes, we moved with great clumsiness through the habitat: totally intrusive outsiders. We had come from the complexity of the West: where one has to study for fifteen years merely to understand somthing of the society that it has created. Now back in the very belly of nature, from which our forebears emerged, we were uneasy as if all around us was an alien land.

After some time we reached a small opening where the bamboo stems had been broken away. Zak and Oswaldo sat down, as the boy with the machete pointed to the end of the clearing. A family of woolly black — almost human — forms were moving about. At first they looked to me like humans dressed in gorilla suits with hidden seams.

A female clutched her baby and rocked it up and down, another picked fleas from her behind with neat precision, using the very tips of her black nails. She radiated absolute satisfaction at ridding herself of the insects.

The male Silverback stamped around restlessly, as if he were waiting for the ladies to get ready to go out. Some other gorillas strolled about like a family on a spring afternoon at Brighton.

Then the male jumped to within six feet of where we stood. He peered: with a stare that seemed to pass right through us.

A glare ran across his face and his eyes were filled with tight round drops. Could these primates have been the original people of Gondwanaland? Perhaps to them the Gond tribe was related. As I stared and wondered many things it felt as if I was being reunited with a long-lost companion whom I had never really known.

Dian Fossey had befriended these creatures. One morning in December 1985 she was found with her skull split open: supposedly the work of poachers. My travels had begun to teach me of the irresponsibility of mankind. I had seen sights of destruction created as a by-product of one form of civilisation.

Ashtrays fashioned from gorillas' hands continue to be made: educated people pay for them. They will pay the price in the future. Man must realise that what he does today shapes the world that he will have to inhabit tomorrow.

The child with the machete led us back towards the edge of the forest. As he hopped through the tall bamboo, guiding us back to the main road, I wondered what would become of that place in his lifetime.

CHAPTER 11

In Search of the Source

'Eyes that look into the darkness,
Tell me where my Sixteen Scores are.'
But the cold stars, twinkling ever,
Said, 'Your Gonds we have not seen them.'

Four men with straight backs passed us and smiled. Each was holding a corpse's limb at shoulder height. The body was concealed under a blanket, except for the feet which poked out from under the covering, pointing downwards.

We continued back towards Ruhengeri which disclosed an assortment of characters in a circus-like procession. Boys with hoops played amongst the long stems of grass which engulfed the edges of the track. Towering trees, with wide green leaves and sprawling branches, gave some cover from the warm drops of rain. Then three more corpses with rigid toes were borne away towards the humpbacked range of volcanoes.

Rwanda, especially before the butchery of 1994's civil conflict, was an unusual country. It felt, somehow, more like an old-fashioned European principality than a remote Central African nation, struggling for development. It seemed inconceivable that such harmony should ever change, as it did so violently in the civil war of 1994. An enchanted place of hills and rolling meadows, it was the sort of domain one might dream of owning, ruling over as one's own kingdom. I began to understand an idea which had once been expounded to me: that presidents-for-life step into their fantasies, actually believing that the nation is their own property.

Marcus was very happy. He spent much of the time re-enacting movements of the gorillas with Zak. At night he would tie the shiny red yo-yo around his waist, lest it be stolen while he slept. It had taken the place of the chicken.

I had decided to go around Lake Victoria, through Uganda, towards Kenya. There were various reasons; not the least being that I yearned to complete my crossing of Gondwanaland's greatest central segment.

Oswaldo burbled that he wanted to track the source of the Nile, which runs from near Jinja right up to Egypt: one of the few rivers in the world to flow northwards. He had read his Bible. Since I had made him participate in a ju-ju rite, he insisted, he should be allowed to see where the Nile starts. The Nile after all, held the reeds where Moses was discovered hidden as a baby. In the knowledge that Oswaldo was from a religious family, I thought that accompanying him to the Nile's source might help him to get over the painful memory of the Babalawo and his Borfima.

A friend in Nairobi, the Kenyan capital, had asked me to pay him a visit. So Oswaldo would be my companion once again. He repeated twice:

'Vee go gooing veesiting, we go eest all the way.'

Zak and Marcus wanted to lurk a little longer in Rwanda's dense foliage. They escorted Oswaldo and me to the main road. We would hitch a ride to Kigali, the capital, situated just west of Rwanda's centre.

When a tractor pulled up, I threw my saddle-bags and Oswaldo's luggage aboard. Then the Patagonian and I turned to wish our companions farewell. But they had already gone.

* * *

When Oswaldo and I crossed the no-man's land into Uganda, I felt the same fear that I had experienced in Zaire.

The immigration men entered our names into a large leatherbound volume and asked politely if we were carrying pornography or explosives. Oswaldo shook his head and collected his kit together. The sky was black as if an artist had painted lines across it with a thick-tipped Chinese brush. Soldiers, no more than fourteen years of age, strutted up and down. Their camouflaged uniforms were belted with straps of hide. The trousers and tunic-cuffs were turned up several times whilst the boys waited to grow bigger.

A character who had a calculator and pencil stowed in his tangled mop of hair took my last Rwandese francs. He pulled out instruments and began to calculate with a wild enthusiasm. Having handed him only a few notes, I was given in return five wads of currency — as thick as bricks. The black-marketeer apologised that only the lowest denomination banknotes were available.

Oswaldo and I were stuffing the near-worthless piles of local currency into our pockets when we heard shouts from the checkpoint. An English-looking man climbed off an antique motor-cycle with a sidecar attached. He stood six foot five and was exceptionally thin. His face was clean-shaven and covered in freckles. The functionary took the man's British Passport and asked if he had either explosives or pornography. He had not. The aging black motorcycle was admired by a line of the teenage conscripts. Then, for the first time, the man turned to where Oswaldo and I were standing. I stopped in my tracks. He, too, looked startled. I walked over and greeted him. Oswaldo had no idea what was going on.

'His name is Denzil Fairfax,' I explained to the Argentine. 'We were at boarding school together in a remote part of England called Dorset. Denzil was my stripe.'

'Stripps?' said Oswaldo, 'Vat dese stripps?' Denzil answered in his low and patient voice, which seemed to hypnotise Oswaldo.

'A *Stripe* is a prefect, a person who is in charge of another.'

Memories of Denzil sitting on my head and throwing punches at my rib cage would always be vivid. The pain had been incidental, for the very fact that the Head of Rowing was reducing me to a pulp would do much for my image. Public schools are like that.

Denzil was on his way to Kampala. He had bought the old Triumph motorbike in Zaire for fifteen dollars and a pair of jeans. Before we had a moment to protest, Oswaldo and I were bundled aboard, and we were tearing around the pot-holes towards the Ugandan capital.

Oswaldo sat in the sidecar; he took my saddle-bags and held them on his lap. A peculiar exhilaration arose from moving so fast into a place so unknown.

Uganda's lush beauty surpassed any other I had seen on the African continent. Innumerable flowers of uncounted species filled one landscape after the next.

We stopped to look for petrol twice on the way to Kampala. It seemed as rare as gold. People had little use for cars, they just walked from one place to another. They had reverted to an almost feudal existence, having been continually beaten down by their presidents-for-life.

But at last the tyranny had ended and a just political regime reigned. It had replaced the same negative type of development as I had seen in Zaire. Only now was the country rebuilding itself, and people were trying to forget their sordid history. Roads had become overgrown, houses lay derelict. But the greatest tragedy was that a warm, hospitable people had become frightened.

The black machine arrived at Kampala as the sun was setting. We took one large room in a rambling hotel near the railway station. The manager showed us to the chamber with some pride. Mildew had until recently covered all four walls, but an industrious soul had systematically scraped it away — leaving only thin vertical lines of greenness which had been missed.

Oswaldo drew the curtains apart to inspect the view. A burst of high-velocity machine-gun fire had left a line of holes, the size of bottle tops, at eye level across the window pane.

Rolled-up sheets of paper plugged the holes. The manager winced, and Oswaldo closed the curtains gingerly, saying nothing.

Kampala had been a battle zone during the fight for supremacy in Uganda. Damage to the capital had been so extensive that years would pass before the scars of war could be erased. Many shop-fronts were still intact, but the shops themselves had been gutted and vandalised. Windows and walls were lavishly sprayed with bullet holes. Spent casings and shells lay about, serving as a reminder of what had passed. This debris surprised me, as the hostilities had in fact ceased some time before.

Amidst the turbulent years of destruction, sporadic periods of rebuilding had occurred. International organisations had left Kampala alone to solve its problems, with the street skirmishes and car bombs, withdrawing their wealth as they went.

Uganda's string of dictators was unequalled by any other African nation. The terror of Milton Obote, Idi Amin and others even became headline news in the West, as one after the other pursued his barbarous reign over the lush East African state.

Amin's coup in 1971 deposed Obote and began one of the most violent periods in all Africa's history. Hundreds of thousands of civilians were dead. The country was left economically destitute, and the people terrified of their master.

Amin forced the Indians to leave, seizing the billion dollars of investment they left behind. Nationalising all that Obote had left in private hands, he squandered the money. While the executions and torture continued, he foolishly invaded Tanzania, his East African neighbour.

Tanzania's unexpected counter-attack delivered a serious blow to Uganda, despite its Libyan military aid. Eventually Idi Amin fled into exile to Libya, before settling in Saudi Arabia. Then Obote returned and a new stage of the terror began.

Brigadier Basilio Okello ousted Obote in 1985, before handing over the presidency to Yoweri Museveni, who began working tirelessly to achieve reform. Museveni, throwing off western beliefs about multiparty states as more applicable to Europe, recognised the primacy of tribal affinities in his planning. He had candidates for parliament stand as independents, and brought members of various ethnic groups into his administration.

Denzil offered to take us to dinner at the Speke Hotel — named after the man famous for discovering the source of the Nile at Jinja. It amused me to hear that an Englishman could be credited with *finding* the origin of the river. As early as 150 AD the Greek astronomer Claudius Ptolemy wrote that the Nile's origin was amongst the Mountains of the Moon, in the Ruwenzori mountains, not so far to the west. Centuries before Speke's arrival in Africa, the Arabs had charted the entire length of the Nile. Not only that, but countless generations of Africans had inhabited the 'unknown' region for centuries.

We ordered lavish dishes from the menu, all of which promptly came. No other guests were patronising the hotel, and so the manager came over and spoke to us.

'It is wonderful that tourists have started to come to our country again,' he said. 'So many bad men fought for this city. So much blood was spilt, we just want to forget all those men and their time. We don't want any more war and killing: you are very welcome in our country.'

There was a charming naivety about him and many other Ugandans that I met. It was more than the desire to please which I had become accustomed to in India or even Zaire. Something about it was almost as if everyone bore the burden of each individual misdeed which caused the past tragedy. I felt safer in Uganda than at any other time. It is an interesting paradox, that the people of this nation are so passive and honest, but they should have been ruled over by a series of such violent and despotic men.

Oswaldo poked me as I tried to draw conclusions. The meal was so cheap that we ordered all four courses again.

Next morning, before the sun had risen above the bullet holes in the windows, Denzil, Oswaldo and I drove out to Entebbe. The famous botanical gardens had borne the brunt of war and neglect. Denzil apologised every so often for tormenting me at school and, sweeping a hand to push back his long hair, he would snort through both nostrils into a very large and grubby handkerchief.

Oswaldo and I took turns sitting in the sidecar. Denzil drove to Entebbe Airport.

Renowned as the scene of the Israeli midnight raid in 1976, Entebbe's chapter of history is hard to forget. Palestinian hijackers took hostage over one hundred Israelis aboard a French aircraft. Three Hercules cargo planes — escorted by Phantom jets — left Israel packed with airborne commandos. Within one hour of landing they had rescued the hostages. In the course of the operation, eleven MiG fighters, supplied to Uganda by the U.S.S.R., were destroyed.

The debris of that attack was still lying about, having been pushed off the runways so that life could get back to normal. One aircraft, it looked like a DC-10, was parked on the tarmac of a taxiway. Covered in green algae, it lay abandoned, I suspected, because the necessary engineers to repair it did not exist.

We took tea in the airport cafeteria, which was open although no flights were expected. A hundred people struggled for good places from which to watch a twelve-inch television screen. Whole families were clustered around the flickering reception of Ugandan television. The cook and cafeteria helpers had deserted their posts and were also crouched around the miracle of technology. Amongst the interference, Michael Jackson was pacing through the robotic steps of his music video 'Thriller'.

Denzil knew a lot about Uganda and its history. He told with great animation of the brutality of Idi Amin and Milton Obote. And he spoke of the burial grounds where the earth was parted and filled with corpses. These were Uganda's killing-fields.

As the sun sank down behind Kampala's concrete buildings, Denzil strapped two jerrycans brimming with petrol onto the sidecar. Oswaldo and I risked instant incineration trapped in that death-seat. Petrol slopped about as we set off at dawn the next day to witness the evil legacy of Amin and Obote. Although I was apprehensive — and at first unwilling — to visit the killing-fields, Denzil maintained that such a trip would be of significance.

For several hours we drove along red mud-tracks bordered with lush vegetation. Once in a while Denzil would pull out a hand-scribbled map. His up-to-date information and interest in such matters as the killing-fields, led me to suppose that the lanky Englishman had unrevealed contacts: perhaps in the Foreign Office. Rather oddly, he seemed reluctant to brief Oswaldo and me as to where the killing-fields were located. When I asked him to give me names and directions for my notebook, he said firmly that these details were irrelevant. Perhaps, I reflected, I had contracted the Developing World paranoia, which almost everywhere holds that newcomers are undoubtedly spies.

At what seemed like the middle of nowhere, Denzil stopped driving, glanced at the tatty map, and switched off the engine.

'We are here,' he said.

An albino boy ran up to the motorbike and screamed when he saw Denzil.

The child plucked up courage, slowly approaching the Englishman and rubbing his fingers through Denzil's long brown hair. Then he chortled, because he had never before felt such a thing. A moment later he touched Denzil's freckles. There were cries from behind us, and the child's mother ran over. She yanked the boy up into her arms, smacked him, and rushed over to a trough to wash his hands. Denzil looked a little disconcerted. The woman had obviously never seen freckles before and thought, quite naturally, that they were due to a disease which might be contagious.

We stayed the night at the back of a teahouse. A fire burned in the middle of the little room. The flames licked at the corrugated iron walls, crackling and squeaking as the fire was fed with a few old pieces of damp wood.

The man who put us up was very old indeed. His name was Albany; and his eyes were rheumy with age. He spoke wearily, as if he had seen the history of the world and all those who had walked upon it. And he told stories of the slaughter.

Albany had seen corpses being dragged into open pits — often by the victim's own children.

In Uganda a generation was stolen by the deeds of tyrannical rule. Albany's raspy words echoed around us. As the flames licked higher than before, the old Ugandan spoke about the lost years of the second Obote reign.

Obote had returned to a people who were beginning to recover from Amin's terror; a people who had not realised that a new dictator had just replaced the last. Albany said that he would rather the truth be told just once, than it never be told at all.

Next morning Albany took us to a leper colony near to the hut in which he lived. I was not sure of the reason for visiting the enclosure and its inhabitants. At first I felt like a voyeur or a child being taken to visit a zoo. Albany knew the lepers well and introduced us to them. Their features and bodies were actually rotting; holes had formed in cheeks, and finger-joints had dropped away.

It was the first time that I had seen serious disease since Bombay. Dry leprosy is not usually as highly contagious as people tend to believe. Oswaldo reached into his pack and pulled out a bag of boiled sweets. They were striped with white and black lines. He handed them to the oldest of the lepers. The joy was no longer expressed in physical demeanour, but in a distinctly higher sense, as if an aura surrounded him.

Few people lived in the region. Visitors were unknown. It was as if the world were trying to leave it alone, in peace.

We walked across a field to buy some milk from a stall. What looked like thick sticks were scattered about, their ends fat and rounded. Skulls were spread about like orbs, some enmossed — others shining brightly — polished by the rain. Many of the bones and skulls were small and delicate; they were those of children and their mothers.

Albany gave us some bananas when we left. He told us to tell our friends that his country had found peace at last. And called out:

'Smile, when you think of us here, because we are smiling for the world.'

The jerrycans were secured and we mounted the black machine. The fuel was hardly the purest: clouds of noxious gases spiralled behind us as we pulled away to seek the source of the Nile.

* * *

A group of white men carrying large sacks were heading towards us. We studied their movements in puzzlement, trying to make out what country they were from. The tallest one moved with a limp in front of the others. Their skin was so white that for a moment I wondered if they were albinos.

The men had in fact come from Jinja's grain mill, where they worked. A second skin of blinding white flour covered each from top to toe.

Denzil left the motorbike with the manager of a backstreet bar who had assured us that he was the right man to take care of the machine. A table took pride of place in the bar at which a school of card-sharps threw down piles of bills, each bearing Milton Obote's face. A monster with eight heads was rearing up from a pinball machine in the middle of the room. Oswaldo tamed it, becoming addicted to the game; until Denzil walked over, picked him up, and threw him outside onto the grass.

The Patagonian and he were very different. One was tall, the other short. One liked knife-throwing, the other was a pacifist. Yet they were fascinated with each other, both respecting, yet each not quite comprehending, the other's viewpoint.

Bicycles were for hire to take visitors to the source of the Nile. Each came equipped with a pedal-man.

I perched on the back of the Chinese-made frame, and it began to gather speed, powered by the gangling body of the Ugandan youth. We passed a golf course on the edge of Lake Victoria where two old colonials were having a vociferous tee off.

Buildings in the 1930s style, neglected statues of Mahatma Gandhi, and small, overgrown Hindu shrines were dotted around. One day in 1972, Idi Amin decided that all the Indians were to leave Uganda. Most went to neighbouring Kenya. One told me later that they were allowed to take no possessions: they crossed the border wearing only their three-piece suits.

Lake Victoria came into view, surrounded in a gaggle of teenage boys and glittering tilapia. The morning's catch had just come in. Scaly fish bellies were being slid into yellow wicker baskets, which were put onto heads and whisked away to market.

Noah, my pedaller, offered to find us a boat so that we might visit the very spot where the Nile is born. He went off and chatted to every boy with a canoe. After lengthy negotiations, we lumbered aboard a craft with three slow leaks. Noah, who insisted on accompanying us, bailed with a jam jar as we pulled out into the expanse of Lake Victoria.

The boat was long and thin. An array of wooden struts held the two sides together, while a child with a paddle propelled us into the middle of the lake.

Noah pointed to a small island and a lone tree which sprouted from the water. He said that the tree was the exact source of the Nile, and that the island moved about according to the moon. As to what he meant, I was unsure. Yet it was something on which he was very emphatic indeed.

Oswaldo gave a short address on his homeland to the occupants of the boat, which he instructed them to tell to their various peoples. The Patagonian was eager to make the most of the auspicious moment. Afterwards Noah asked me exactly what my friend had said. When I admitted that I had no idea at all, Noah burst out laughing and ran off to tell his friends.

The Owen Falls Dam raged as Denzil's little black Triumph ran across the road bridge towards the Kenyan border. At a checkpoint, at Tororo, on the border we were received with great courtesy and hospitality. A cluster of young women, who wore coloured cotton dresses with pointed shoulders, stood about chatting to the soldiers. A bucket of hard-boiled eggs and packets of biscuits — which tasted of grit — were passed round at the border post. The officials lounged beneath a wide acacia, smoking cigarettes from pink cartons.

Out of all the countries I had visited, Uganda was the hardest to leave. A curious sense seemed to bond all Ugandans together. As if it developed like an extended family which is united by hard times.

The supply of cash that I had brought from London was running out. Somehow I had to contact my bank there to send more money from my account. Although concerned that problems would inevitably arise, I was reassured that very soon I would be with Mich — my childhood friend — in Nairobi.

Before crossing into Kenya, we had a last bottle of Coca-Cola in a rowdy café. At the bottom of the bottle there was an inch of black silt. Swirling the remaining fluid around this deposit, I leant my head back to drink. As I did this, my eyes caught on a few words scrawled across a blackboard on the café's wall. Each letter was carefully formed. It read:

As for me, God will help we all in the judgement day for the work we doing today. And also God will help human being more than anything in the world. He is our guide and he we love.

CHAPTER 12

Beowulf and Buckweed

'Lingo hear, your Gonds are asses,
Eating cats, and mice, and bandicoots,
Eating pigs, and cows, and buffaloes;
Filthy wretches! wherefore as me? . . .'

In the early afternoon we reached the edge of Nairobi. A dented sign announced:

Welcome To The Green City In The Sun.

Breaking with our tradition, we stayed in a rather extravagant hotel in Westlands, a suburb where many Indians and European expatriates live. My travelling companions had refused to put up with the bug-infested rooms with no windows which they thought I favoured. I would have preferred luxury, but was living on a tight budget. The sword money would not last for ever: and Gondwanaland extended, after all, to the farthest reaches of South America.

Denzil had negotiated with the hotel's manager and swapped his motorbike for lodgings for us all. He was delighted, secretly confiding that the vehicle would only be good for a few more miles.

I telephoned Mich, who was attending the Kenyatta University. We arranged to meet in the centre of town.

Bus number 118 was very full. Oswaldo dangled from a window and yelled with exhilaration as the driver swerved around the huge roundabout near Tom Mboya Road. It was hard getting used to metropolitan life once again. Buildings stretched twenty storeys into the vast African sky, and had lifts that worked. Tour guides herded flocks of package 'safari' tourists from one souvenir shop to the next; as the bustle of suit-clad commuters hurried home. My companions were thrilled to be in a big city once again. Denzil ran off towards Woolworth's and Oswaldo hugged a businessman from Argentina.

At the Thorn Tree Café outside the New Stanley Hotel we met Mich. He had changed considerably from the twelve-year-old whom I had known many years before. Built like a Marine, with a square body and a shaven head, his hands were as wide as soup plates.

Mich had roamed the trouble-spots of the world with his father. A military man, his father was, as he put it, 'A Colonel — the Full Bird', now stationed at the Pentagon. They were always at loggerheads. Mich's father had expected his son to follow in his footsteps and join the Marines. But Mich was dedicated to other causes. He loved animals and detested war. His favourite creature was a ferret called Buckweed. The two had been almost inseparable. But, before coming to Africa, Mich had been forced to leave Buckweed with the Full Bird: who hated animals and loved war. I dreaded the consequences.

Mich invited me to see Kenyatta University. We took a *matatu*, a private van, out to Kahawa, which is on the road to Thika. At the matatu-stop on Moi Avenue hundreds of people ran into the road as soon as any of the private vans approached.

In Africa seldom is there queueing: a surge of arms and legs push against each other, in the hope of squeezing aboard. A woman forced her head towards my face. As the bushy mop of hair obstructed my nose and mouth, I began to suffocate. Forget-me-nots were embroidered on her dress. I wriggled in horror that they should be the last thing I would see before finally collapsing.

The bus plied a course through the military base at Kahawa, until it reached the University grounds. A sly move on the part of the government, it was said, to ensure that the University was constructed beside a military base. Student demonstrations in past years had caused various Kenyan universities to close and a gigantic backlog of students to develop.

Kenyatta University was very spread out. Students crisscrossed the campus along the sand-covered paths as if they had a definite purpose. I asked Mich why he had not bought a bicycle. He shook his head and said,

'Nah, I'd just look rich . . . people here don't have as much as we do. I brought all these clothes from the States, but usually I wear the same pair of pants and just a couple of the shirts.'

I asked what the drop-out rate was.

'Man, if a guy dropped out he'd be throwing away his life. Kenya has the highest population growth in the world. You know, it's funny . . . when I was in the States I used to grumble all the time at what I had. At Virginia Tech we had multi-million dollar wind tunnels and we weren't happy. But just look at our physics lab over there . . .'

He motioned towards a pair of huts with tin roofs.

Mich shared a room with two others. Three beds were pushed up against the walls, leaving just about enough space for two people to stand in the surrounding area. Mich pointed to a duffle bag and said:

'That's where Jimmy keeps his stuff; Kennedy doesn't have anything but what he wears. I've got enough equipment to kit out an army. These guys have become closer than my brothers; they've taught me so much by their example of modesty.'

Above Mich's bed was hung a framed picture of his ferret, Buckweed, and a three-toed sloth. As I was admiring them, the door swung open. Kennedy stumbled in and we were introduced. He stuck out one of the largest hands I have ever seen: bigger even than Mich's. It seemed to grip at my whole arm. He was wearing shorts and was agitated for some reason.

'What's wrong with you?' asked Mich.

'Well, I don't want to bother you, because your friend has come. But I remembered that yesterday was your birthday . . .' Kennedy rummaged under his bed. He pulled something out wrapped in a page of the *Times of Kenya*. 'I didn't forget, but it took longer than I had hoped to make you a gift.' He held out the small package and Mich took it.

'Open it. I made it myself.'

Mich unwrapped the paper which was scrunched up at the edges. A pouch made from denim was revealed. Mich examined it with praise, opening it for a moment, as if he expected something inside.

'It's for Buckweed,' said Kennedy.

'I shall treasure this, but you cut up your jeans,' Mich said.

'I don't mind wearing shorts,' Kennedy replied, laughing.

He sat on his bed and picked up a Mills and Boon romance. We left him to read and Mich offered to take me to eat dinner.

* * *

Mich had given me the address of a place in Eastleigh — an overcrowded suburb of Nairobi. From this secret establishment one could telephone, at a low fixed rate, anywhere in the world and talk for as long as one liked. We took bus 106 out to Eastleigh — where Ethiopians and Somalis are the majority — to meet our contact, whose name was Francis.

A river of oozing mud was surging down the main street of Eastleigh. Oswaldo took charge of the scribbled directions and navigated us passed the Disco Day and Night Club to the house where Francis lived.

A doorway led to a passage and then to a house with dry mud walls. We entered the main room and Francis greeted us. His teeth were many shapes, and rather unusual in that most of them were twisted at right angles to what would have been their normal positions. And as he talked, he used them to strip bark from stems of *mira*, a bitter-tasting plant containing amphetamine, which is legal in Kenya.

Half the room was curtained off. I could see the shadow of a woman breast-feeding an infant on the other side. Francis handed each of us a book of international dialling codes and pulled a handkerchief away, revealing an extremely modern telephone with digital display. It sat upon a stack of international directories. I rang my bank in London and persuaded them to wire some money from my account to a bank in Nairobi.

Oswaldo took the telephone next. The hut in Eastleigh was miraculously connected to Oswaldo's village in Patagonia. Oswaldo's eyes filled with tears of joy; but after a few moments of conversation his voice trembled and he stared into space. He put down the phone and whispered:

'My Papa dying last week. Dey burying heem tooday in mi veelage.'

The bank cashier counted out several hundred purple notes. With a sweep of his tongue, he coated each finger in a layer of sticky saliva. The lubrication aided the counting process. Then he smiled broadly.

My bank had successfully transferred some money to Nairobi but, on arrival, the funds had been automatically changed into Kenyan shillings. I pleaded that, since the sum had been sent in sterling, it should paid out in sterling. The manager shook his head and suggested that I hasten to a quiet, discreet foreign-owned bank in a suburb of the capital.

It was one P.M. — on the last Friday of the month — by the time I arrived there, and this circumspect branch was being mobbed by five thousand people, all of them trying to cash their pay cheques. When I jumped up and down in the middle of the crowds, the mob paid no attention, but swept over me like a wave rushing shoreward. An elderly American queuing up was creasing back page three of Robert Ruark's *Uhuru*. I told him my story, weakly hoping to win his friendship and sympathy. He looked up for a moment and said,

'Gard, man, ya should go to Botswana if ya think this is bad!'

Having decided to use other tactics, I burrowed under the waves of legs, and threw myself on the mercy of the most senior clerk I could find. He counted out twenty forms, mumbling,

'You can start by filling these in.'

Snatching a ballpoint from the official's hair, I wrote furiously, hardly lifting the pen from the page.

The sheets were accepted with grave formality, and the officer himself climbed on a chair to place them atop a pile. Then he unbuttoned his shirt another notch to reveal a navel filled with sweat. After which he removed his left shoe and began to exhibit its fine stitching to his colleague at the next desk.

When I banged my fist on the table, he looked up in annoyed shock, handed me another batch of forms, and told me to shut up. A man in a boiler suit crawled over to me from under the desk. He was groping about with a screwdriver trying to mend the electric fans. I refused to fill any more forms. The official replaced his shoe and almost showed some pity. He commended me on my own footwear, then said I was to meet him at the telephone box behind the bank at three that afternoon.

At five-thirty P.M. I was still waiting and was beginning to wonder what exactly was going on. A group of men in long black coats were watching me, as if they had been told to do so. Was it usual policy to meet clients at the telephone box? The long black coats moved closer and I went inside the box. A moment later there was a tap on my shoulder and the bank officer addressed me: 'Thank you for waiting . . .' he began.

I butted in, 'What are those men doing staring at me from over there?'

'Don't worry, they're waiting for one of my colleagues.'

'The gentlemen who process the forms would like you to pay them some money. It will speed the wheels of your case.'

I reeled in surprise, at first, on learning that bank officers could be corrupt. But then, instead of condemning the system, I realised the possibilities, and asked:

'How much?'

'A thousand shillings.'

'I'll give you five hundred.'

'They might take seven hundred.'

'Six hundred and it's a deal!' I shouted.

'I'll see what I can do,' he replied, shuffling away. He returned an hour later with the necessary signatures.

Oswaldo met me under the Thorn Tree. He looked a little happier, and said that Denzil had taken him to an astrologer who told his fortune. Then Denzil had gone off to see his elderly great-aunt who lived in Nairobi. A decrepit Indian soothsayer, with a face as creased as an elephant's belly, had seen Oswaldo's future. The phantoms and spirits which he had conjured up had pledged that Oswaldo's future was to be mystical and great. I was shocked that the Patagonian would bow to magic provided it predicted *good* things. It all seemed very hypocritical, especially after Oswaldo had refused to feed the Babalawo's Borfima.

'What are the details, Oswaldo?' I couldn't help asking.

'Dey remain seecrets, meng, till five yeers passing. Nice man give me magica stoone to protekting me fameely and Oswaldo.'

'What does it look like?'

His hand fished about in the tight jeans pocket and pulled out a yellow piece of stone. A pentagram was etched into its face. He held it close to his chest and shut his eyes. Images of Rajasthan and the alchemist's assistant were hard to suppress. Could another of Bhindu's brothers be working from above a bicycle shop somewhere in Nairobi?

Denzil's great-aunt invited us all to watch Beowulf. A local boys' school was putting it on as an opera, for a limited period only. Mich, who was helping Kennedy with his studies, apologised for not attending. At eight that evening, great-aunt Rosela, Oswaldo, Denzil and I found ourselves sitting in the front row of a draughty school hall.

Boys dressed as witches and princesses pranced about, shouting out lines from the great Anglo-Saxon epic. Oswaldo, who was sitting next to great-aunt Rosela, was called upon to explain what was happening, as she was more than a little short-sighted. The South American was at a loss for words as he had no idea of the events, either. Irritated by the slowness of the plot, great-aunt Rosela banged her stick on the ground, croaking for a gin and tonic.

After the play, we applauded until our hands stung; and great-aunt Rosela invited us to a cocktail party. One of her oldest friends, another widow, was returning Home: to England, to retire to a country cottage. The expatriate enclave awaited us.

Oswaldo entertained a select group of elderly and captivated European ladies at the soirée. He filled their glasses liberally from a bottle of Gordon's gin, gallantly escorting them about the room on his arm. All the time he spoke of Patagonia.

Having escaped from an expert in molluscs — who had cornered me under a long portrait of an early settler riding a zebra — I sidled over to Oswaldo. Suddenly, and without warning, he dug the stiletto from his boot and threw it at the feet of one of the women. Gin glasses clinked and fake pearls clattered as all stared down in horror.

The dagger was embedded in the parquet flooring, through the body of a large winged insect which had been killed outright. The mollusc-man strode over and picked the creature up, caressing the corpse with his fingertips.

Aunt Rosela and the other widows swooned in disbelief at the prowess of the gallant Patagonian. Miss Lambeth-Whitely became quite wheezy and lay for a moment on a sofa. Miss Finklefirn produced a fat cigar from her handbag, and stuck it between Oswaldo's lips. She announced that it had belonged to her departed husband, Archie, and he would definitely have liked a Patagonian to have it. Oswaldo lit it and choked on the smoke, but persisted until his face turned crimson.

Miss Lambeth-Whitely had the sort of voice that can break glass or embarrass one at a church function. As Oswaldo topped her glass up she twitched, blushed, and shrieked:

'Oh, you are a naughty little Latin, aren't you?'

Denzil and I withdrew to the kitchen. Mama Wanjiru, the

maid, shuffled around us on leathery toes, giggling. We licked out the bowls she had used to make cake icing, as a string of orders in high-pitched, mispronounced Swahili emanated from the other room.

Miss Finklefirn, who was soon to depart Africa, passed around slabs of chocolate fudge cake. The mollusc-man had interred the murdered insect and returned to swallow lumps of gooey chocolate. He gave me a pernicious stare as if I had abetted the execution of helpless wildlife. I turned to Miss Finklefirn and asked politely why she was leaving Kenya after so many years. She stopped passing out cake, and looked me straight in the eye.

'Young man,' she said, 'I have been here forty-two years and quite frankly can no longer stand all those blacks!'

⋆ ⋆ ⋆

Kennedy and I became firm friends. Although he was from Nairobi, his father had a small decorating business in Marsabit which, he imparted in a whisper, was on the verge of bankruptcy. Kennedy invited me to drive north into the wilds of Samburuland and up to Marsabit itself to deliver some paints to the construction project. I had wanted to visit the northern regions of Kenya for a long time. For it was there, near a small town called Maralal, that the most formidable English explorer still resided: his name, Wilfred Thesiger. The Afghans had been proud to receive him in our country. I wanted to return the compliment to him, in his own adopted home.

Oswaldo and Denzil were far too busy to leave Nairobi. They had become instant socialites. Great-aunt Rosela and Miss Finklefirn wined and dined them in a most unconventional manner. When they were not playing golf, they were playing bridge, and when they were not playing bridge they slurped at gin and tonics in the Muthaiga Club's bar. The canny old dames taught Oswaldo to shuffle cards like a Las Vegas croupier, which he liked very much.

Kennedy drove the dilapidated silver pick-up through the

groves of blazing jacaranda out on the road to Thika. Stands selling fowls, pineapples and Tusker beer died away as we left the city's outskirts. A cluster of pots containing purple paint bumped about behind as we sped northwards. All was engulfed in a bright yellow light.

The sun beat down and I groaned about the extreme heat. I longed to gulp chilled water, or to suck at a cube of ice. Kennedy said that it was quite normal for nomadic people who graze their cattle on the plains of the Rift Valley never to have seen ice. Some drinks rattled about at the back of the pick-up in a cooler, covered with several large lumps of ice. When we next saw a Masai woman walking, from what seemed to be nowhere to nowhere, Kennedy stopped the pick-up.

'What are you doing?'

'Look at this,' he replied and, fishing out one of the melting pieces of ice, he presented it to the woman.

One might have thought that she would be grateful at seeing such a wonderful thing for the first time: but her response was quite unexpected by me. She screeched and dropped the shiny block on the ground.

'Why did she do that?' I asked Kennedy, in an almost angry tone.

'She has never felt coldness like that,' he said; 'For her cold means night and night means danger.'

The Masai woman looked at us with intense distaste: as if we had been performing magic. She turned her back and began to walk away from us towards the distant emptiness.

The road was little more than a dust track as it broke across into the northern hemisphere. I stared out of the window and, for a moment, thought I was seeing the whole world spread before me.

Giant termite mounds sprang up out of the desert savannah, and birds with bright tail feathers darted about. Kennedy realised that I had been affected by the power of the place.

Kennedy said: 'Tahir, this is where life itself began. Its energy filled our bones with marrow.'

At Isiolo we ate a roast chicken divided down the breastbone. Kennedy would not start until I was ready to have a second helping. His uncontrollable laughter revealed a set of teeth stained dark brown by the high fluoride content of Nairobi's water. When I washed the grease from my hands, Kennedy scurried away and paid for the meal. I argued that I ought to pay. He replied: 'When the river flows through your land, you may feed the fish.'

The silver Datsun began to move once again, and we entered Samburuland. A pair of warriors flagged us down. Although they looked like members of the Masai tribe, their adornments were quite different. Kennedy said that originally the Samburu had been the same tribe as the Masai, but they split away and ventured to the northern territories. The two jumped into the back of the truck and banged the signal to start on the roof.

Zebra and ostriches took shade under Afzelia 'magic bean' trees, whose giant pods dangled down above their heads. The warriors seemed contented, as if they were surveying all that was theirs. Then there was another bang of a palm hitting the roof and Kennedy stopped. The Samburus clambered out and walked resolutely off into the desert — as if to a pressing appointment in the middle of nowhere.

'This is the land of the Samburu,' said Kennedy. 'For them, there is no middle, no beginning or end. For them it's as you see our planet. It is round.'

* * *

When we arrived at Maralal, Kennedy ambled off to meet some old acquaintances, and I asked at the petrol station where I might find Wilfred Thesiger.

'Ah, you mean *Mizee Juu*,' said the clerk; 'Follow that track out of Maralal and continue up the hill to the big house.'

Ten minutes later I found myself sitting beside the great explorer, invited to a rather late lunch.

'I hate cooking and I always have,' said Thesiger as he stared into a dish of over-cooked goat stew.

As we sat in the sun-room of his green-roofed shack I observed the great man carefully. Wrapped neatly in a fraying Gieves and Hawkes jacket, Thesiger began to tell me about his most extraordinary life.

Widely acknowleged as the last of the great explorers, his knowledge of the Middle East and Africa was encyclopaedic. Indeed, he was perhaps the only man alive to be revered as a legend in both East and West.

'You're the first Afghan we've had up here!' Thesiger panted as he led me on a tour of the shack. 'This is Bush Baby, and that over there is Laputa. He came to me many years ago with the words "My name is Tommy Gun, please give me a real name." So I did.'

Thesiger pounced on one of the children of his adopted Samburu family, crying out, 'Do you know where Afghanistan is?' The infant looked up at the towering Englishman and whispered, 'I think it's near Germany, *Mizee Juu*.'

Thesiger shook his head in regret that the child should have such little geographical knowledge.

'We are a long way from Germany, let alone Afghanistan,' I said weakly. But the old explorer was not satisfied. 'I'm going to get my maps out later!' he threatened, as the child scampered away to play with his hoop.

'This is the best house in the world!' cried Thesiger as he led me from one room to the next, 'Well, it's the best house in Maralal at least.'

A scattered herd of zebra lingered in the valley below, languid as if scarcely able to move in the tremendous heat. The valley had once, not long before, been covered with trees that gave shade to the goats and droves of wild animals.

'There's a disease that attacks the juniper trees, the top first, then the affliction spreads downwards,' said Thesiger, as we looked out towards Maralal. 'I see nothing stopping it killing the whole forest over there. No one has done anything about it. I don't know if they could.'

The old explorer swept his arm in an arc and said sadly, 'As far as you can see was once forest. Now it's all dead.'

Change has ravished many lands to which Wilfred Thesiger had travelled in his long and distinguished life. Yet, unlike so many explorers and adventurers before him, he had borne witness to the changes in landscape and society.

'It is a great mistake to go back to a place,' he said, staring at the fibres of his jacket. 'I was horrified to go back to Arabia.'

Wilfred Thesiger was born in 1910 in Abyssinia, now Ethiopia. It was there that his father was instrumental in helping Ras Tafari, later to become Emperor Haile Selassie, to the throne. This influenced Thesiger's whole life. His earliest years in Abyssinia cultivated a passion for the wild; a passion which Thesiger never relinquished. His remarkable books are, of course, classics.

Although he had a flat in Chelsea, London, it seemed as if he dreaded the prospect of returning to the industrialised world.

'I go *home* on leave once a year,' he said. 'The housekeeper who I had for forty-seven years is no longer with me.'

Haile Selassie never forgot the services that Thesiger's father had given him. Thesiger, while studying at Oxford in the late 1920s, was invited to call upon the potentate. 'I said to him,' remarked Thesiger recalling the events some sixty years before, ' "There is one thing that I want to do more than any other . . . that is, to return to your country." '

The wish was granted soon after: Thesiger was the only westerner personally invited to the Emperor's coronation. 'The most decisive thing I ever did was when I made that trip to Abyssinia. I took a rifle with me and went on to the Danakil Country. After that there was no question of settling down to a nine-to-five job.'

'God I hate cars!' roared Thesiger suddenly. He had been stirred from his reminiscences by the sound of a Land Rover braving the dry river bed. 'The biggest misfortune in human history was the invention of the internal combustion engine!' he barked. 'Cars diminish the world and rob it of its diversity!'

Thesiger slipped back into his memories once more.

'The years I spent with the Bedu were by far the most important years of my life,' he said. 'I went to them deciding that there would be no concessions: I was going to live as a Bedu.'

Indeed, he accomplished exactly that. His travels with the Bedouins, and two crossings of *Rub' al Khali*, the Empty Quarter of the Arabian desert, made him a legend in his own lifetime. His travels brought him face to face with despondency, danger, and starvation.

'The desert is a place of almost unbelievable hardship,' muttered Thesiger, leaning back into a tattered armchair. 'There was constant anxiety that the camels would collapse. If it hadn't been for the Bedu, the journeys would have been a meaningless penance.'

The Bedouins' unfaltering belief in themselves, as well as their unsurpassed generosity, gained Thesiger's undying respect. 'The challenge of the desert kept them on their toes,' he said. 'They accepted no one as their equal . . . they would say, "I am Bedu and the cold does not matter to me." '

Thesiger's memories, as clear as his piercing gaze, spanned eighty years. One moment he would be recounting details of his first trip to India, in 1917; and the next he would be speaking of hunger in Arabia.

'I remember one day,' he recounted, 'we were longing to eat the hare we'd caught that morning. We hadn't tasted meat for ages. I kept suggesting that we stop and cook it there and then. But each time the answer was that we could only rest when there was water for the camels. At last a suitable spot was found. The camels drank and we cooked the hare. I can still smell it now, it was a smell from paradise.

'Just before we were about to begin eating, someone noticed three Arabs approaching in the distance. When they arrived the hare was presented to them. One of our party said "Please feast, it is a blessed day that you have come." '

As the old explorer conjured his recollections before me, the door was flung open. In its frame was hunched an aged Samburu woman. Completely blind, she had been led up the hillside by a child. She and Thesiger were old friends.

She stumbled into the room and began to embrace me, kissing my hands. Multi-coloured beads adorned her neck, and her ear-lobes had been cut in the traditional Samburu manner. I looked over to Thesiger. He let out a roar and shouted,

'She thinks you're me!'

The herd of zebra moved about uneasily in the valley as if a predator were nearby. It was almost too hot to move. I was very lightly dressed, yet sat palpitating in the tremendous heat. Sweat ran down my face as I took in the indefatigable explorer's tales.

Pausing for a moment, Thesiger glanced over to where I was slumped. An apparition had begun to haunt me, blotting out all else. It was a glass of freezing cold water with tiny droplets of condensation on the sides. My head began to spin at the very thought of gulping such a deliciously cold liquid. Thesiger pulled his Savile Row jacket closer about him, as if an icy chill had run down his spine. He rearranged himself in the armchair and said, softly, 'Let's have a nice hot cup of tea shall we?'

* * *

Marsabit is a dusty enclave in the desert. Kennedy's schedule forced us to travel further northwards to attend to his family's business. I had left the great explorer — now retired — vowing to return if time allowed.

Samburu warriors were lounging about, chewing on roots and trying to keep cool. Some plaited their hair, covering it with red ochre. We were about the same age and for a moment I contrasted our lives. Was it possible to compare them? We had been exposed to such different aspects of life, yet being with them I felt a common link.

Kennedy drove to the building site so that we could deliver the paint to the foreman. His name was Julius. He wore pink wellington boots and greeted us with a grin which seemed to bisect his face. We were escorted behind a row of unfinished houses. Julius stopped frequently to point out the quality of the workmanship and the materials used. I praised both, and handfuls of soft insulation asbestos were brought for me to fondle and appreciate.

The buildings were at an early stage of construction: still having no roofs or doors. However, painting had begun, and now we had delivered the top coat it would be used immediately.

In a *banda*, a small round hut, we were given tea. Two-litre tins of bronze emulsion were drawn together in a circle so that we might sit, cushioned with wads of fluffy white asbestos fibres. With the collapse of the asbestos market in the west, stocks of the hazardous material had been shrewdly sold to developing nations.

The world was warm yet seemed remote, as the sun fell behind a row of the unfinished houses. I sipped the hot sweet tea, no longer bothering to scrape off the black film of drowned insects from its surface.

Julius stood up and exclaimed in a deep, proud voice that Kennedy and I were invited to his home. We were to be the guests of honour.

Big Ben looked down at me from a faded postcard on one wall. We had been hurried away to rest in Julius' house. He was happy that I noticed the card and said:

'My friend, Francis, is in London. He sends me pictures and I pack up special maize-flour porridge, *ugali*, which he likes to get.'

A goat was led into the kitchen: it skipped along with a degree of curiosity. Then there was the glint of a knife in the moonlight and it was announced that dinner was soon to be served. The foreman's young son was paraded in front of us and prodded, to demonstrate an unusual talent. A beer bottle was handed to him and he removed the top with his milk teeth. Julius was proud of the boy.

He cleared his throat and announced that there would be no salt with the meal. It was far too dangerous to venture out to the shop after dark. Four people had already been killed that month by elephants running amok.

The oil lamp was dimmed and a large tray bearing a whole goat was trundled in. The animal had acute rigour mortis. A limb was hacked off and presented to me. It was absolutely raw. I held the hoof in my fingers and tried to look pleased. The other three legs stood perpendicular to the corpse and were removed with some degree of surgical precision, Julius using a rather blunt hatchet. I pretended to gnaw enthusiastically, before exclaiming that I was far too full to eat another bite.

A bed was made up, its pillows plump with asbestos and newspaper, and I lay down to sleep. As I drifted off, a picture of Rick and Gracie Schmetman rolled in front of my eyes. Each was wrapped in a golden raincoat with transparent buttons. Rick looked at Gracie and Gracie looked at me. Then they both shook their heads slowly, in disappointment.

* * *

Back in Nairobi, a flock of ravens had crossed Oswaldo's path and he knew that he was cursed. As we sat at the Impala bar in Westlands, drinking mango juice from moulded Chinese glasses, he spoke tenderly:

'Meng, Patagonia calleng me. Dose eyes mounteens at me hoome waiteng me.'

The news of his father's death had been a severe blow to the Patagonian and, although he had obtained new strength from the talisman, it was clearly not enough. His left eye had developed a disconcerting twitch and from time to time his top lip ruffled upwards for no reason at all. Concern for omens occupied his time. We began to take elaborate routes around the town as he trod on every crack and avoided ladders, old women and black cats. Sometimes he would sit and stare into space, his eyelashes would quiver as if he were remembering Patagonia, of whose beauty he so frequently spoke.

Then, one day, he put his hand on my arm while we were walking, as his feet juggled with the crazed paving:

'Chappy, came to South America . . .' he said; 'Vee goo Amazon, vee goo leoopard hunting! Yoo like us Latin peeples . . . vee crazee meng!'

Images of lost cities, jungles thicker than any on earth, and visions of mountains made of ice, ran through my mind. The thought of venturing to the last piece of the Gondwanaland puzzle began to tug. I told Oswaldo of my thoughts.

'Vats Goondwannahland?' he asked, screwing up his face.

'Well,' I explained, 'scientists say that once, long, long ago, India, Africa and South America formed one giant continent. This was called Gondwanaland.'

The Patagonian seemed confused.

'But that's not all!' I cried, hoping to recapture his attention, which was flagging. 'You see, this super-continent got its name from a mysterious, barbaric tribe who used to live in Central India . . . they were called the Gonds.'

Without warning, Oswaldo suddenly slapped me on the back. As I recoiled from the blow, he chortled,

'Khey chippy, Patagonia once coled *Patagondia* . . . mean 'foot of dee Gonds' eat ees home of dee Gonds, chap!'

Oswaldo had a point: I was quite ready to be sure. Patagonia could have evolved from Patagondia. This remote region of southern Argentina might indeed have played a key role in the Gondwanaland story. I glanced at Oswaldo. Smiling broadly, with his arms akimbo, he was revelling in his new role as an amateur philologist.

Oswaldo's link between Patagonia and the Gonds almost seemed plausible. I would certainly try to look into the connection, once having reached the area.

But my interest in Macumba still superseded any other. I was enthralled that such a cult existed and was growing; a creed whose heritage was based in three continents. I had not told Oswaldo much of Macumba, as my curiosity for it might have upset him. Yet I was determined to learn more of this fantastic Brazilian art. I knew no other way to get the compelling itch of curiosity out of my system.

I pledged that I would venture across the continent from the north to the southern edge: and yes, I would journey to Patagonia, where my extraordinary companion had been born.

* * *

Mich and Denzil had lost all their money gambling with some card sharps in Nairobi's International Casino. They mumbled that a Mafia element had short-changed them. Now, sick of city vices, they wanted to leave that very night for the hills. I suspected an ulterior motive for such a speedy getaway. Mich broke down under interrogation and said:

'Those Sicilians gave us till tomorrow to pay our debts . . . otherwise they would take *necessary action*.'

'How much do you owe?' I asked.

'Nine,' said Mich.

'Nine hundred shillings?'

'No, nine thousand shillings.'

'And . . .' murmured Denzil 'a side bet of two camels and a race horse with another player.'

The first *matatu* leaving Nairobi was heading towards Ngorengore, a small town west of Narok. Mich managed to send a message to Kennedy of our whereabouts. I tagged along to give moral support. Fifteen bodies and thirty chickens pressed tightly together as the *matatu* wound down into the Great Rift Valley.

It was very late by the time Ngorengore's single street-lamp lit our descent down the rutted road. Oswaldo, Mich, Denzil and I huddled in one clump, wondering what to do. A man wearing dark glasses and 1973 silver disco boots whistled and we followed. His name was Basil. In a strange way, he resembled a crocodile. Taking pity on our motley group, he invited us to come and stay in his hut, to meet his family, and to share with them what little they had.

A yellow tin can was passed to me and in the darkness I began to drink. It contained a muddy brown mixture: a special homemade potion, concocted from fruit, I was told, within the very black walls of the room in which we sat. Basil was jubilant when I complimented him on the brew,

'It'll make you potent forever and women will run to your side,' he said.

But he stopped speaking as I began to chew on the grit at the bottom. The lumps would not grind up and so I swallowed what felt like bits of broken glass. Basil said that we were to stay for ever and become his new children. We thanked him in chorus. He wore a three-piece suit. I could make out the lines of wide stripes which rolled up and down the cloth, undulating around the creases, giving it character. When he noticed me looking in admiration at the silver disco boot strapped firmly to each foot, he removed one and handed it to me for closer inspection. Here, as elsewhere in the Developing World, boots and shoes are talking-points, for they bespeak sophistication, and even relative wealth.

Three women in the one-room dwelling lolled about and giggled, as if in confusion at everything that was said or done. I was not sure whether they were Basil's sisters, wives or even his daughters, but it hardly mattered, as everyone was having such a nice time.

The yellow tin can was taken away and refilled with a new

potion. It was hot, and the vapours which poured off made my head spin. This was *changa'a*, a drink prepared locally. I managed to avoid it, as the women climbed over each other to get to the liquid.

At that moment the babies appeared. Their small, round torsos were passed from one lap to the next, as they passed water with surprising frequency.

The tea-chest table was removed and Basil announced that it was time to dance. Denzil passed out cigarettes, hoping this would frustrate Basil's intention. Basil grabbed the carton and lit two. He drew in smoke from alternate hands. The women were too drunk to appreciate his skill. They lit cigarettes and started to choke, violently. They had obviously never smoked before.

As the confined chamber filled with tobacco smoke, the babies screamed as one. The largest of the women pulled me up to dance. Her enormous breasts closed in around me, engulfing me like an amoeba, against the wall. I shouted out. No one heard me, except for a baby who threw up with excitement. Then, in one movement, another of the women stripped off all her clothes and ran around the room. No one showed any surprise at all. Only I stared in dread. She plucked a yellow dress from beneath an infant and put it on. She looked like a marigold. When I told her this, she tried to drag me into a corner.

Basil said he had a secret to show us. He went to one corner of the room and removed a large piece of dry mud from a cavity in the wall. He turned back, holding a shiny, brightly coloured object in his palm.

'This comes from Ethiopia,' Basil began. 'An Ethiopian chief gave it to me in exchange for four cockerels.'

He held it out at arms' length with confidence: almost as if the object radiated an invisible power. We sat in silence and stared at the cube. Was it a new kind of magical device, perhaps in some way related to the Borfima? Each of the six sides was made up of nine coloured squares: it slowly penetrated my fuddled brain that it was a Rubik cube.

'I, too, was surprised when I saw this magic block,' Basil continued, 'it seemed a very odd thing; then, after many days, I understood the power that it has. Shall I tell you the secret?'

Mich and Oswaldo nodded, mesmerised by Basil's cube.

'When I move one of the sides, it may seem a very small thing that happens. But when the colours turn over at the body of a sick person, he is healed. Those little children who run about in here were all covered in a rash. One of the ladies used to shout out at night, another had a bad fever.'

'Is it really that easy?' asked Mich.

Basil looked deep into his eyes and said:

'No. I close my eyes and must say some words of magic. It is only then that the spell will be made.'

The next morning a row of ill people loitered outside the hut. Mich rearranged a set of five stones around under a cloth. In his trick, one of the stones magically appeared above the cloth. The woman in the marigold dress sat and watched for hours. Now and again she prodded Mich's legs, suggesting that he go round to the back of the hut with her.

Basil's makeshift clinic was really thriving. He stumbled about in his disco boots, between lines of bodies which were scattered outside the hut. Each patient paid one shilling and was given a sip of changa'a.

On our fourth day a whirling cloud of dust approached at speed from the distance. It cut between the mud houses of the town and I recognised the pick-up's driver. It was Kennedy. He greeted us, then led Mich aside.

They returned a few minutes later to where we were sitting. Mich's eyes were bulging with tears; he clasped Kennedy's shoulder. I asked him later what had moved him so. He replied:

'Kennedy came out here to offer me all his savings. He knew that my debt must be very big.'

'How much did he have?' I asked.

'Nine hundred and thirty-four shillings. He said that his father would give me another five thousand, but it would take a week before they could sell their animals to raise the money. Of course I couldn't take it.'

Denzil and Mich said they would stay with Basil until things in Nairobi quietened down.

Oswaldo, Kennedy and I climbed into the cab of the little silver pick-up and sped along towards the capital. I stared at the ground as it ran by beneath the car's shadow. We entered the expanse of the Great Rift Valley, where human life, it was said, began.

Suspicious now of anything with the word 'Great' in its title, I had learned my lesson from the Great Thar Desert.

The Great Rift Valley surrounded us in all directions until the earth curved away.

In the late afternoon we ascended one of the steep slopes of Ngong and sat on the grass to watch the world. A lone thorn tree stood as the last perpendicular object before the horizon. Vultures and eagles rode high on the thermals and swooped past each other in diagonal lines.

At that moment I felt the force which embraces the African continent — the power which bonds man to nature and nature to mankind. Kennedy came over to where I sat and whispered,

'There is a story in East Africa,' he said. 'One day a Luo herdsman was leading his cattle across the valley in search of water and new grass. His name was Joseph. In the far distance he noticed a tall warrior approaching. The cattle grew restless and moved their feet in circles when the tall man arrived. The two men were from the same tribe and embraced each other. Joseph said to the tall warrior, "Why have you returned to this place?" The other replied, "I went far away to live with those people in the north. It was a very nice place, and eh, I would have liked to stay there very much."

' "But what made you come back?" asked Joseph.

' "You see," said the other, "I had seen this sight before I left and the memory tormented me. I had to come back, for I need it as a cheetah needs meat." '

Kennedy turned and pointed far across the Great Rift Valley and continued, 'Tahir, those two Luo warriors were standing where we now sit. Like the tall one, you will return. The memory of all this will draw you back, Africa is now your real home.'

Oswaldo, Kennedy and I sat for a long time, looking to where the savannah became the sky. I thought over what Kennedy had said. Then I smiled.

PART THREE: WEST GONDWANALAND

South America

Caracas
Ciudad Bolivar
Angel Falls
SOUTH AMERICA
Negro
Branco
Manaus
Amazon
Fortaleza
Recife
Salvador
Brasilia
Sao Paulo
Buenos Aires
San Carlos de Bariloche

CHAPTER 13

Beyond the Devil's Teeth

Then they rose and followed Lingo,
Followed onwards to the forest,
From the mountain Dewalgiri,
Followed on till night descended.

Jesús poured himself a beer and blew the foam from the top. The corners of his mouth were turned up, so that it seemed that he was smiling even when he was not. Before drinking from the glass of the *Polar* lager, he tipped a little liquid onto the dusty café floor.

'Are the flies bothering you?' I asked.

'No,' said Jesús, 'it is for the saints.'

We sat on the veranda of a Café Popular in Ciudad Bolivar: on the southern banks of the Orinoco. The sky suddenly turned inky black and the Venezuelan rains gushed down.

I had come in search of Macumba. The cult's existence had intrigued me since Blake had first spoken of it on his roof in Bombay. And I was eager to learn more and understand the mechanics of a society whose roots were imbedded so interculturally.

The route from East Africa had been straightforward enough. A cheap courier flight had taken me from Jomo Kenyatta International Airport, at Nairobi, to Amsterdam. From there, I had flown standby to Miami, in time to catch a direct, discounted flight to the Venezuelan capital.

Brazil was my target, in particular its Amazonian capital: Manaus. I was careful not to reveal the reason for my quest to anyone. Previous experience had shown that esoteric matters are either derided by most people, or else tend to scare them.

Even from Oswaldo, whom I planned to visit in Patagonia, I had kept secret my thoughts, my deep fascination for Macumba.

A child selling cigarettes crawled under an amphibious army truck and kept his chin high, waiting for the rain to cease. His friend pushed a tub of purple ice cream under one of the wheel arches and climbed in after it. Jesús took a gulp of the lager, and continued with his stories.

We had met on the bus from Caracas, the Venezuelan capital. He had pressed his tanned fingers tightly into mine, laughing through a bearded mouth, exclaiming that our friendship would last forever.

Giant moths fluttered above the crowded café life, taking refuge from the tropical storm. One landed on the pelt of a dead cat, which hung high up on a wall: its wings matched perfectly with the cat's matted fur, and it was invisible for a moment.

Jesús cut me a piece of *cachapas*, a maize pancake filled with white cheese. It had been, he said, a favourite dish of the country's liberator, Simon Bolivar. He offered the rest of the pancake to a table full of soldiers who sat next to us. One stood guard, his hands gripped around a nine-millimetre UZI machine-gun, while the others drank beer and played draughts. It all seemed so like Africa: the beer and the tropical rains, and nature's domination of the land.

Jesús talked for hours about his country.

'Yes, of course there is corruption here,' he said, 'but there is corruption everywhere. God gave Venezuela all the minerals it would ever need: he gave us oil and aluminium, mangrove bark and tonka beans. Education is free and there are ten universities in the country. Bolivar would be pleased if he came back now. My father wants me to join him in business. He has a little land that farms balata gum. You must come and meet him and stay with us.'

Putting down my drink — a tall glass of coconut milk — I broke in: 'Jesús, I have to go southwards. I am heading for Belo Horizonte, in Brazil. My friend Oswaldo Rodriguez

Oswaldo gave me a letter of introduction to his cousin who lives there. Then I want to go south, to Buenos Aires and beyond: to walk amongst the ice mountains of Patagonia.'

'Where have you come from?' Jesús inquired.

'From the east.'

'Did you go to that place . . . "India?" ' asked Jesús.

'Yes, I stayed there for a long time.'

'What are the people like?'

'Well,' I began, 'the first thing is that there are so many of them, almost nine hundred million.'

Jesús looked at me as if I were mad, 'In Venezuela,' he said, 'we have seventeen million people!'

'They are fine once you get used to them. But they have some unconventional customs and traditions.'

'What do you mean?' said Jesús pouring himself another beer.

'Hindu people revere cows as sacred . . . they worship them.'

'Worship them?' Jesús yelled. 'In Venezuela, we don't worship cows, we barbecue them! India must be an amusing place: tell me more!'

'There is a God called Ganesh,' I began. 'He has the head of an elephant and the body of a man. He's got four arms and rides upon a mouse.'

Jesús started to roll about, crippled with laughter.

'These customs might seem peculiar but they are very ancient. People have worshipped cows in India for four thousand years. I find such ideas strange as well, but I respect them, if only for their longevity.'

The Venezuelan nodded in agreement and wiped the tears from his eyes.

'We may not have as many people, but this is a big continent. And, remember, the map might look very pretty, but its colours can deceive!'

I promised that I would return to talk with Jesús again after leaving Patagonia. It all seemed so easy. Jesús' watery green eyes rolled, perhaps in awe at my naive confidence. Then he fell off his chair. For he was very drunk indeed.

As I walked back to the Roma Hotel, winged insects of all types buzzed around the street lamps, and wide-bodied lizards scuffled around my feet. The hotel's owner was asleep in the garden, stretched out on a rope bed. I opened the door of my room. There was no lock, and the hinges squeaked as I pressed the door inwards.

Since my travels in West Africa I preferred not to turn on the light before I slept: it only revealed where the biggest of the insects were and attracted more creatures around the bulb. The bed was large and the pillow moulded around my head as I lay down to sleep.

There was the sound of a cricket moving restlessly on my bed. I edged away and was just about to drift into sleep, when a hand lunged down against the sheets and squashed the insect and its noise with a single blow. I leapt up and ran to the light switch. A stubby figure was sitting up. He had almond eyes and one-inch bristles radiated sparsely from his face in all directions.

'Herro,' he lisped, 'my name is Kiato.'

He stared at me and blinked, almost as if telling me his name explained why he was sleeping in my bed. Fumbling for a pair of wire-framed glasses, he slowly unscrewed his eyes which had been blinded by the light.

'The managel said I could stay with you, I am flom Japan,' he said, through a slight American accent; 'Does that bother you?'

'No, since you're here you might as well stay.' I was too exhausted to argue, and made a mental note to claim half my money back in the morning. 'I have to leave early, anyway. I am going to El Dorado and then towards Brazil,' I said.

'Learry? That's where I'm going. The bus reaves at six,' said Kiato.

I turned off the light.

No sooner, it felt, had my head touched the pillow, than Kiato shook me and said that it was time to leave. When travelling alone it can sometimes be hard to refuse company.

At the bus station people lounged around eating purple ice cream and drinking pineapple juice. There was a shout: a man was running towards me through the damp morning air. He waved a piece of paper and moved with wide athletic strides.

'Amigo Tahir, mi amigo!' he called.

It was Jesús. He gave me his address so that I could find him on my return. It was time to get on the bus. As I stepped aboard, Jesús handed me a leather pouch.

'They are tonka beans,' he gasped; 'they will bring you your fortune.'

We shook hands and the bus moved away towards El Dorado.

Oil processing plants and *nodding donkeys*, for pumping oil to the surface, mingled with the jungle and lined the route. The landscape was identical to that of Uganda. Berries and fruits of all colours weighed down the branches of rubbery trees, which sprouted from the brick-red earth. Kiato whistled and took pictures of all he saw with an autofocus Minolta. He was, he said, from Kyoto, the ancient Imperial Japanese capital.

'I studied at the Amelican school in Tokyo,' he stammered. 'My father wanted me to work for his company. So I went to the ailport and took a fright to Guatemara. It's best not to algue with him, just to reave.'

Kiato stopped speaking. Then we both stared in horror at our first encounter with serious deforestation. One hillside after the next lay barren, like shaven scalps. The oncoming lane of the newly macadamised road carried massive tree-bearing trucks towards the ports. It was as if the very soul of Venezuela was being exchanged for yet another petrochemical processing plant. A receding line of jungle was the only witness.

Kiato was now too shaken to take photographs. He moved about uneasily, put the camera on his lap, and said,

'My country buys the wood and gives Venezuera technorogy to exproit its minelars in exchange. I am ashamed of what I see, knowing that my people are to brame.'

Kiato spoke wonderful English, but it took a while to become adept at recognising problems with the letters, 'L' and 'R', a tendency that struck quite randomly. Sometimes I would confuse him, for fun, by asking: 'Do you mean 'L' as in Rome?' to which he would reply, 'No, I mean 'R' as in London!'

The bus' brakes were slammed on and we all trooped out at a military checkpoint. Our passports and malaria tablets were scrutinised by an officer with two red shoulder-stripes — attached with safety-pins. Another soldier touch-typed in triplicate and handed the bus driver a permit to proceed.

More than a hundred butterflies were squashed against the radiator grille. Some were still moving like dying soldiers on a battlefield, their pink and blue wings twitching in minute movements.

Eight hours later we reached El Dorado. It was a place surpassed by its reputation and would have been easy to miss. Surely this was not El Dorado, the lost city of gold? I suspected that it was not: a lost city would be more glamorous, of that I was certain.

Two men and a dog lay out asleep in the full scorching afternoon sun. I had the feeling that I was stepping down onto a film set. The dog woke up, barked at Kiato, and waddled away, to sit in the shade. We moved into a hotel with no visible name, off the main square. The room, which was despicably filthy, had a defective fan and was divided in two by a spotted plastic table covering. Yet, curiously, I was surprised to find that the bathroom, down the hall, was immaculate. Paintings of romantic French landscapes hung on the walls, freshly laundered towels were waiting to be used and, the shower emitted a geyser-like jet of water. Puzzled that such a dingy rest-house should offer impeccable bathing facilities, I made enquiries. An assistant to the manager confided the reason. He said that when the gold-miners arrive back to El Dorado — city of sin — the first thing on their minds is a long, soothing shower. After spending weeks without washing, the bodies of these gold-miners or prospectors are awash with traces of the precious metal. Conniving landlords install filtration systems and high-pressure showers to relieve them of the grains of gold.

Kiato wanted to see one thing more than anything else: the Angel Falls. They are said to have the longest drop in the world: over three thousand two hundred feet, and are on the Churun river, a tributary of the Caroni.

Kiato's guide book said that an old German and his Guyanese wife led expeditions to the Falls. The weather-worn trailblazer, however, was asleep on the veranda of his house when we found him. And he had led no trips into the jungle for over ten years.

At the town's small airport a hammock had been slung between a six-seater Cessna 206 and a tree. Inside was Roberto, the pilot. Although he had no map, he said that he knew the route and agreed to take us to the Angel Falls. But the problem was the weather. Storms were forecast for the following two days; Roberto would contact us at the right time. We thanked him and went to eat spaghetti.

The café in the centre of town was square-shaped and trapped the heat, as if designed by an oven-maker. Those around us gulped down glass after glass of warm dark lager. It was almost as if a spell had been cast to ensure the room was always baking hot, inducing the clientele to consume ever larger quantities of alcoholic liquid.

Waving my arms about, I tried to distract the unnaturally large population of flies which were swarming above my plate of over-cooked pasta. The insects were certainly breeding well in the damp café heat: and lived long, robust lives on Bolognese sauce.

A man at the next table passed me a part of his newspaper to swat the insects. One fly, larger than the others, had landed on the wall next to where I sat. Rolling up the paper, I aimed, then lunged with all my strength. The fly died a sudden death. As I scraped its remains from the cement, I noticed something curious. An almost spherical object, like a gourd, dyed blue and decorated with etched vertical lines, hung from a nail in the wall. I took it down to inspect it closer.

The man who had given me his newspaper was watching me. I glanced at him, half expecting an explanation of the object. He folded the remaining pages of his paper and laid it down, and said slowly:

'Macumba.'

I sat up, startled by the word.

'I want to know more on this Macumba; can you advise me how I might learn more?' I asked eagerly.

'What you are holding comes from Brazil,' said the man, in excellent English, 'although Macumba does exist in Venezuela. That comes from Manaus, in Amazonas. It's designed to give protection to everyone who comes here, and to make sure that no catastrophes happen in this little café.'

'What actually *is* Macumba?' I asked.

'It's a belief that developed in Brazil, although much of what it counts as sacred originated in Africa. When slaves were taken to South America by the Portuguese, they brought with them their ancient gods. Those gods, and their knowledge of magic, herbs and nature, are at the centre of what is called Macumba now. Macumba concentrates on spirit possession.'

The man lit a cigar and sucked hard on it. I invited him to sit with me. And, as soon as he had sat, he began to speak again:

'I became interested in Macumba, Umbanda and Candomblé when I was living in southern Brazil. Many of my friends took part in the ceremonies at the time, and one of my closest colleagues at work was a medium.'

'Who or what possesses the mediums?' I asked.

'Usually the gods of the Nigerian Yoruba tribe. They are known as *Orishas*, and it is thought that they control everything that happens to us and around us. You must pay homage to them and worship them, and then they will be happy and make circumstances favourable towards you. If you want to make them very happy you can let them enter your body.

'There were problems when the slaves came to Brazil, because the Portuguese wanted to make them Catholic. The Africans did a very ingenious thing. They pretended to be worshipping the Catholic saints, yet really they were praying to their own gods. Each of the gods was assigned the image of a Catholic saint.'

'Is Macumba used to cause harm?' I asked.

'Are you referring to Black Magic?'

'Yes, that type of thing.'

'No, Macumba itself is rarely used to inflict pain. That isn't the nature of it. It has come to be used very widely throughout South and North America — often known as *Santeria*: for it does something very important. It acts as a system that gives social, psychological, and even medicinal aid. It also helps people relieve themselves of stress.

'But there is a cult which is known for its evil practices. It exists mainly in Cuba and is known as *Mayombero*. Its spells can maim, or put an end to life: they are designed eventually to destroy. Mayombero works in league with the Devil, whilst Macumba works with God.'

'I want to find out more about Macumba,' I said. 'Where can I find a group that practises it?'

'I heard recently that Manaus has a lot of ceremonies going on; why don't you try there? Failing that, Belem is famous for its special kind of rites.' He pulled a visiting card from his pocket and clicked it down before me. The gentleman nodded politely and, as I scanned the card's neat italic script, he left the cafe. It read: *Professor Francisco Fernander*.

* * *

Kiato took pictures of a little boy who was dressed in a colourful Hawaiian shirt. His mother sat down next to us and began to chat. Her name was Maria. She had long, jet-black hair, alabaster-white skin, and eyes the deep-blue colour of the finest lapis-lazuli.

At thirteen she had been married in Caracas, then had left her husband and settled in El Dorado. I asked what she did all day long.

'I take care of people,' she said. 'You know, this town revolves around mining gold. That's the only reason anyone's here at all. At night the prospectors would spend everything on beer and prostitutes, so I take care of their money for them. They trust me.'

Every few moments she would wave or turn to greet someone: she seemed to be very popular. We walked around the town with Maria as she collected money and noted down figures on a blue pad. She would introduce us to people, slipping in a side comment like, 'he killed his wife' or 'watch your wallets.'

One man, called Princess, was delighted that Maria had brought two young men for him to meet. He winked and removed his shirt so that I could admire his biceps. Kiato shuffled to the door uneasily. Princess said his job was to wash the prison guards' uniforms and darn their socks. Sometimes he made dresses in his spare time. Maria whispered that he performed other duties too. He blushed, and we left.

I had read Henri Charriere's work *Papillon* and been moved by his story. Papillon had been incarcerated at El Dorado prison after leaving Devil's Island in Guyana. When I asked Maria if it was possible to get into the prison, she became serious all of a sudden, 'Do you *really* want to go?' she asked.

I replied that I did.

'Then I shall see what I can do.'

By the end of the afternoon we seemed to have met everyone in El Dorado. There was not much to do, so we went to eat more spaghetti. Kiato set up a solar charger to replenish the batteries for his camera. Eventually I heard Maria calling my name, and turned around. She was sitting in a black Ford Sierra Cosworth. Such a splendid car — easily capable of one hundred and fifty miles an hour — looked very peculiar in such a dilapidated place as El Dorado.

Kiato and I climbed into the back and breathed in the odour of the cool leather seats. A young man was at the wheel. He pulled up in front of a bar at the edge of town.

Maria went inside, and soon returned with a fat, bald man who was very drunk. He was pushed into the back with Kiato and me, his face slouched against the window. He writhed and muttered as if in a state of delirium.

'Okay, now we can go to the prison,' said Maria.

'Who's the drunk?'

'He's thc head of security.'

Five miles from El Dorado we tore across a wooden truss bridge, as the young driver demonstrated the full capacity of his machine.

'This is *La Colonia*, as the prison is known,' said Maria. 'It's surrounded by the *man-eating river*: there are so many piranha in these parts.'

At the checkpoint, the police chief was prodded and he managed to salute with his left hand before throwing up over the white leather upholstery. A row of uniformed guards saluted back and raised a barrier.

Eight hundred men were serving sentences at El Dorado Prison. They hung about, chatting and making little souvenirs to be sold to the few tourists who visit El Dorado.

Some cheered when they saw Maria and she blew them kisses. Various sections of the prison were pointed out. One wing was set aside for homosexuals, another for the most dangerous men: that was where Papillon had been. A couple of rather unenthusiastic offenders were painting the high-security area bright yellow.

Maria said that one man in particular would like to speak to us. We walked through gates with iron bars and locks that clicked behind us. Under the wide branches of a tropical tree we met Leroy. He had been sent here thirteen years before, convicted of murder, and was the only prisoner who spoke English. His voice wavered as he spoke to us. Now and again he chuckled loudly and his head shook from side to side.

'You can't imagine how it is for me to speak English,' he said. 'To use these words is like being able to breathe again. At first when I was locked up, away from my home country, Trinidad, I used to talk to myself in English. Even, oh, until a few years ago, then I gave it up. There's seven more years left, but I should get out before that for good behaviour. The guards here like me and are kind. I brew them fermented drinks and they sometimes give me cigarettes.'

'Is there anything we can bling you, Reloy?' Kiato asked.

'Nothing I need, I'm used to it here.' Then he thought for a moment and said gently, 'But there is one small thing that I've been craving for a very long time.'

'Anything; what is it?' I asked him.

'It might seem strange, but could you say the word "melodramatic" out aloud?'

Giant moths flapped like bats above our heads at El Dorado's most popular bar. The insects tried in desperation to obtain camouflage on the walls. Music blared from two colossal speakers. I hoped it was below the decibel level necessary to perforate eardrums. The habitat had been created by the ruthless clientele native to El Dorado.

When a teenager of a more refined aspect sauntered over, declaring that he knew a quieter place, we needed no further persuasion to follow. His name was Hubert.

El Dorado seemed an unlikely place for luxury to exist. The last thing I had expected was for the door of a discotheque to be swung open by a white bouncer in a dinner-jacket.

He stood square in the door frame like a peg in a hole, taking the last drags from a very pungent cigarette with no filter. The room was dark and insipid. Air conditioning units rumbled in each corner, producing an arctic environment.

Hubert, Kiato and I made for a corner booth and sat. Hubert snapped his fingers and a forty-dollar bottle of Bacardi arrived on a silver tray.

Kiato and I glanced at each other in surprise as Hubert threw down a wad of new bolivar notes and motioned the waiter away. We had been living on no more than two dollars each a day. Hubert swallowed a glass full of the neat white rum and left. He said that he was going to get some women. He never came back.

The elite crowd of El Dorado swanned languidly about on the disco dance floor which dominated the nightclub.

Kiato started talking to a man at the bar, whose friend was also out hunting for women. We offered him some of Hubert's rum and he sat with us. His head was bald; a thick red beard sprang from his face and bounced against his chest when he spoke. It impressed Kiato enormously as his own beard was very sparse.

The friend, who had been looking for women, returned. He looked like a desperado, and dragged me out, telling me to keep an eye out for under-age girls.

My lungs seemed to seize up when we entered the humid evening air. Two whale-like creatures approached us. My companion kissed his fingertips and nudged me in the ribs. I wondered for a moment if we were looking at the same women. They ambled up, both looking as if they might be suffering from the latter stages of some unpleasant, nameless and virulent illness.

Both had revolving, roving eyes.

The desperado leapt about with joy. He started to pull the heftier woman towards an overflowing gutter. Protesting, I returned to the disco.

A few minutes later the wild man returned to the icy

air-conditioned atmosphere and came over to where I sat. The huge women loomed behind with unsure steps. Kiato and the red-bearded man were horrified, and blamed me for the desperado's choice.

The larger woman pulled me up to dance. As she acclimatised to the arctic surroundings — romping about — the nature of her movements began to alarm me.

But the dance ended very suddenly. The record was removed and the strobe turned off. Without any words, everyone from the disco moved outside. The time was exactly three A.M. People were walking towards a dark back street from all over town.

A man shepherded everyone into one of the shops. I recognised him: it was Princess, the laundry-man. An audience had assembled, all eager to get a glimpse of the action. Still not understanding what was going on, I asked the bald, red-bearded man.

'Don't you know?' he said. 'You must be from far away; Princess's fashion shows are famous.'

'Are they always held at this time of night?' I asked.

'Of course they are!' said the mouth swamped in red bristles.

Girls more beautiful than I had seen before paraded about in dresses of red and green. As they twirled around, the crowd clapped and whistled and Princess beamed with pride.

When I was leaving the shop, Maria came over to me and whispered:

'Now you have seen El Dorado. Now I think you know why I stay here.'

We were woken late. A little urchin girl brought word from Roberto, the pilot, that the weather had cleared and he was ready to fly to the Angel Falls. Kiato and I entered the bright sunshine and the innocence of day. There was no sign of the prostitutes and alcohol. Princess was darning socks again; and pots of spaghetti were being brought to the boil at the café.

At the airport Roberto slipped from his hammock and stretched.

'It's a great day for flying,' he said, pulling on a pair of worn Levi's jeans.

We spoke for a while. I asked how he came to speak such good English. In El Dorado, few seemed to know the language.

'I'm from British Guyana. Started flying in Canada back in sixty-six. There isn't much call for a pilot these days. I ferry gold-miners around mostly, to the less accessible areas of the jungle.'

'Have you seen the Angel Falls before?' Kiato asked.

'Yup, but not for about twenty years. They're beyond the *Devil's Teeth*; shouldn't be too hard to find.'

We walked to the plane. Three men were hoisting two forty-gallon drums of petrol up into the fuselage.

Roberto put out his cigarette and muttered, 'Probably best not to smoke around those babies. You don't mind if we drop them off at the Mission along the way?'

There was no choice. I climbed into the co-pilot seat, which was jammed at the most forward position. This made it impossible to use the foot-operated rudder controls if I had wanted to. Kiato was wedged in the rear of the aircraft, his face squashed against the window, and with a slow-leaking oil drum between him and the exit. We exchanged looks of dismay as Roberto turned into the wind, pushed in the throttle, and slid back the stick. The Cessna 206 felt very heavy indeed. As my seat soaked up the petrol like a sponge, I forced myself to stop imagining a gloriously explosive end. Kiato hummed. His face was tight and paralysed with fear.

The Cessna's controls were still very familiar. When I was seventeen, my father had sent me off to learn to fly. Biff, the most relaxed pilot in history, had taught me to solo a similar Cessna over the swamps of north-west Florida. The one hard rule Biff had ground into me was that one must always have an emergency landing-spot in mind. Roberto set the direction indicator and adjusted the altimeter. Two thousand feet below, the jungle sprawled out in all directions. One tree's canopy merged into the next. Where would we land if there was a crisis? I plucked up courage and asked Roberto. Pulling out a silver hip-flask from his back pocket, he opened it with his teeth, and drained it dry. Then he cackled with deranged laughter.

The flying bomb proceeded for more than half an hour over dense jungle. From time to time palaeozoic rock formations jutted from the jungle floor. The Cessna buzzed like a moth between giant flat-topped cliffs, sprouting like mushrooms from between the trees. Roberto pointed to a clearing in the distance where a large white building stood. It was the Mission. Circling twice, we landed into the wind. The forty-gallon tanks were carried away.

An Indian dialect was spoken by the people who lived at the Mission. They had become used to the insects which infested everything. Slapping one's legs would leave a pair of blood-streaked hands.

Soon the irritation of insect bites was a memory. Roberto pushed the throttle in again and we soared high above the bumpy grass strip.

Small mining communities could be spotted on the banks of some rivers; their panning turned the water yellow. Roberto pulled the stick further back and we climbed to six thousand feet. The crumbling mountains, covered in green forest, gave way to spectacular gorges.

Roberto put his hand on my knee. His voice trembling, he shouted,

'Below are the *Devil's Teeth*: the entrance to the canyon of the Angel Falls.'

It was as if we were venturing into a primeval land where dinosaurs and extinct monsters still roamed. The stone walls of the canyon were grey and crumbled with age. Our Cessna soared like an eagle round and around. Then, whilst banking steeply, we caught a first glimpse of the Angel Falls.

They plunged from the Caroni river down to the jungle floor. The distance of their vault was so great that the water turned into mist halfway down. I could understand how the American aviator, Jimmy Angel, might have felt on discovering the Falls in 1935.

Kiato's camera clicked. He, Roberto, and I whooped with wild exhilaration. We circled around the canyon four times.

Roberto was now, for some reason, very relaxed. He took his hands from the control column and fumbled for his own camera. The Cessna's nose began to fall. The altimeter's hands started to wind downwards. The trees grew bigger and bigger. As the engine made a tortured, droning noise, I grabbed the stick — gently easing it back.

Roberto banked left, and we flew through the Devil's Teeth and out from that prehistoric land — back into our own time.

On the return flight to El Dorado we stopped at a mining village to collect some prospectors. A cut-throat looking bunch of men, they were hardened by the gruelling conditions of their jungle work. Their hands were rough and calloused, and their burnt, worn faces were mostly hidden beneath tattered beards. Each clutched a nugget of gold. Rubbing their palms together in their relief at escaping the jungle for a time, they chatted of their favourite prostitutes who would be awaiting them in El Dorado.

When we landed, Kiato and I left Roberto and walked back into town. We were both silent. Our minds had been captured by the force of nature.

There was time for one last bowl of spaghetti before the bus bound for Kilometro 88 arrived in the square. I looked round at El Dorado — that most extraordinary place — and climbed aboard.

Kilometro 88 was about as exciting as its name suggests. The town was almost an exact replica of El Dorado. Kiato and I took shelter from the torrential rain in a cavernous drinking house. In the bar, which was hung with bunting, I pulled up a beer-stained chair. Just before sitting, I noticed the beer stains were moving. A pair of eyes amongst the stains blinked.

Almost every free surface in the room was covered with giant moths, which were perfectly camouflaged in the sordid atmosphere. The floor seemed to be littered with piles of decaying brown leaves, which twitched even though there was no breeze.

Kiato ordered a large steak with macaroni piled on top. The bus to Santa Elena, at the Brazilian border, arrived as he sucked up the first pieces of pasta. There was no hurry to bolt the food. The driver and passengers waited courteously until we were ready to leave.

For fifteen hours the silver bus laboured towards Brazil. When it rained, water drenched us, seeping through a thousand holes in the ceiling. When it became dark we ploughed on at three miles an hour. The driver's friend walked in front, guiding the way and forcing all wandering animals to clear the road.

Just before noon the next day the bus pulled into Santa Elena; the town had a sense of greater social cohesion than El Dorado or Kilometro 88. It seemed as if people resided there because they really wanted to be there.

Old crones sat in doorways knitting, and their grandchildren played in the dirt at their feet.

The previous week had seen the heaviest rain in the region for a very long time. A major bridge en route to Manaus, the Amazonian capital, had been washed away two days before. It would be at least a month before repairs were completed.

Under a magnificent statue of Simon Bolivar, an assorted group of travellers had gathered. Kiato sat down and waited for them to introduce themselves. Like us, they were heading towards Manaus. And, like us, they had heard of the bridge which had been washed away.

The tallest was called Rudolf van den Bosch-Drakenburgh. Standing six foot two, he had a Daks tweed jacket over his shoulders, and wore a paisley-patterned silk cravat, knee-length breeches, and riding boots.

'What's all this nonsense about?' he began in a light Dutch accent, 'Luigi, get my brogues!'

A monstrously large creature unpacked clothes from an antique sea trunk. Although taller than the Dutchman, he lacked any air of sophistication. His clothing was tattered, his hair was oily and unkept, and his severely sunburnt face was peppered with grotesque sores.

'The suede ones or the black pair?' he asked gently, ducking with subservience.

Luigi was a batman and general factotum to den Bosch-Drakenburgh. Foamy saliva filtered through one corner of his mouth, dripping onto his torn shirt front. He had not adapted to the climate well. Originally from Galway, in western Ireland, he was now living in Shepherd's Bush, London, where, he assured me, a good pint of Guinness was to be had. It remained a mystery why an Irishman, even though resident at Shepherd's Bush, had a traditionally Italian name. Yet perhaps even more mysterious was the reason for his utter subservience to Rudolf, who had gained complete domination over the Irishman. Luigi seemed to crave a sadistic master.

Kiato demonstrated how to use the solar battery-charger to another man, who sat beside him. He was thin and his face was drawn and white. He was a Russian named Yuri.

We spoke for a long time and, out of the three, Yuri's comments and expressions were by far the most interesting to me. He had been born in Volgograd, the only son of Orthodox Jewish parents.

'My father died when I was eight,' he said. 'And for my mother there was great prejudice against her for being Jewish and a widow.' He lit a Belmont cigarette before continuing in his poetic English. 'I studied English and German in Moscow.

It was so wonderful to be in that city, you can't imagine. My mother was very proud, I think. Then in 1982, when I was twenty, the Red Army sent me to Afghanistan. The initial eagerness soon evaporated. They told us lies, they said that we would be fighting the Americans! Can you believe that?'

'Where were you stationed?' I asked.

'At first near Kandahar. I thought that was bad. The rations would often be cut in half because the Mujahedin had hit the supply convoy to our base.

'Then one spring morning my unit was moved to fight in the hopeless offensive against Commander Ahmad Shah, at the Panjshir Valley. Many of my friends were killed. Others committed suicide, or went mad because of bad treatment or drinking engine coolant: there was no alcohol. We were like rats in a cage, shaking with terror whenever the rockets fell like rain. I vowed that when I got free I would see something of this world. Twelve months later I was sent back to Moscow. There had been no news from my mother for over half that time. Then I found out that she had died from depression a month before.'

* * *

Rudolf, the Dutchman held still as Luigi's clumsy hands fumbled, trying to tie the plaited leather laces of his brogues. Having acquired exit stamps from a small police outpost, we walked towards the Brazilian border. A truck with no bonnet picked us up and dropped us at the frontier army post. Rudolf spelt out his various titles to an officer who wrote them all in the register.

The officer's face was three inches from the page. Crouching with concentration, he formed each letter individually, using a blunt pencil. A gust of wind shook the tree above, and an avocado fell to the ground. The officer dropped the pencil and scampered over to the fruit. Another produced a knife and they split it in two.

Luigi hauled Kiato off to look for toads, saying that toad-spotting was a popular sport in his native town. The rest of us took shelter from the evening rains and slept our first night in Brazil.

At six the next morning clouds of blue smoke drew closer with a noise like an approaching tank. A truck with no exhaust-pipe trundled up. Two blonde German girls were riding in the back. They pulled us up and we set off for the bridge which had been washed away.

All but Kiato and I were strong swimmers, and were confident that we would be able to cross the water. Luigi passed around handfuls of toads, and snuggled up to the Germans, who were called Elaine and Seline. They looked uneasy as the Irishman jerked something from his jacket pocket. He pulled out a creature, as large as his palm, with eight furry legs which moved in opposite directions.

The girls screamed, and Elaine punched Luigi, who — recoiling from the force of the blow — dropped the spider on Seline's lap. Rudolf stretched out and struck Luigi on the other side of his face. Wrapped in gloom, Luigi edged over to where Kiato sat.

The truck pressed on, deeper into the jungle. Snakes slid across the road, monkeys and colourful birds moved amongst the greenery, and called out from the forest. The pot-holed track ended where the water began. A hammock had been slung from one petrol tanker to another, and a workman was cradled in it, asleep. At the river's bank the current was fast moving. Forty metres separated us from the other side.

Luigi crouched on all fours without being instructed to do so. Rudolf sat on his arched back and removed his shoes. It seemed natural for the Irishman to assume this position, leading me to suspect that the two men had been together for a long time. Kiato and Yuri went off to look for something to use as a float. Somewhere in my saddle-bags I found a hundred and fifty feet of parachute cord.

Rudolf took charge. Handing the line to Luigi, he told him to swim across the river and tie it to something on the other side. The Irishman, who was evidently embarrassed at removing his clothes in public, dived in — the cord in his mouth — and swam to the other side completely dressed. The German girls looked at him as if he were mad. In an easy movement, each stripped off all her clothes and leapt naked into the water.

A mechanism for hoisting the packs across the water was slowly developed. Yuri had found an inner tube. It was attached to the line. Rudolf commanded Luigi to swim across with every pack. As always, he was compelled to obey. The two complemented each other perfectly: one was a sadist, the other resigned to a life of masochism. Each was dependent on the other.

The inner tube, which had a slow leak, was pressed deep into the water by the weight of Rudolf's trunk. The Dutchman removed his cravat, but refused to undress. He said that he was light enough to ride aboard the trunk. We all watched. Rudolf's twitching lips strained to be confident.

The Irishman tugged gently at the line. The tube, trunk, and master, glided across the choppy surface of the river. Halfway over, Rudolf began to shake. He scrabbled to keep level. But the well-travelled sea trunk, which had begun to list badly, slid into the river like a sinking ship. The Dutchman went with it. Kiato, Yuri and I cheered. The German girls whistled and shrieked with laughter. Only Luigi looked sad. Either he sincerely cared for Rudolf's safety, or — as I suspected — he knew that he would be beaten.

Elaine and I walked ahead of the party. We both wanted to keep at a distance from Rudolf, who was in a very bad mood indeed.

Along the red sand track we strode, splashing through the puddles of rainwater. Elaine talked of her life. I was impressed by the great strength of her character. Sweat dripped into her eyes as she spoke.

'I don't understand weakness,' she said. 'I've always believed that if one person in the world can achieve something, then there's no reason why I, or others, can't do the same. I don't know how someone like that Irish guy can put up with being treated that way.'

We both glanced round to see Luigi stumbling slowly under the weight of Rudolf's sodden trunk and his own pack. Foam oozed from both corners of his mouth, and his thick mop of black hair stood on end. The Irishman was like an animal trained by a lion tamer; but in a distressing way had become addicted to the torture.

Shouts of joy broke the monotony of Luigi's groans. Yuri had spotted a small round hut at the point where the straight red sand road met the skyline. Rudolf was complaining that he had blisters and was thirsty. Indeed, we were all utterly exhausted, having walked for five hours.

The evening air was thick with mosquitos. The owner of the round hut gave us some hot water and pointed to a group of trees from which we could sling hammocks. Rudolf ordered the proprietor to give him a chair. When comfortably seated, he made Luigi bathe, bandage, and dry his blistered toes.

Yuri and I stared up at the night sky. His voice trembled in awe as we watched shooting stars cascade across the galaxy.

'In Volgograd, I had a telescope,' he said. 'It was the only escape from a childhood of oppression. Every night I would sit and watch satellites spinning through space. It's strange that here, far from Russia, I see the same stars. It's wonderful to think that people all over the earth stare up and see the same planets, the same constellations. Yet at the time you feel a very personal sensation, as if they are invisible to all but you.'

He pointed at the constellations, slowly naming each in turn, and speaking of the new ones — of the southern hemisphere region — which he had not seen before.

A generator rumbled in the background. The man in the hut moved in the flickering light of a black and white television. A broad satellite dish fixed to the top of a tree trapped pictures beamed from Boa Vista. Dallas — the American soap opera — was starting, and the Amazon night had just begun.

Kiato had mastered the art of sleeping perfectly still in his hammock — something which I was incapable of doing. As I floundered about, experimenting with random positions, Kiato had analysed the problems. A colony of ants shared my hammock. They climbed around my body and explored the creases of my skin.

In the middle of the night, my hammock turned inside out and I was thrown face down onto the ground. The grass was warm and smelt of liquorice, and I felt closer to nature than I had ever done before. I dreamt of Papillon's tale and of the Angel Falls.

As the sun rose over the jungle treetops, I sensed a snout snuffling up my trouser leg. At first I tried to ignore it, but the probing persisted. I opened one eye, then the other. The spiny nose of an ant-eater was foraging up my trousers for breakfast. It was very happy. I could feel the warmth of its mouth and the lapping of its rasping tongue, sucking up the insect colony to which I had become host.

A little girl with bright blonde hair ran out of the hut shouting, 'Oscar, Oscar, you are very naughty!'

Grabbing the ant-eater's snout, she dragged the creature away to play with her in a ditch.

The jungle turned into low-lying green savannah as we continued pacing deeper into Brazil. The landscape bore an uncanny resemblance to that of Africa. People waved and whistled, and had the same air of open hospitality as the friends I had left from Dakar to Ngong. Once joined to Africa, now thousands of miles away, this was the last segment of the puzzle that had formed Gondwanaland.

We entered Boa Vista in the late afternoon. Kiato, who had drunk stream water the night before, was feeling very ill. Cramps stunned his abdomen every ten minutes and he was drenched with sweat. He started a course of antibiotics, swearing he was strong enough to continue to Manaus.

Yuri and the two German girls decided to rest in Boa Vista for a few days.

The road southwards to Manaus had only been recently completed, yet it was already washed away. Nature had reclaimed it for herself. The fastest way to the Amazonian capital was by boat — which left from Caracarai — on the Rio Branco.

Yuri shook my hand as Kiato and I mounted a bus bound for Caracarai.

'Never forget,' he said, 'that we inherit the world and all her problems. Walk softly upon the earth and you will achieve great things.' It seemed a very philosophical, very Russian, departure.

Kiato lay down and slept most of the way until we reached Caracarai. He seemed to be getting a little better. Rudolf fed us with red boiled sweets, as the Irish batman sat and sulked. The bag of sweets passed him by.

'Doesn't Luigi like sugary things?' I asked.

'No,' was the reply, 'they're bad for his teeth. I don't let him indulge. You'd expect him to thank me, but he was brought up without manners.'

Luigi's eyes were as wide as fish bowls. His lips were cracked and swollen, and a coarse rash had developed under his chin. He looked at Rudolf, then a single tear ran from the corner of his left eye towards his lips.

A lone riverboat bobbed up and down on the Rio Branco. She was called the *Rio Uaquiry*. We climbed up a steep plank from the shore onto her dull boards. The captain said he was leaving that night for Manaus. The journey would take three days. He could provide food along the way for a small price.

A pair of cocks were fighting in the street which ran to the jetty. And a huddle of dogs sat gnawing at a buffalo's head outside the butcher's shop. Hammocks of all colours were displayed on a fence: a boy with a kite was their salesman. I bought a yellow hammock for myself and a packet of chicken soup powder for Kiato.

Back at the boat three blond men were ascending the gang-plank. Each had an athletic build, and carried a surf-board. I recognised them immediately as native Californians of the *surfer* variety.

'Hey Pops, is this tub heading for Manaus?' one of them called out. Rudolf donned a blue cravat, slipped on his riding boots and came to introduce himself.

'My name is Rudolf van den Bosch-Drakenburgh . . . I am from Holland, and this is Luigi, my assistant.'

'Oh man, that's great. I'm Marvin, this is Leo and Pete.' The men shook hands and the Californians told their tale.

'We came overland from Los Angeles. We bought this great car in L.A. for fifty bucks and started to drive south, but after thirty miles she caught fire and burnt out. So we left her and hitched through Central America as far as here.'

I slung my hammock and asked Marvin why they had brought surf-boards to central Brazil. Marvin looked at me, then at his two friends. I had the feeling that I had asked an idiotic question. Pete swept back his long blond locks of hair and replied, 'Dude, we've come to surf the Amazon!'

'Guys, this is one awesome tub!' shouted Leo and Marvin simultaneously. They set about making a pirate flag. A skull and crossed bones were sketched out on an old shirt, which was hoisted up on the flagpole.

The boat had two decks. It was forty feet long and half as wide. At nine that evening, diesel fumes belched upwards and the engine gave out a spluttering groan.

A single bulb flickered above the captain's dining table and he invited us to come and eat. A dish of hard-boiled eggs, dried beef and rice, was passed around. Kiato threw up as soon as his eyes saw food.

Marvin sat beside me and began to tell of grotesque diseases endemic to Amazonas. Disease — in particular bubonic plague — was his only interest other than surfing. As there was one plate and only a single spoon, we took it in turns to eat. The glass was passed from one hand to the next, like the witch sisters sharing a single eye.

After the meal, the captain, whose name was César, offered to take me to the bridge.

César relieved his eight-year-old son at the helm. As the craft broke through new waters of the Rio Branco, César made jokes and drew long breaths through a cigarette.

'I have never left Amazonas,' he said. 'But I want my boy to travel when he is older. He must see the wonders of the world.

'You know, I sent my son to school in Caracarai and they tried to tell him about all kinds of imaginary animals. One, they said, was like a horse, but was covered in stripes! Can you believe it?' he exclaimed, spinning the boat's wheel through his fingers. 'I was worried that his teacher was telling him lies, so I went to meet the man. "What is all this rubbish you're telling my son?" I demanded. "Have you ever seen such creatures with your own eyes?" I asked him. He had not, so I brought the boy to live with me on the boat. When he's old enough I'll give him money and send him away to see the world. Then he can come and teach proper knowledge, not fairy-tales, in the school at Caracarai.'

CHAPTER 14

Opera in the Jungle

And the Alligator Pusé,
Looming long upon the water,
Bore the Gonds into the torrent,
Through the black and roaring water . . .

The map was bright green and had blue lines running across its folds. There were few place-names and no roads. I remembered all the fuss in London about saving the rain forest. It had never seemed particularly important as I rushed to catch the tube, or battled down crowded Oxford Street on a Thursday late-shopping night. But, as the twin-decked river boat cut down the Rio Branco towards Manaus, I could feel real nature all around. I had never encountered a region so utterly free from humankind.

Every so often, vast areas would lie cleared. Tree stumps stretched as far as the eye could see, their roots clutching like tentacles into the red soil. The trunks of great trees were being loaded onto long trailers. Twigs and vegetation blazed in fires which were dotted about.

Each branch divided into smaller branches: and they divided into twigs, which split still further. They looked like the bronchioles in a lung. But then, as fire engulfed them, their capacity to breathe was destroyed.

The surfers were sitting around Kiato. Marvin had studied pathology and knew which bits of the patient's body to prod and poke. Pete pulled back Kiato's eyelids and shone the penlite into his pupils.

'Guys, is this gonna do any good?' cried Kiato as he wriggled on the upper deck.

'I don't believe this!' said Pete, his mouth gaping open in

disbelief. 'Look at the way his iris twitches . . . that's awesome, I think there's definite evidence of a paranormal presence.'

'What are you getting at, Pete?' I asked.

'I'm writing a thesis on perceived paranormal manifestations in Los Angeles' suburban population. Your friend here has the same nervous eye movements as some of my most advanced patients. I'd like to examine him further.'

At that moment, as we crouched over Kiato, he spewed out the contents of his stomach. Partially-digested chicken soup, and what had once been locally-canned corned beef, dripped from our faces. It slithered onto the deck and César came to protest at the mess. Leo went back to reading his book.

'Looks like he's gonna live,' he said.

Hollowed-out tree trunks, basic canoes, would approach our vessel from the dense canopy of the jungle: the paddlers wanted to trade meat and fresh fruit. The following afternoon, three wild boar were shown to César. They scurried about the hollowed-log craft, looking for an escape route.

César nodded and, with one blow, a machete had sliced off all three heads. Blood shot into the air and the carcases were washed in the river. A gut parasite several feet long wriggled from the flesh of one, and slithered away into the water. Another man hoisted a load of date-shaped berries aboard. They and the boars' bodies were taken away to be cooked.

Leo called out over the side to the boars' executioner. They motioned to each other and both laughed. One of the boar heads was thrown up to Leo as a gift. He hurried into one corner of the boat to dissect the skull with a chisel and mallet on loan from César.

Early that evening we crossed into the southern hemisphere. Birds with red bills flew overhead to roost in the tall trees; monkeys chattered deep in the jungle undergrowth. César's son had poached two of the boars. Their partially boiled flesh was served up to complement the meat of a small unidentifiable rodent. The food was passed around.

César chewed at a lump of boar's heart which was deep red and exceedingly muscular. The bones in the boar meat had been crushed, using the mallet. Consequently there were sharp splinters in the meat which everyone spat out onto the floor. Although I managed to avoid the boar, a sliver from the unknown rodent gashed the inside of my right cheek.

The berries on stems were mashed up. As the juice was collected, César said that it would ferment in a couple of days. I sat at the helm with him while he steered the little white craft to where the Rio Branco met the Rio Negro. The water grew dark and pushed about under the flat-bottomed boat. Storm clouds formed and, in an awesome display of nature's force, it began to pour with torrential, blinding, monsoon-like rain.

Rudolf spent much of the passage reading aloud from the works of Leo Tolstoy. Luigi sat at his feet and listened. He was forbidden to ask questions. The contents of the Dutchman's coffer were hung in the sunshine to dry, after their immersion in the river.

The belongings which Rudolf had chosen for such an expedition — and had transported to South America on the boat from Rotterdam — were quite astonishing. Five washing-lines criss-crossed the upper deck, weighted down by numerous sets of evening dress: both tails and dinner suits. On top of the trunk, selected items were laid out to dry. They included a bowler hat made, it said inside, by *Frederick Harold of Wimbledon*; an extensive amount of hardbacked reading material; a ceremonial sword; a very large wooden shield, emblazoned with a coat of arms; and the steel scaled-down model of a battleship.

'Malingerers!' cried Rudolf, catching me gawping at his possessions. 'Look at that stupid slit-eyed little whipster. Hasn't done an honest day's work in his life! All he can do is shirk about, pretending he's sick.'

Before I could defend Kiato's honour, Marvin walked over.

In a single movement he picked up the Dutchman by the neck and tossed him into the water. Then he returned to his book.

Muffled cries could be heard as Rudolf van den Bosch-Drakenburgh started to swim through the piranha-infested water towards the boat. As Luigi grabbed at his master, there were tears in his eyes. Was it possible to convert a masochist into a sadist? I wondered, and watched as Rudolf took his anger out on the Irishman from Shepherd's Bush. Perhaps it was not.

* * *

The Rio Negro's current grew faster as we moved between the large islands in her midst. River barges became more frequent and I realised that Manaus was drawing near.

The first signs of civilisation were the sprawling shanty towns whose wooden shacks spread for miles along the river's banks. Some children were splashing about in the oily black water. They laughed as we approached, their dark brown eyes framed in angelic faces. César threw a rope to the shore.

A flight of steps was cut into the soft purple bank and we climbed up one by one. Kiato led the way between houses built on stilts. Piles of broken television sets were guarded by anxious children, as if frightened that we had come to rob them of their family's assets. Pete shook hands with a line of smiling infants. Each was covered from head to toe in the slimy purple clay. Two of them began to fight over a dead cat which they had found. Children and babies squirmed about wherever one looked. Every woman held a child. Infant bodies were being scrubbed in tin baths, and bananas were stuffed down their throats by exhausted mothers.

Kiato removed his shirt at the King Henry Hotel. Then he spent an hour writing postcards to his family in Kyoto.

We had arrived in Manaus: capital of Amazonas, centre of Macumba.

Whenever possible I would creep away in search of contacts

which might introduce me to a Macumba group. Kiato was very inquisitive of my interest in the darker alleys of the town. But I was determined to keep all knowledge of my fascination away from him. I was adamant that he should be shielded from any possible danger by his innocence. I remembered Oswaldo and the Babalawo.

Rudolf had read that one needed the Mayor's permission to enter the famous botanical garden. He set off immediately, with Luigi in tow, to contact such a powerful pillar of society.

We had taken accommodation in a green container box in the rougher area of Manaus. Kiato assured me that this bargain could not be passed by. One green container, such as are used for commercial cargoes, was piled on top of another: a spiral staircase linked them together. The group of six containers was grandly named the King Henry Hotel. I suspected that the real profit of the establishment derived from its manifest activity as a bordello.

Shadowy figures trampled up and down the spiral steps both day and night. Whenever I dared to leave our windowless box, a group of naked Amazonian women sitting beside the stairs fluttered their eyelids, motioning towards another windowless green-walled room.

Then Rudolf returned. Overcome by heatstroke, he lay supine on a smelly black mattress for three days. Luigi poured water from a jug into his master's mouth, and fanned him with the *Life and Work of Leo Tolstoy*. The Mayor had left town.

Manaus lies in the deepest part of the Amazon basin. At the turn of the century, the city became the world's rubber capital. It was in those days that Amazonian trees supplied the world with *caoutchouc*, the sap from which rubber is made. Prosperity resulted in an extraordinary flamboyance.

Monstrous buildings had been constructed in European

styles, under the guidance of a handful of super-affluent rubber barons. The stage of the *Teatro Amazonas*, the opera house, was once graced by the world's finest singers and dancers. They would perform to a thousand people at a time, drowning out the sounds of the jungle night.

The cathedral stared down at a city bathed in pomposity and an ornamental opulence — a city that depended on the jungle — but was disconnected from it.

When rubber trees were exported and successfully grown in Malaya, the empire of the rubber barons collapsed. Their great city lies dormant now, surrounded by a wall of jungle on every side.

Kiato and I wandered about the cobbled streets in awe. In the main square, next to the university, a band was playing New Orleans jazz on an ornate Portuguese bandstand. Stuffed piranha fish were sold door-to-door by an old seaman with scarred ridges across his face. We sat at Café Florentina and sucked up bowls of fettucine. Kiato laughed; he was well again. He sketched the tiled Portugese façades and tittered when I complimented him on his skill. Then we took refuge from the afternoon heat in the great cathedral.

Generations of misbehaving children had carved their initials into the hardwood pews. Yellow sunlight poured in through the open doorway and illuminated the walls. They and the ceiling were adorned by frescos in the classical style.

The latest Japanese technology was displayed at every shop. In an effort to popularise Amazonas, the government had declared Manaus a duty-free zone. Video cameras and notebook computers were demonstrated by hard-sell salesmen, of the type one finds in New York or Hong Kong.

Microchip equipment of the greatest sophistication is assembled by cheap labour in factories deep in Amazonas. Paradoxically, Manaus is a city that — until recently — had no airport of any size and no road linking it to the outside world.

Outside the opera house, the evening game of bingo was

being set up. Kiato pushed a wad of notes towards the bearded woman in charge, and was handed a stack of bingo cards. An hour or so later he wandered away with the first, second and third prizes: three live chickens.

Back at the green box Marvin was boasting. He held up a large X-ray, exclaiming that every bone from his thumb to his elbow had shattered while punching a barkeeper. The fight had arisen when the surfer made a pass at the barman's wife. Putting his Hawaiian surfboard under his good arm, he left for Panama to have the bones properly set.

Kiato gave Marvin one of the chickens and a handful of grain to feed it. We gave another to Rudolf, who threw it into the corridor late at night, roaring that it kept him awake. Kiato was grieved when, the next morning, he discovered a line of prostitutes sitting down to a roast chicken breakfast.

The hole in my cheek, caused by the unknown rodent's bone, became infected. One of the women, whose giant eye was often pressed against the crack in my door, took me aside. She rubbed roots from two plants on her hands and stuffed her fingertips into my mouth. As I choked for air, she forced the nails, with black beneath, deeper down my throat. When I managed to ask what she was doing, she cackled and winked. Then she strutted off to solicit customers and, strangely enough, the infection soon ceased.

Three black panthers lay on their backs at the military zoo. They were too fat to move. The big cats and boas were fed a diet which looked like the zoo's smaller mammals. The panthers chewed engagingly at a collection of sundried bones as the heat of the afternoon reached its peak.

Kiato posed for a picture. Suddenly, he took to his heels screaming as I focused my camera. On turning I saw a leopard stalking towards me. A conscript dived at the enormous tail just as muscular back legs clenched to jump. He led the animal away for another meal, saying, 'I told you about escaping before!'

* * *

A lot of time was spent pursuing my quest for Macumba. Some locals shrieked when they heard the very word uttered; others simply shrugged or shook their heads. At the back of bars I had loitered, trying to make a contact. I had spoken to street-cleaners, to workmen, and even to a terrified lady missionary, but no one could help me.

Kiato had begun to suspect that I had an ulterior motive for what I assured him were sorties to meet the people of Manaus. In desperation I went down to the fish market.

Fish of all shapes lay belly-up in the heat of the cavernous market hall. The early evening light streamed down through multi-coloured windows — stained by the Portuguese many years before. The stench reminded me of the tilapia at the source of the Nile.

On one bench a pile of eels and other creatures twisted about awkwardly, before being hacked into even-sized lumps. Their blood dripped to the floor where it congealed in a few seconds.

At one end of the hall a group of three or four men sat about smoking. Each had a pair of flip-flops moulded to his feet; and each was drenched in blood as if he had taken a mortal blow. I sidled up. A sack was dusted off and laid down so that I might sit for a while. We talked of fish and the heat and then of fish again. The men were happy that I should want to spend time in their city.

On meeting someone for the first time, the moment comes when one has done with the pleasantries, and either says nothing, or embarks on a major new subject of conversation. As we sat, the men smoked and the reek of rotting fish surrounded us. It was then that I decided to test for a knowledge of Macumba.

'Someone was telling me,' I began with the usual unease, 'that Brazil, and in particular Amazonas, is famous for some old idea called . . .' I paused to check that I still had the men's attention: they stared into my eyes, waiting for the word; 'something called *Macumba*.'

The man covered in the most blood — the foreman — nodded slowly. He had learnt English while working as a taxi driver in Miami.

'My friend,' he said, 'a word may be simple but its meaning may fill many long books.'

The butchers looked at me enquiringly and then the foreman began to speak again:

'Remember that you must have a reason to follow a quest; you must understand why you are choosing to explore something, even if it is hidden behind the veil of a pretty little word.'

The foreman and his colleagues seemed to realise that my interest in Macumba had not come about recently. It was almost as if they sensed that the thing had become an obsession. I replied:

'I do understand the importance of this belief, and I have come to learn more of it and to pay my respects to it.'

The men glanced at each other through telepathic silence. Then the foreman spoke again:

'Come here just before midnight. The market will be closed, so stand in front of the main doorway. I shall meet you here.'

He stood up, stamped out his cigarette, and led the group back to work.

Strolling back to the King Henry Hotel, I thought about my conversation with the men. It had all happened so easily: I had the feeling that one day I would look back and realise how naive I had been.

Kiato had found some second-hand Japanese children's books in a hat shop near the hotel. He said that their owner had been selling them as decoration, they had been very cheap.

'The guy said they were Kolean! Can you berieve that he thought Japanese was Kolean?' he said, bursting into laughter. Then he began to sing a selection of his favourite Japanese nursery rhymes aloud, before stopping abruptly in mid-sentence.

He peered up from above the vertical lines of text, narrowed his eyes until they were no more than a slit, and said accusingly:

'Have you been eating fish?'

Luiz was the man that Marvin had hit. Although the disagreement still stood, the surfers suggested that if we change money we should — for the best rates — do it with him. Luiz lived up a staircase in a darkened house. There was no sign of him at the residence, which would not have been out of place in a Hitchcock thriller.

Luiz's wife said that we should wait. Her name was Claudia. She was only twenty years old and sat with us talking. Long brown hair flowed down the edges of her face.

She had a mischievous smile and dimpled cheeks.

'My husband is much older than me,' she began in passable English, 'he works so much, but I still have fun.'

'How do you enjoy yourself in Manaus?' I asked.

'I go to discolandia . . . and so many good parties in Manaus. Then there are my lovers . . .'

'Rovels!' said Kiato, 'but you're so young, have you had more than one?'

'Yes,' said Claudia, wriggling about, 'I've had nine; would you like to see their pictures?'

We nodded and she gathered up two armfuls of photographs, each neatly displayed in its own frame. She named them one by one: army officers and businessmen, doctors and pilots.

'This was Sergio, he was so adorable; and this one is Leo, he knew exactly how to touch a girl; oh, naughty little François, see how he stares up, those eyes drive me crazy . . .'

'What does your husband think?' burst out Kiato.

'He's used to my ways, but he gets so jealous. I don't know why.'

'Our friend, an American, had a fight with him,' I said.

'The big one?' she said clasping her cheeks. 'Was he very hurt? I shall never forgive Luiz for that.'

A baby screamed in the other room. It was a lonely, pitiful cry.

'That's your baby?' I asked. She blushed.

'Yes, his name is Sergio.' She went to bring the child, and continued to speak.

'Of course it made Luiz very unhappy at first when he saw that his own child was black. I managed to persuade him that sometimes, even to white parents, a black child is born.'

'Did he believe you?' I asked weakly.

'Yes, deep down Luiz is a sweetie. But I named the boy after his real father, I shall never forget that brave, wonderful man.'

Claudia lit another Hollywood cigarette each time the last had burnt down. She squirmed about on the tattered sofa, sitting with her knees pressed up against her chin, and told at length of discolandia and her friends.

Sergio's huge brown eyes swam in his face. His dark skin was soft and rubbed against the bare floorboards as he crawled about. A fat ginger cat appeared and the two began to spar. Sergio stuck one of the paws in his mouth, screwed up his face, and sucked.

It was then that Luiz arrived. His body seemed as broad as it was tall. Two enormous arms sprouted from his shoulders and led to hands capable of wicked deeds. We were taken to the bathroom, where wads of notes were counted at speed. I stared up at Luiz's crude, barbaric features: a nose deformed, no doubt, by many bar brawls, a cauliflower ear and eyes as cold as ice.

'In future,' he growled, 'make sure you don't talk to my wife, she's got enough to do without your distraction!'

Kiato and I bowed in unison, and we returned down the ill-lit stairs and back onto the street.

Kiato discovered that under his bed the air was cooler. Although the ground was infested with all manner of creeping things, he was prepared to sacrifice relative comfort to remain cool. At eleven-thirty that evening I slipped on my shoes and silently crept from the green box — leaving Kiato snoring beneath his bed.

Outside the King Henry Hotel a group of men were lounging about. I suspected that they had been customers of the women who worked inside. As I walked by them I smelt their marijuana and heard their laughs as they discussed which woman each had visited.

A figure was lounging with his back pressed to the main gates of the fish hall. He chewed at the end of a cigarette restlessly. I checked my watch, it was five to twelve. The man stood up straight, pushed his hand into mine, and said:

'So you came, my friend! My name is Alfonso: stick close to me and then you will learn.'

The former Miami taxi-driver had kept the appointment. Now the working apron had been replaced by a spotted white shirt and a pair of white trousers which reflected the moonlight.

Alfonso led me down a street behind the fish market where rows of boarded-up shops housed their sleeping owners. As we walked through the alleyways, which radiated in all directions, Alfonso clicked his heels on the cobblestones, and hummed a tune. His left foot tended to drag slightly.

'Have you hurt your foot?' I asked.

Alfonso stopped humming, and I could hear the tap of his boots more clearly. He breathed in deeper as we began to ascend a gradient. The clicking grew more irregular.

'About ten years ago,' he said, 'I was in a car crash when I was living in Belem. A bus smashed into my friend's jeep. He was killed outright and I was left — thought to be dead by the people who found me. My foot was broken in six places . . . the doctors wanted to cut it off. They said it would never heal properly and I'd be better without it.' Alfonso paused: he pulled a cigarette from a soft pack, threw it in the air, and caught it between his teeth. 'No way was I going to let anyone chop my foot off,' he said, 'so I checked out of the hospital and, in desperation, I went to see an acquaintance whom I knew to practice Macumba. I'd never taken it seriously, but I was ready to try anything. My friend took me to a *Babalawo*, a healer . . . for eight days I stayed in his care and we prayed every hour to the *Orishas*.'

Babalawo, the word was more than familiar. Oswaldo's face came to mind, looking at me harshly, his forehead knotted with disappointment. Alfonso had more to say:

'Macumba has great power. My foot is fine, see the proof! Respect it and it will respect you. But if you look towards it lightly, or don't take it seriously, the consequences will be very terrible.'

Agreeing to remember his words, I promised to stay by him.

A narrow doorway was concealed behind what seemed to be a mulberry tree. There was the faint smell of its fruit — a smell that sent my thoughts back to Peshawar.

Alfonso paused for a few seconds outside the doorway.

'Is everything all right?' I felt distinctly nervous.

'There is something different . . .' muttered the Brazilian.

'Is it because I'm here?' I asked.

'No, it's not you . . . it's something else, some strong force that isn't human. I've only felt it once before . . .' Alfonso seemed quite dazed, giving me cause me to wonder whether accompanying him was such a sensible idea. It was almost as if he were frightened of this power.

'C'mon,' he said at last, noticing my concern, 'they'll be waiting for us.'

I followed him through the doorway into a courtyard. My feet trod exactly where his had. At the far end of the rectangular yard a curtain covered an arched doorway. We proceeded towards it. As we made the fifteen paces or so, I caught one last scent of the mulberries. Alfonso reached for the curtain but, before his fingers had touched the cloth, it was pulled aside from within. We stepped across the threshold and entered the Macumba shrine.

Nothing had prepared me for the layout of the chamber, or for the atmosphere of the ceremony which was about to take place. I still wonder why I should have been permitted, as a complete alien to the society, to be present at such an orthodox Macumba ritual. Perhaps the reason was so that I, as someone who had come from Europe, might witness the unassailable energy and dynamism that is so deeply embedded in this faith.

Alfonso began to remove his clothes. He passed me a loincloth and told me to put it on. Having wrapped the blue fabric around my waist, I placed my clothes on the floor together with the other bundles. It was only then that my eyes fully adjusted to the candlelight. I slowly scanned the room and its occupants.

Twelve figures were seated in a circle on the dark floorboards. Each was dressed as I now was, in a bluish cloth. No one moved, but sat with crossed legs and closed eyes. Alfonso and I assumed our place in the circle. I noticed that four of the twelve were women, they were covered by tunics made from the same blue material as the men wore.

The chamber was lit by several dozen candles, which too seemed blue in colour. They had been placed randomly, and illuminated almost every part of the room. Only one corner was shrouded in darkness.

Shadows flickered about the room like phantoms. They were distorted where the low ceiling met each wall. A large frieze, which seemed to be of some Biblical scene, was half-consumed by the shadows. It was if the saints depicted had been possessed by the roaming spirits.

One corner was more decorated and illuminated than any other part of the room. Seven statues had been arranged on a raised platform; and in the candlelight I noticed that each had been painted with intricate detail. Four of these forms were familiar. One was the Virgin Mary, and beside her was Saint Christopher, then Christ on the Cross, and what seemed to be Saint Peter. The other three figurines did not look like Catholic saints. Although they were finely crafted, their features were harder and rougher than those of the angelic-looking Catholic saints which I knew.

The largest of these non-Catholic statues had been painted with concentric blue circles. His bare chest had the broadest design. On his face the features were almost completely obscured by the arrangement of circles: which were centred about each eye. His left hand clutched what I made out to be a rock; the fingers of his right hand were locked around a bow.

Alfonso stood up and went over to the dark corner, returning a moment later with a hide-covered drum. Two of the other men did the same. Then, sitting once again, they beat out a rhythm in unison. The palms of their hands struck the drums with a force the sound of which sent shivers down my back. Each hand was raised up to eye-level and then thundered down on the hide. The blows grew faster and more powerful. Sweat streamed from Alfonso's face, and I could almost feel the energy pour out though his arms and the palms of his hands.

The other members of the circle began to clap their hands as one. I was the only person not creating noise. As I wondered what to do, a giant figure appeared from the dark corner. I realised later that a small antechamber led off from the corner.

As soon as the huge man showed himself to those gathered, they stiffened. The chamber was suddenly plunged into silence, as the giant took his place in the centre of our circle. He knelt on the floor in an odd posture. His knees dug into the boards and his feet splayed outwards.

Alfonso began to thump at his drum gently. They were slow, solid beats, that acted as some kind of introduction for the priest. For this was, without doubt, the Babalawo: and he was about to speak.

A man of some fifty years, his dark skin had been painted elaborately. Blue circles, similar to yet smaller than those of the deity on the altar, covered him. Each eye was encircled by five concentric rings. But strangest of all were the tattoos on the back of each hand. They depicted a kind of spider's web which had trapped all manner of creatures. In the candlelight it was not possible to make out much of the detail. As I tried to focus on these designs, the hands moved around each other and clapped together slowly. It was then that the members of the circle began to sing.

Alfonso and one of the women hummed to the words of the group. The sound that they created was like that of a dragonfly, a buzzing sound, made by humming while pressing the tongue onto the roof of the mouth.

As I listened to these droning tones and the rhythmic song of the group, and saw the shadows play about the chamber's walls, I began to fall into a stupor.

The Babalawo squatted and turned round and around. As he revolved, pivoted to one spot, he cried out the words: '*Dai-umba! Dai-umba!*'. Then, rising to his feet, he went over to the altar, spread his arms out, and repeated the cry, over and over again: '*Dai-umba! Dai-umba!*'

One of the group made for the antechamber, returning a few moments later with a live chicken in each hand. The birds were held by the feet and hung upside-down. They made no effort to escape. The drumming began once more; soft taps to the hides generated a dull thudding sound. The Babalawo lit one last candle at the altar. He placed it in the centre of the ring of devotees, who had started to produce buzzing sounds again.

The man sitting on the other side of Alfonso stood up and joined the priest in the centre of the ring. His head had been shaven, except for about two inches of hair at the back, above the collar. He sat obediently next to the Babalawo, who reached for a bag tied to his waist. I watched in silence as a small quantity of the pouch's ointment was applied to the crown of the shaven man's head. This man was about to undergo part of his formal initiation.

Various dark dried leaves were rubbed into the chest of the neophyte, who sat upright with his eyes tightly closed. The drumming continued and was accompanied by the dragonfly sounds of the rest of the group. I sensed Alfonso close to me. Although we had only just met, it was reassuring that he was there. Yet a single image of the fish market kept springing to mind: Alfonso and his workmates standing before me, drenched in blood.

The candidate began to writhe about. His body squirmed and twisted as he entered a state of silent convulsion. The ring of followers seethed forward, their shadows roaming the walls as they moved. One of the chickens' heads was suddenly torn off by the priest's hands. A long spurt of blood gushed and the Babalawo directed it towards the neophyte's lips. He lapped at the blood which covered his face, chest and loins. As Alfonso explained later, it was not the man himself drinking, but the spirit which had possessed him.

The Babalawo changed his tone towards the new initiate, addressing him with great veneration. He welcomed the *Orisha* to our world, and into the body of the neophyte. Then, as we sat now silent and transfixed, the priest began a conversation with the spirit. The words he uttered were not Portuguese, the usual language of Brazil; indeed, they did not even sound like Yoruba words. For it was an Amerindian deity who had been invoked, and it was his language that the Babalawo now used.

The initiate's eyes were wide open, but the eyeballs had rolled upwards. He crawled about in the centre of our circle, murmuring through the voice of the god.

The other chicken was decapitated and offered as refreshment. The initiate sucked up the blood with a crazed ecstasy. Blood dripped from his face onto his belly.

Then, as the humming began again, the neophyte leapt to his feet and spun in circles. The priest motioned with his bloodied hands and a goat was brought from the anteroom. The animal bleated continuously as it entered the candlelight. Alfonso beat a solid rhythm from his drum and the Babalawo began to stab at the goat's jugular. The beast kicked its legs and wriggled as the priest grabbed hold and plunged the pocket-knife's blade deeper into the wound.

The initiate twisted as if in a rage. He yelled in a voice coarser than thunder: '*Dai-raamatoo! Dai-raamatoo!*'

The Babalawo, who was saturated in the dead goat's blood, presented the sacrificed animal to the Orisha. Through the novice, the Orisha drank for what seemed an age: locking his mouth onto the fatal wound.

I had not realised that the ceremony had only just begun. What I had already witnessed seemed horrific at the time. For, as the Macumba priest produced ointments, potions, and more animals to slaughter, my stomach churned and I felt more and more nauseated.

Alfonso was next to me throughout. His presence alone represented the outside world. I had met him in the fish market: and the image of him there haunted me.

In the course of the rites, the Babalawo turned to me. His creased and painted face, splattered with blood, reflected the candlelight and the shadows of the chamber. He seemed interested that I had come; but he did not show any suspicion why I should want to attend. Before I assumed an active role in this most sinister of Macumba rites, the Babalawo made me swear an oath. Alfonso explained his orders and, after him, I repeated the pledge: solemnly promising not to reveal the knowledge imparted to me.

Alfonso touched my arm as we were leaving. The sun was bringing natural light back to Manaus. We walked slowly towards the fish market: the town seemed very different from when I had left it. 'Always honour the Orishas,' said Alfonso softly, 'and they will honour you in return.'

* * *

Rudolf lay in a state of delirium in the green box next to mine. Sweat dripped from his brow and evaporated as it came in contact with the floor. There was no sign of Luigi. Where was he? I could not believe that the Irishman would desert his master, especially in a crisis.

Rudolf began to whine and bark like a dog.

'Luigi!' he cried. 'Where are you, Luigi?'

It was painful to see a sadist without his disconsolate prey. I was sure that somewhere, not too far away, Luigi would be pining for punishment.

With a vacant expression, the delirious Dutchman reverted to child-like prattle. And in English. Why not in Dutch? I never discovered.

'My mother wanted to call me Lucas . . . but father would have nothing of it. He said I was to have the name of a real man. Don't worry mother, I shall be home soon. We shall dine at the Amstel when I return . . . when I return . . .'

The words echoed around the green box. 'Rodolfo Oswaldo Raffaele Pierre Philibert Gugliemi, I will bear your name and do it justice.'

Had Rudolf been named after Rudolf Valentino, whose real name he repeated over and over again?

A naked woman came to say that the police had arrested a man from London for stealing. We would have to go and pay his fine. I realised that it must be Luigi.

Kiato and I sat in the chief's office at the police station. Piles of unopened letters were strewn about on a large school-master's desk. Lists covered the walls and a peaked cap hung on a hook. A secretary sat in one corner and slowly picked out the details of the offence on an antique Olivetti. Luigi was brought from his cell and made to stand in front of us. He stood accused of robbing a chemist's shop that morning. A man in blue suede shoes was asleep in the middle of the floor. One hundred and fifty-three bottles of Campari had been arranged around his foetal form. He lay quite still while Luigi explained what had happened.

'I took the medicine from the chemist without paying the full amount by mistake. It was my fault.'

His face melted with shame and despair. The officer-in-charge reached down, picked a bottle of aperitif from the floor and poured himself a drink.

'The fine will be twenty American dollars. You may pay and leave.'

The woman who had cured the hole in my cheek was sent for. She twirled round and round in Rudolf's green box, clapping her hands, and shuffled from one wall to the next. She was fairly drunk. I explained that Rudolf's fever seemed very serious and perhaps she could treat him. The woman looked at me and then at Rudolf. She removed his shirt and trousers and pushed her hands across his chest.

'He's so muscular,' she said.

'Is there anything you can do?' I asked.

'Of course,' was the reply. She soaked the stems of two dried plants in water and I propped him up as she gave the potion to Rudolf to drink.

He called out in delirium, 'Mother, mother, you know how I hate schnapps!' Then he lay back, inert.

The woman gulped down the rest of the elixir and lay down next to Rudolf. Both sprawled out on the bed, comatose, with Luigi at their feet.

CHAPTER 15

For the Need of a Thneed

Then they travelled through the forest,
Over mountains, over valley,
To the Glens of Seven Mountains,
To the Twelve Hills in the valleys.
There remained with Holy Lingo.

The sun rose over Brasilia and its red desert sand. No birds sang, no leaves rustled in the morning breeze. An eerie silence engulfed Brazil's ghost-town capital. Kiato and I rubbed our eyes and wondered if it was all a bad dream. Our hotel was in sector S2MW-702 of the world's most planned, but perhaps most dead, city.

An assortment of unscheduled flights, begged on executive jets, on crop-dusters, aerobatic planes, and on long distance buses, had brought us from Amazonas to the nation's capital.

Brasilia is like an experiment that went terribly wrong. It incorporates the idea that man is happy living shrouded in concrete, in the middle of a desert. A former President of Brazil, Juscelino Kubitschek, seemed to think it the perfect solution to unite the country economically and politically. As Head of State, he had ordered Brasilia to be constructed: a myriad paper-pushers and politicians were banished to his new capital. The city was opened in April 1960.

Arriving on a weekend decades later, Kiato and I found the multi-lane highways and concrete monoliths all but deserted. At the weekends everyone of consequence jetted off to Rio or Sao Paulo.

On the journey from Manaus southwards to Brasilia I had caught Rudolf's mysterious fever. I had been delirious for most of the trip. My dreams were dominated by the priest-like woman who had brewed a potion to dispel all ills. My face pressed against endless bus windows as my eyes absorbed the contours of the road. Kiato frog-marched me from one vehicle to the next, poured chicken soup down my throat and always made sure that mine was the seat away from the draught. He was adept at begging rides for himself and his 'dying friend'.

On a bus nearing Brasilia I was slipping in and out of consciousness. My eyeballs felt as if they revolved in an opposite directions. Kiato found me, incredibly, a small bar of white chocolate. Until that moment, I had craved it with a desperate longing: its name had been the only word on my lips. When the bus stopped he had risked being left behind, in the hope that tasting the sweetmeat would bring me back from the edge of death. He whispered my name, and I turned, my mouth foaming and my face twisted into a paranoid mask.

'Tahil,' he said softly, 'I have blought you something special.'

He held out the bar, coated in a crinkled red wrapper, cupping it in his hands as if it were a few drops of holy water. Glancing at the chocolate and then at him, my eyes burning as I saw what seemed an enemy with poison, I screamed:

'Kiato, you bastard! Just leave me alone. I never want to see you again!'

* * *

The bus to Belo Horizonte stopped every hour for a similar amount of time. My fever had cleared, but I felt like a limp rag. We approached the city through a darkened suburb. It could have been anywhere, perhaps Africa or India: we were just passing through, visitors to that land.

At the bus station a tall figure in a black leather jacket waved. I handed him the letter written all that time before by his cousin, Oswaldo Rodriguez Oswaldo. The tall, clean-shaven figure wrapped his arms around my back and squeezed.

'Have been waiting for you, hombre!' he said in a rubbery voice. 'I am Leonardo Domingo de Rosas. Oswaldo wrote to me saying you're arriving. I have met every bus in the last three days. Many buses, amigo.'

He laughed like a hyena and then stared deep into my bloodshot eyes with almost psychopathic friendliness.

'I will show you my city, then we shall go to other places. I will take you to *Ouro Preto* . . . the city of Black Gold.' He paused for dramatic effect and waited for us to gasp. 'I have made a schedule and we have not a moment to lose.'

Our watches were synchronised and we set off, down the ramp from the bus station towards his house.

Coffee as thick as treacle was poured into thimble-sized glasses and passed around. Leonardo still lived at home. His mother, a decent-looking woman, made subtle hints that perhaps he should move out as he was well over thirty. Grey-haired, bespectacled and kindly in manner, she caught me in a questioning glance. First she looked at my unshaven face, then at my shabby, unwashed clothes: as if to say, 'Why can't Leonardo have *respectable* friends?'

At the far end of the table a silent man crouched solemnly over a plate of simple peasant food: rice and beans.

'Who's that?' I asked.

'That's Justo, he's my stepfather,' replied Leonardo coldly. 'He and my mother got married ten years ago . . . in that time Justo has only spoken to me twice.' Leonardo pulled a face at the man, then changed the subject. He was eager to hear stories of his little cousin, Oswaldo.

'That madman and me grew up together,' he said. 'Does he still keep a dagger down his cowboy boot, which he never takes off?' When I answered that he did, Leonardo looked at his watch and laughed for seven seconds.

'We must be very organised so that you get to see everything in the time you stay with me,' he said. 'Firstly you must change out of those crazy jungle rags and get some proper clothes.'

We were driven straight to a shopping centre and kitted out with suitable accoutrements for day and night disco dancing.

Kiato disappeared into a changing room. A creature emerged, dressed from top to bottom in luminescent red leather.

'Wow hombres, that's nice, isn't it?' cried Leonardo.

Black and gold threads ran vertically down the front and back of the suit which he chose for me. A waistcoat embroidered with purple sequins was worn beneath.

'Girls gonna go crazy when they see you chappies!' the Brazilian shrieked as we sped off towards *Upstairs*, the hottest discotheque in town.

Leonardo secured a large crucifix around his neck with a heavy gold chain.

'*Agua, agua!* When the girls know you guys are foreign they'll be fighting for you,' he said.

Kiato pushed back the giant red leather cuffs of his outfit and we marched into *Upstairs*.

Three hundred people, sitting at tables adorned with cut glass, silver and starched napery, each wearing neat dinner dress, turned around. Kiato stopped dead in his tracks. I pulled my jacket closed to hide the purple sequin waistcoat. Leonardo scanned the room with a tortured expression. He walked to the bar and ordered a drink: gulping it down in one. Then, looking me straight in the eye, he whispered:

'Sunday night, old people night, poppy!'

The next morning was the one that we had been waiting for. Leonardo was to take us to Ouro Preto . . . the city of Black Gold. His younger brother, Julio, turned up in an Italian sports car. He grinned incessantly and chortled 'Shall I take you to see poor people? I know where some live!'

Leonardo told his brother to behave. We piled into the alcohol-run car and drove out of the city. Julio, a well known parachute champion in Brazil, spoke about his narrow escapes.

Leonardo cut him short.

'Don't talk to me about escapes, Julio! I decided to learn 'cos you were getting all those girls,' he grumbled. 'I turned up early in the morning. The instructor told me to wait as he was just going up to jump. I watched his plane go up and level off. Then a man in a black suit jumped out. He fell and fell. I watched, wondering when the 'chute would open. He kept falling and went through the roof of a house. There was a terrible mess and they made me clear it up. That's not very nice of them is it, amigo?'

We drove for several hours until signs for Rio de Janeiro came up on the highway. Leonardo, in his enthusiasm for the adventure, had driven in the wrong direction. It was nearly evening when we finally arrived at Ouro Preto.

The town was filled with churches and monuments. Ouro Preto had been the Portuguese colonial mountain base, where many Republicans had been executed. For it was there that the first Brazilian rebellion against the Portuguese was started. And, in the town square, the first martyr of the rebellion — the white bearded victim known as *Tiradentes* ('The Tooth-puller') was savagely executed. Clothes and manacles for the infant slaves were on display in the Inconfidécia, a great baroque building, which is now the museum of Ouro Preto. At one time the home of the Municipal Congress, the building was started in 1748, but only completed in 1846.

Leonardo made sure that we commented on each item before moving to the next.

The architecture of Ouro Preto was staggering. Portugal's most eminent artists and artisans worked for decades to construct the town's dozen magnificent churches, and its fine public buildings. Perhaps the greatest virtuoso ever to toil at Ouro Preto was a crippled mulatto sculptor named Aleijadinho. Although unmatched in his sculptural talent, his own facial features grew ever more hideously deformed. The disfigurement, which were put down to his 'diseased blood' was unfortunate, particularly as Aleijadinho lusted zealously after any woman he saw. As the deformity grew steadily worse, the maestro took

The jungle bus packed with passengers at Isiolo, Kenya.

An island that is said to move according to the moon, on Lake Victoria, at the source of the Nile.

A wolf-dog sits obediently i
the Patagonian Highlands.

The frozen landscape of Patagonia.

to wearing a sack over his head, so as not to frighten away those who glanced at him. At last, as Aleijadinho lost all co-ordination, his assistants resorted to tying the hammer and chisel to his hands using leather thongs. But observers of Aleijadinho — Ouro Preto's finest artist — said that as his outer ugliness grew more horrible, so the beauty of his sculpture increased.

Kiato had gone into a decline following the humiliation of *Upstairs*. He staggered about in the red leather outfit, moaning woefully, complaining of our 'Ross of Face'. He seemed to take the episode so seriously that, for a moment, I had feared he would commit *seppuku* — Japanese ritual suicide.

Leonardo marched us up and down the cobbled streets with the ruthlessness of a Nazi leader. We felt obliged to follow, even when he stepped into an underground bar.

The owner of the tavern, who revealed himself to be a communist, ran off, asking us to take charge. He said there was a party at the other end of town. Julio sidled up to customers, taking their orders and mixing them exotic cocktails. He made up the prices as he went along, allowing those he liked to have drinks on the house. We were involved in several fights.

Time dragged by very slowly.

At three the next morning the communist returned. He led Kiato into a hidden vault and handed him a human skull in payment for our assistance. Leonardo — who was jealous — forced Kiato to return the skull, as he held the crucifix high in the air, with the words:

'This city of Black Gold can be dangerous! It has a history like that, *burrito*. Never take a skull from a stranger and you will live a nice life.'

Leonardo dragged us to Sao Paulo to see the shopping malls. At the bus station a family was huddled at the bottom of an escalator. They had come from the countryside with their belongings in a single smallish brown box. The father looked at the mother and they both scratched their heads. Why were the stairs moving? And since they were moving, how were people expected to get on? Kiato showed them how, as the mother choked with fright at the enormous complexity of simply climbing some stairs.

Leonardo marched us from one super deluxe concrete complex to another, demonstrating the modernity of Brazil.

'Brazil is a great country!' he shouted to make himself heard above Sao Paulo's grating traffic. 'This makes for a nice sightseeing doesn't it, chap?' We agreed that it did as we were led onwards between the buses and cars to admire the city's drainage system.

In a suburb of a suburb lived Thomas. He had studied with Leonardo, and invited us to meet his family. Sweet tea was poured and shortcake slices passed from one person to the next. Thomas had been lucky enough to study abroad with Leonardo, in Bournemouth. He spoke of that coastal town with reverence, as if it were a magical place filled with royalty and palaces.

'Ah, Baornemowth,' he said in a dreamy voice as if for those few months he had touched paradise. 'I miss the *Alcatraz* disco. It's where I met my fiancée.'

It seemed that Bournemouth was somehow an extension of Brazilian territory. All the Brazilian students I met had either come from or were going to Bournemouth.

Leonardo's stepfather, Justo, had an apartment in Guaruja, a beach town near Sao Paulo. I proposed that we stay there for a few days to get out of the city. Leonardo supported the plan and we jumped on a bus.

The road to Guaruja passed through some of the world's most dramatic and beautiful tropical scenery. One valley replaced another, mountains were overhung with creepers and rubbery plants. Wild birds, their beaks striped with colour, squawked from the undergrowth and Kiato captured all he saw on film.

The road snaked around mountain passes, and waterfalls

poured down either side. Then we drove down into Cubatao.

The sky was black with industrial smog. Rivers still flowed in abundance, but they ran in fluorescent, polluted greens and bright oranges. The trees had been felled and their stumps stretched for miles. There were no sounds of life save for the roaring of the turbines from the innumerable factories. Chimneys spewed noxious gases into the atmosphere, their bright colours mixed with the dense black pollution of death.

I stared in horror and was ashamed of even my own small share in the culture of the West. It reminded me of a book — by Dr. Seuss — called the *Lorax*, which I had read as a child.

Its story told of a land where Truffula trees grew in their thousands, Humming-Fish hummed and Bar-ba-loot bears played in the sunshine. This was paradise. But one day the Once-ler arrived. He chopped down a Truffula tree and knitted a *Thneed*. His Thneed sold.

Soon everyone wanted a Thneed. All the Truffula trees were chopped down and the Lorax appeared. He, as the spirit of nature, asked the Once-ler to stop. But the Once-ler cut down the last Truffula tree. He looked around to see the sky was polluted and the rivers clogged with mud; the Humming-Fish and the Bar-ba-loots had all gone. The land of the Lorax was destroyed, and looked exactly like what faced us now, in Cubatao.

I told the story of the Lorax to Leonardo, in the hope that he would understand the destruction of his countryside.

'What is those Thneeds, mate?' he said.

'Leonardo, don't you realise that Brazil's being destroyed. Look at all those chimneys out there!' I cried.

'But hombre, we have to pay our foreign debt,' he said. I pointed to the fluorescent green rivers and the throbbing factories which had created them, and shouted:

'Who owns all those monstrous processing plants, who the hell would be deranged and evil enough as to own factories like those?'

Leonardo stooped his head slightly, blushed, and said:
'My stepfather Justo does, Justo owns them.'

Kiato made sandcastles on the beach at Guaruja while helicopters passed high overhead — flying towards a string of private islands — like yachts moored offshore. A few miles away, in Cubatao, children are regularly born with brain damage. They live short painful lives in what is thought to be the world's most polluted city.

The mansions on the private islands have their front windows pointing towards the ocean: so that the rich will not witness the poverty they create. I thought constantly of the Lorax whose land was destroyed by the greed of a Once-ler, for the lack of a Thneed.

Brazilians are well known for their willingness to have fun. Even so, some looked twice when they saw our group of three young men — dressed in fraying, sequined waistcoats and red leather trousers — slouching on the beach.

Leonardo was now overcome with shame as my continual railing against the polluters took effect. His country's beauty was being ravaged as day and night discotheques softened the population's minds and shook the very foundations of city life. He stood up and rubbed at the patches of damp sand on his clothes, then walked off alone. Kiato and I returned to the apartment, sensing that we ought to leave Leonardo to himself. Realising that it would be hard for such a person to come to terms with his nation's troubles, I feared the worst.

An ant-like figure, viewed from the apartment window, moved with haste along the promenade of the beach two hours later. It made for our apartment block. I came away from the window as the door burst open. Leonardo, crippled with exhaustion, shrieked a few disjointed syllables before collapsing:

'Partee-ng, to-ga partee-ng!' He had seen several women,

apparently wrapped tightly in togas, heading towards a downtown bar. *Everyone*, it was obvious — Leonardo swore — would be there.

'Such things is tradition in Guaruja!' he cried.

The Brazilian had obviously found it impossible to contemplate matters of a serious nature for long: matters of importance not only to him, but to all his countrymen.

Starched sheets were pulled from the beds and Leonardo wound the makeshift togas around each of us. I was reluctant to participate, locked in a sombre mood.

Leonardo grinned and wet down his hair at the same time. Before I knew it, I, too, was soon wriggling about under the layers of white cloth. Like Kiato, I was bitter at the Brazilian for forcing us to wear our disco clothes underneath.

We walked down the dank corridors and the steep steps to the street. Another Brazilian night was under way. The metal tips of Leonardo's alligator skin shoes from Miami clicked along. We stumbled forward — like three certified madmen in our white strait-jackets — towards the toga party.

A strange darkness hung within the bar's four walls. We shuffled inside in single file. It was then that I smelt a familiar odour: that of Bombay's local *biri* cigarettes. I made out a few syllables of Hindi being spoken at the bar. Leonardo pinched me and pointed. A group of women were lined up against one wall as if waiting for a firing-squad to arrive. Each was swathed in an embroidered saree; a red felt *bindi* was pressed onto each frowning forehead. They stared at us as we gaped back at them. Then they wobbled their heads from side to side in smiling admiration of our outfits.

Perhaps Leonardo's mistake at taking a saree to be a toga was forgivable. He thought it very peculiar indeed that it was only the women who were wrapped in togas, while the men huddled in one corner in western dress. So he sidled up to the widest of the women and attempted to make polite conversation to put them at ease. Her saree was partly concealed beneath a voluminous navy trench coat, and a luminous pair of Reebok running shoes adorned her size ten feet.

Bowls of blancmange were brought by a gangling waiter. The large Indian lady tilted back her head and let a great quantity of the runny confection slide down her oesophagus. Kiato's eyes bulged in amazement at the volume of her internal digestive tract. A little of the creamy blancmange dripped down the front of the lady's navy trench coat. Rubbing the drops into the fabric, she whispered:

'Eat, my coat, eat!'

Leonardo dominated the small dance floor with carefully choreographed movements; made within the constriction of a tightly-wrapped bed sheet. He thrived on the attention of the Indian tour group, who had just arrived from Bombay. That was, when we had convinced them that we were not eunuch transvestites. Kiato became pally with the wide lady in the trench coat. They told stories to each other. Kiato told her about *Sumo*, Japanese wresting, and his appreciation of it.

Then he admired a cornelian ring she was wearing. She twisted the silver band round on her finger.

'This is a magic ring,' she said. 'It brings good fortune to any who wear it. For my whole life I wanted to come to Brazil, and now I have had my wish: see I am here!' She translated a faint Hindi inscription from the bezel:

Glory to he who holds me, luck and fortune to that one,
When I have aided you give me to another,
Let him benefit from my charm.'

Kiato touched the ring and closed his eyes. His fingers trembled as if they drew a magical force from the centre of the stone. The lady pulled the collar of her coat tight to her neck and said to him:

'My wishes have come true. I must now pass on this magic

ring. Remember to respect the spell, then protection and wishes will be yours.'

Leonardo spun round and around like a cross between a whirling dervish and a Cossack dancer somewhat out of control. Each wall was lined with clapping spectators, whose applause echoed like thunder in the smoke-filled bar. Kiato felt guilty at taking the Indian lady's ring, but she had forced it upon him. It was unlucky, she said, to keep it after it had done its work.

In this atmosphere of insanity — as we fumbled about in bed sheets — Leonardo gave the key of the apartment to a young couple. They said that they wanted to be alone. Leonardo's head seemed to split in two as he howled with laughter.

The dancing continued and the wide lady removed her heavy coat and danced *lambada* with Kiato. My sequined waistcoat had become like a second skin, bonded by sweat. At five A.M. a bouncer threw us all out onto the street.

The clicking of the alligator shoes led the way back to the apartment. When the door was opened, Kiato was the first to enter. There was no sign of the young couple. There was no sign of anyone. The ornaments had been taken from above the fireplace, and all our bags were gone. The alligator shoes stopped tapping across the parquet and Leonardo stood motionless. I threw my bed sheet on the couch and sat beside it. Leonardo broke the silence:

'They were not from Guaruja, mates; local people are friendly.'

He sat next to me with his hands clasped about his ears. I patted him on the back, but deep down I knew that I could never forgive him.

It was not the fact that my camera had been stolen, nor that my saddle-bags were gone. But the thought of having nothing to wear but a set of fluorescent disco clothes, made my hands want to close around Leonardo's neck. Kiato breathed on his wishing ring. I waited for our bags to spontaneously appear. They did not.

'It's rucky,' Kiato began, 'that I hid our passports and money before going out.' He held up the pouches of notes.

'Leonardo,' I said, 'I'm sorry this has happened but I have to leave and go far from here.'

'Ret's go to Algentina as soon as it gets right!' shouted Kiato. His words brought a glimmer of hope back to the depressed atmosphere.

'How can you, the dearest friends of my little cousin, ever forgive me?' asked Leonardo despondently.

Then, plucking the alligator shoes from his feet, Leonardo handed them to me at arm's length. There was a faint smell of foot odour.

'Take these,' he said. 'They are my most treasured possession. I don't want forgiveness or pity, but just to be your friend.'

It was a miserable moment. I said that we could not leave our host and comrade barefoot as well as clad in disco paraphernalia. He must keep the shoes. Besides they were far too small. He smiled broadly as if to cement our friendship, and the next morning we left for Argentina.

CHAPTER 16

The Mountains of Blue Ice

Thus he taught them, Holy Lingo;
And his last words then he uttered —
'Keep your promise to the Turtle,
To the River-Turtle Damé;
To the Gods I now am going.'

The basin in our room at the Hotel Ushuaia, in Buenos Aires, was as long as a cattle trough. Crafted by Shanks of England, it reeked of an era when Argentina had been one of the richest nations on earth. Three beds were separated by pieces of mahogany furniture painted with cream gloss; a set of French windows opened out onto Avenida Cordoba and the bedspreads, with embroidered blue flowers, felt uncannily soft to the touch.

Kiato picked up the solid black telephone and ordered room service. His words ran down the line and a few moments later a lad in a pill-box hat knocked at the door.

We had travelled for days and nights on a journey where one bus had stopped when another had begun. Sequins and red leather, stained and sodden, still hung from our crippled forms.

Kiato sat in the basin and stared hard into the mirror. His eyes were bloodshot, and his manner was like that of an ex-convict, attempting to get to grips with freedom after a very long time.

Two days were spent lying on our backs and learning to adjust our spines from a chronic sitting position. Out of our hibernation we finally came, out into the bright sunshine of downtown Buenos Aires. My waistcoat was reversed to hide the motley sequin pattern. Kiato could not take the disapproving looks from every passer-by. His red leather disco outfit, which was more than torn and worn, smelt of many things, including long-distance bus terminals.

Scott Joplin's tune 'The Entertainer' permeated out from a large departmental store. The building's long windows were filled with sophisticated costumes. Silk ties, tweed jackets and an assortment of bags and cases — sculpted in the finest leather — had been artistically arranged. I looked up to see the name of this marvellous shop. It read quite simply: *Harrods*.

An army of assistants appeared with tapes in their fingers and pencils behind their ears. One took away our disco clothes at arm's length, his face contorted with disgust.

We strolled about the town in crisp starched shirts, and gaped in disbelief at the components of this almost European capital. The buildings might have been in Paris or London, the farrago and bustle of people like that of New York. I felt more at home there than in any other place. An almost eastern courtesy enveloped the society, as did a sensation that one could live there in contentment forever.

Argentina's enormous former prosperity based upon meat and wheat — which had existed until the middle of the century — was reflected in the extent and grandeur of the avenues, and the façades which run along them. Ladies strutted about in wide-brimmed hats or with parasols and their escorts held open the doors to small cafés. But the signs of a former malevolent totalitarianism abounded.

In the Plaza de Mayo, *Las Madres* trudged through the Thursday afternoon sunshine, bearing like crosses the portraits of long-lost sons. The dirty war of the 1970s had stolen a generation.

But the nation's fortunes were being restored — by the astonishing work of one man: President Carlos Menem. Born in the province of La Rioja, Menem schooled himself in law and economics. But he yearned for democracy and equal rights for his people, and for all citizens of Argentina. Three years after being elected as the Governor of La Rioja, in 1973, Dr. Menem was imprisoned by the military government. When his five years of imprisonment came to an end, Menem continued his political career, finally being elected as President of The Republic, in 1989.

A man of enormous integrity and ability, Menem has transformed Argentina's collapsed economy to become the prosperous leader of South America once again. There are no longer 'telephone number' inflation rates, but a robust and dynamic economy. As we walked about Buenos Aires, I felt proud for the people of Argentina: they had a cultured country, and a strong, just man to lead it.

Tea was poured into china cups with real saucers beneath at the Richmond Tea House on Avenida Florida. A young lady took off her tweed coat and slowly stroked back her rich auburn hair. Lipstick was fresh on her lips. Her dilated eyes gazed lovingly, across the green leather-topped table, into those of her date. Wc had seen such sights but rarely, if at all, for many months.

Foxes ran from dogs and from horsemen clad in red, in paintings across the walls. The young couple fed each other crumbs of teacake and whispered secrets from mouth to ear. Beside them two gaunt women clutched at their cheeks and swapped their gossip across the green leather. Kiato leaned back into the rounded chair and smiled. He rubbed at the bezel of his cornelian band and said,

'My wish of paladise has come. You learry are a magicar ling.'

Below the tea-room Argentines of all ages were playing chess and drinking beer. The air was thick with cigar smoke, as slouched figures, old and young, pushed carved pieces from one square to the next.

At the far wall a crouched but somehow imperious figure was moving two queens in succession towards a sole black pawn. He was large and familiar. Opposite him Luigi, the Irishman from Shepherd's Bush, pushed his single chess piece in random terrified movements.

Luigi saw me and bounded up like a Great Dane, embracing Kiato and myself warmly. Rudolf van den Bosch-Drackenburgh seemed astounded to see us. Then he produced a set of manicured nails for me to shake.

'Bet you never expected to see me again,' Rudolf began in a very confident manner. 'You left me with that drunk witch!'

'Did she cure you?' I asked.

'Cure me?' said Rudolf. 'I couldn't get rid of the damn woman. She was besotted with me. There was only one thing to do.' He stopped speaking and I bent forward to hear the secret.

'What was that?' asked Kiato.

'I gave her a bottle of my musk aftershave which she took a liking to. She drank half of it and poured the other half over her head. I had to give her my Swiss Army penknife with sixteen blades as well.'

'Actually,' butted in Luigi in a frail voice, 'it was *my* Swiss Army penknife.'

'Shut up, you Irish idiot!' said Rudolf.

Luigi's face dropped for a moment, then he nuzzled up to Kiato, elated that he was with friends once again.

Rudolf led the way down Avenida Nueve de Julio, one of the widest streets in the world. He seemed to have an encyclopaedic knowledge of Argentine history and events. Plucking up courage, I asked how he had acquired such a gigantic amount of information, challenging him at the same moment on his always flawless English. Rudolf caught me in his steely stare, pausing for a moment. His jaws parted, and he said coldly:

'I read.'

Oswaldo's tales of Patagonia and its ice mountains were more vivid in my mind than ever. I had told them over and over to Kiato and he, too, was heartened at the prospect of a new adventure.

I longed to walk in Patagonia and see my old friend Oswaldo. Resisting Luigi's whines that we should all go to dance at the Hippopotamus Club, we went to buy train tickets for Bariloche instead.

Rudolf looked up from a hardback copy of *The House of Dread*, by Dostoevsky, and said that he had no intention of being cold. Luigi looked at his master in clear anticipation that he might be allowed to make the trip.

'You are forbidden to go anywhere without my permission,' said the Dutchman.

Luigi cringed deeply and asked:

'Then do I have your permission to go with them to Patagonia?' Rudolf looked the stooping masochist up and down. He narrowed his eyes and slowly mouthed the word, 'No'.

Next evening Kiato and I left the Hotel Ushuaia. We went to the railway station for the eleven o'clock train to San Carlos de Bariloche. I crawled down onto the floor to sleep beneath the seats. The wheels ground on the tracks a few inches below my head. And the faint smell of shoe leather and cigarette ends made me cough as I lay stretched out. Feet of all kinds tripped over my legs during the night.

At six A.M. the sun rose and a waiter in crimson garb rushed through the carriage calling,

'Cafay-Cafay Oy-Cafay! Cafay-Cafay Oy-Cafay!'

Juggling an urn and cups like skittles, he moved down the aisle. Children scampered from one seat to the next, avoiding the floor. Their mothers sat about sucking *maté* through a *bombilla*, straw. The tea-like drink is made from the leaves and green shoots of the *yerba maté* tree — *Ilex paraguayensis*, a kind of holly which grows in north-eastern Argentina. A sealed cup, with a bombilla tube often embedded in it, is passed from one person to the next.

Out on the pampas, cattle ran from *gauchos*; and the sun rose high above the scrub, which had replaced the greenery of Buenos

Aires in the night. The train hummed as we sped across the boundless plains of Argentina.

From time to time it would pull to a stop and various characters would climb aboard. Some would sit before descending a few miles on. Others would stand at the front of the carriage with bags of marvels and cry their wares. The audience was captivated by frequent demonstrations of useful objects. One man exhibited a device to stamp patties from a pound of minced meat. Another sold knitted table-cloths covered in geometric designs.

At one such stop an elderly gentleman with red sideburns, and a flat cloth cap, climbed aboard. He removed his checked green overcoat and a very worn pair of rubber galoshes, then sat next to me. I smiled and he began to read a book in English. I tilted my head unobtrusively, so as to be able to make out the small lettering on the spine. It read, *Eskimo-English Dictionary*, and was by Rev. Edmund J. Peck. The gentleman noticed my interest. I cricked my neck in straightening it, guiltily, at speed; he peered over his half-moon bifocals and introduced himself as Morris Meadowcroft, from Grimsby.

Now retired, Mr. Meadowcroft was indulging in his favourite hobby of fifty years: train-spotting.

'There's nothing better than taking a long train ride with a good book,' he said.

'Is an Eskimo-English dictionary as interesting as it looks?' I asked politely.

'*Interesting*?' he said. 'This is a marvellous edition, simply marvellous! Of course, we must now bear in mind that it is not Eskimo, but Inuit.'

'Are there any simple phrases that you could teach me, should I ever need them?' I asked.

Morris Meadowcroft beamed with joy that I was showing a regard for his marvellous edition. He scanned a page and his forehead crumpled into troughs.

'What about *Passijaksavngijutiksarsivok*, to start with?' he said.

'What on ealth does that mean?' Kiato asked.

'*He finds cause for an excuse*', was the answer from the train-spotter from Grimsby. He continued . . .

'*Pattingovokit*, means, *he is tired of eating marrow. Iglovikamepok*, stands for *he is in the snow house*. Or what about *Kannilerungnarpok*?'

'What does that mean?' I inquired.

Morris Meadowcroft looked serious for a moment and then said:

'*It may snow*.'

The cabin lights were switched on when it became dark. Morris Meadowcroft stepped down the ladder in the middle of nowhere. With the checked green overcoat coat on his shoulders, rubber galoshes on his feet, and the Eskimo-English dictionary under one arm, he seemed prepared for anything.

It was Kiato's turn to sleep on the floor. He stretched out and murmured disjointed syllables, apparently in Eskimo and Japanese, before falling asleep.

As I lay on my back and watched the moon shine from above the flat Argentine landscape, I thought for a moment about all the unusual characters I had met. What surprises were there still in store? The next day we would sleep in Patagonia.

Kiato woke up in the middle of the night and said he could smell snow. An icy wind gusted down the centre of the carriage. We peered through a frosted window: there was a blizzard outside. I went to the lavatory and slipped about on the skating-rink floor. Kiato's knees seized up with cold and we huddled together in our starched cotton shirts: as always, unprepared for what was about to come.

Bariloche sits on Lake Nahuel Huapi, and is mirrored within her waters. We walked from the railway station towards the cluster of wooden houses of Swiss design, a few miles from the

Chilean border. Oswaldo's village was a little higher in the mountains. I went to the post office and rang his house. When he heard my voice, he screamed with laughter. Within the hour, Kiato and I found ourselves bundled up and sitting in front of a crackling log fire. Oswaldo crushed my ribs and chortled three times. I had never seen him happier.

'Yoo crazee chappy!' he gurgled. 'Yoo gooing to love Patagonia, dese ees me hoome, dese ees your hoome. Vee all gonna live together in Patagonia!'

Oswaldo's mother — a female version of her son — rocked back and forth in one corner of the room. She moved two long knitting needles about each other with a degree of expertise.

'Mama gonna made yoo dee sweatering soots,' said Oswaldo, 'dose seellee seetee cloothes not for Patagonia.'

Kiato rasped his fingers over the flames; he had never once complained at having all his possessions stolen. He turned to Oswaldo and asked if we could walk amongst the ice mountains.

'Vee walk over every one meng!' shouted the Patagonian.

Five layers of blankets sheltered me as I slept. Yet only the hardest concentration ensured that I did not move at all, and thus remained warm.

Suddenly, a stream of yellow light pushed into the room as the door slowly swung open. Oswaldo crept in with plates of boiled salt cod — *Bacalao* — broth, and a heap of what seemed to be itchy horsehair sweaters. I fumbled for Kiato's watch: it was three A.M.

'Oswaldo, is it really necessary to get up this early?' I groaned.

'Caramba! Everyone getteng up eerly in Patagonia. Hooray, vee gooing on expeedition. Today vee walking on dee bloo mounteens.'

I gulped a pint of chicken broth, but my stomach was clenched asleep. And the back of my neck was rasped by the horsehair sweater as I pulled it over my head. But outside the snow was falling and we knew that warm clothes would be a necessity.

A van with bald tyres — and rusting snow-chains wrapped around them — pulled up. Kiato and I were bundled into the back. Two burly creatures lounged in the front, chain-smoking. Oswaldo murmured some syllables in a local dialect. The chains slid across the slush, and we moved out towards the mountains of blue ice.

The driver had a peg-leg and looked like a pirate; his companion had a bird's nest beard, which obscured much of his face. A one-legged mountaineer? Before I had seen India I would have thought such a thing impossible. Yet Maindra Pal, with one leg, at 49 climbed the Himalayas. He broke a world record, scaling Mount Abi-Gamin, 24,140 feet. Something in common for the two Gondwanaland extremes.

From time to time we would have to jump out and push the vehicle for a mile or so up the steeper parts of the icy track. Whenever I moaned, a hip-flask of chicken broth was handed to me — in the apparent belief that one taste of such an elixir would cure my discomfort. The soup contained Jaborandi, a South American aromatic herb which causes, as I soon discovered, sweating and salivation.

The Pegleg and his friend, who boasted that they were trained guides, would lead the trek.

'Can we drive all the way to the ice mountains?' I asked.

'No Señor,' was the pirate's answer.

'Where will we stop?' I asked. The Pegleg looked around. There was thick forest on three sides and an endless wall of snow on the fourth. He switched off the engine and mumbled,

'Okay here, caballeros.'

We ploughed through what seemed to be a cross between bamboo and bracken. Oswaldo told tall tales of a mythical jabberwock that was said to lurk amongst the fibrous stems. He reminded me that Zak had spoken of a colossal mythical creature — a toxodont — which was thought still to roam the highlands. Kiato believed every word. He soon spotted giant footprints which he claimed were those of a great pachyderm.

I dared not reveal to him Zak's description of a toxodont — which he had alleged was of the rhinoceros family — only with coarser hair. Even without these details Kiato grew very worried indeed.

Streams ran under a layer of ice which had trapped fallen leaves as it froze. Where the forest's canopy was tightly-knit, a carpet of fine green moss cushioned each footstep.

So this was Patagonia, the place of which Oswaldo had spoken as we had tramped across those African lands. He had been right to be so proud of his homeland.

One waterfall cascaded into another, tumbling down into a pool carved from the forest's floor. Oswaldo wanted me to see everything: he seemed almost to point to each frozen berry, each twig that we passed.

'Dees ees Patagonia!' he repeated, over and over. As Kiato put it, he was 'positivery leverring' in it.

Pegleg knocked on the door of a shack which broke the undergrowth's symmetry. A youth, whose beard was just starting to come through, pulled back the door, as a little fresh snow fell from the lintel. Three wolf-like dogs leapt out and sniffed around our ankles. The boy called for them to sit. Their orange eyes burned in grey-white faces, as they pranced about in defiance of all command.

'They're three-quarters wolf and one quarter dog,' said the boy as we sat about an open fire drying our socks. 'I raised them from day-old puppies, they're supposed to obey me, but they always pretend not to understand.'

The Pegleg said that darkness tended to fall suddenly, and even though it was now only late afternoon, it would be wise to spend the night in the shack. My feet were freezing — water had seeped in around them — and the horsehair sweater had rubbed the skin from my neck.

I lay back and breathed in the smell of melting plastic. Kiato fished Oswaldo's hiking boot from the flames. Deformed with heat, a taper of noxious fumes rose from where the laces had been.

When I asked the young man about his life, with Oswaldo translating, he responded to my questions in a lethargic manner, which seemed quite characteristic in Patagonia. It was an attitude that Oswaldo did not have: perhaps this lack of it had caused him to travel elsewhere. We gulped as much chicken broth as our stomachs could take, then bedded down for the night. One of the puppies clambered about on a set of over-sized paws, wanting to be cuddled. He crawled into Oswaldo's sleeping bag and whined all night.

In the morning the wolf-dogs nuzzled between the boy's legs as he sat. He asked if I had ever visited *Caleeforneeah*. I said that I had.

'I'm going there,' he replied. I perked up a little, surprised and pleased that he wanted to travel.

'When are you going?' I asked. He thought for a moment, rubbed his chin, and replied vaguely,

'Oh, any day now.'

Oswaldo was eager to hurry out again into the forest. He had secured the damaged shoe to his sock-covered foot with string. The wolf-dogs howling behind, we pressed on into the bracken.

Soon there was silence again, but for the crunching of our shoes on the icy ground. We moved in single file, each stepping in the footprints of the one in front. Pegleg was at the head of the party: he claimed to know the layout of all Patagonia. His best friend, the man with the bird's nest beard, was second. The two were inseparable, and chattered away in what sounded like a slurred and garbled dialect.

Kiato, Oswaldo and I stumbled along behind the two professionals: we were new to the trekking business.

The snow-covered path, that had weaved through the forest and bracken, suddenly divided. One fork led towards the sound of gushing water. We took the second branch. After five minutes the trail came to an abrupt end. A rock-face sheered upwards.

At first it seemed obvious that the experts had brought us the wrong way. Kiato and I turned round and started to walk back to the junction. Pegleg whistled like a parrot and pointed to the top of the bluff. Then he began to climb.

Forty feet above the ground, Oswaldo clung spread-eagled and whimpering to the rock-face. The two old Patagonians had scaled the precipice effortlessly and had left the rest of the party wobbling in their wake.

Ten feet below Oswaldo, Kiato's left cheek was pressed against the bare rock. His fingers grappled for niches, as he began to recite lines from a Buddhist prayer. My hands wrestled for the same nooks as Kiato's feet and, in a moment of agony, my fingers and his boots agreed on the same holes. In my anguish I gaped upwards. Some sixty feet above, the two old professionals were roaring with laughter.

It was noon by the time we had overcome our fear and conquered the rock-face.

In the distance we could now see the precipitous slopes of a gigantic glacier rising even higher upwards. We stood gazing, captivated by its beauty and the brilliance of its aquamarine form. Oswaldo, who had instantly forgotten the terror of his rock-climbing experience, started to sprint towards the peak, screaming in Spanish. He ran and ran until all we could see was an ant-like speck. I was nervous that he had finally lost all sanity. Then he suddenly disappeared. No one rushed to help him.

The snow grew deeper and more compact as we crossed a wide plain and neared the glacier. We trudged in a single line towards the ice mountain. I wondered what we would do when we got there. We tramped on, past a heap clothed in horsehair and embedded in a drift. It was Oswaldo. He lay face-down, hoping that we would take pity on him. Each of us carried on, hardened by the expedition, and united only in our belief in the survival of the fittest. Oswaldo realised that we would not stop and solemnly joined the rear of the column.

The idea of trekking back, and scaling down the rock-face was most unwelcome. At least the rough sweater no longer rasped at my neck — it was lubricated copiously with perspiration. Kiato and I were suffering from acute headaches, having not fully acclimatised to the Patagonian elevation. The jaborandi and the effort had dehydrated me. I stumbled over to the man with the bird's nest beard and pleaded for a sip of water. The old Patagonian lit a new cigarette with the butt of the last and pointed to the ground.

'Drink that!' he said.

Oswaldo pulled out a neatly furled umbrella: his mother had forced him to bring it along. Like her son, she seemed to have no understanding or knowledge of the dire climatic conditions present in her native Patagonia. As we each took our first uneasy steps on the edge of the glacier's back, Oswaldo poked about for crevasses. The umbrella had suddenly become an invaluable tool, and Oswaldo pretended that he had brought it along especially for that purpose.

Some time after mounting the glacier we reached a severe fissure in its surface, about two feet across. Although not a fully-fledged crevasse, the furrow was a distinct hazard, especially to us amateurs in the party. The bank on which we stood was higher than the one on the other side. In single file we clenched knees and jumped. A great sense of achievement accompanied the landing. But then Kiato, who had made a brief study of the icy structure, realised that — as the two banks were of differing heights — it would be impossible to return by this route. When the point was raised, the guides said that we would be using another route to exit the glacier.

By late afternoon we were all exhausted. Pegleg said that we should camp for the night. It was a popular plan. I offered to start putting up the tents. Pegleg looked at me blankly and shook his head. There were no tents. Only Oswaldo had one. I felt dissociated: at the same time, being part of such an ill-equipped expedition now felt quite normal, and characteristic of my jaunts through Gondwanaland.

Kiato and I stood speechless, wondering what the odds of survival would be against dying of exposure or frostbite. Oswaldo broke the silence.

'Een Patagonia,' he said, 'meng soo stroong need noo teents!' He was obviously trying to conceal the fact that the tents had been forgotten in the enthusiasm for the expedition.

The Pegleg, grinning, now removed his grubby pack and brought out three rather tattered lightweight tents. I had not appreciated his joke.

An area of snow was cleared and, shamed by the hoax of the veterans, we arranged the camp. The bird's nest man, smirking, gave Kiato and me small but adequate sleeping-bags. Oswaldo had his own homemade sleeping-bag: partly knitted and partly formed from black bin liners, it was padded with down.

The sun went down and with the night came bitter coldness.

As usual on a trip that lacks preparation, one of the group tried to rectify things by posing a solution to relieve the discomfort. Oswaldo had read about the prison of Alcatraz. He explained the special method of sleeping in the steel-floored isolation block. The body's weight is rested only on the elbows, knees and toes — thus keeping direct contact with the ground to a minimum.

Kiato, Oswaldo and I wriggled to stay balanced in the new position. This was made all the harder as we were shrouded in sleeping-bags. There are no words with which to describe such inexorable cold. It was impossible to sleep.

As the snores of the man with the bird's nest beard growled around us, images of my travels entertained me. I thought of Prideep and Osman in Bombay: would they still remember me if I ever returned? I was sure they would. No doubt Blake was still training the vultures to do tricks, and Abdul the Warrior was probably crooning over his glass lampshade from

Birmingham at that very moment. Perhaps Zak and Marcus had discovered their mythical animals, and Luigi had escaped from Rudolf's clutches. Kennedy's face merged with that of Jesús; then the features of all those I had met ran together. It had been an extraordinary expedition, and I had crossed Gondwanaland, right to its southernmost tip.

By the morning I had lost all feeling in my legs. Kiato, who tried to straighten out his back, was sure that it would be permanently arched following a night in the Alcatraz position. Our guides began chain-smoking well before dawn. They had slept solidly and were eager to get going. Oswaldo refused to go anywhere until he had eaten.

We warmed up some of the powerfully smelling *bacalao*, and forced down a little more chicken broth. The mountaineers imparted that most of the provisions had been left behind. This time they were telling the truth. Oswaldo was about to throw a tantrum, but I sensed that he realised it would use up valuable energy.

The man with the bird's nest beard emptied the contents of his pack onto the ice. He had run out of cigarettes and was very miserable. As he stooped to stuff the junk back into the bag, I noticed a small bottle made from brown glass. I picked it up. It had no label.

'What's in here?' I asked.

The mass of beard looked up and the man answered me slowly and clearly in perfect English, a language which he had not spoken before:

'That's the antivenom for a Desert Death Adder's bite.'

I thought for a second and remembered that Desert Death Adders are only found in Australia, and then only in the scorching heat. I told him. He stood completely still. Then, staring me straight in the eye, his chapped lips slowly parted, and he said:

'You never know.'

Again, we formed a single file and began to slip our haphazard path across the ice.

After an hour or so, Pegleg signalled for us to stop. A new emotion contorted his face. It was that of fear. He pointed downwards: three feet in front, the glacier ended abruptly in a crevasse. Kiato, Oswaldo and I exchanged glances of horror. There was no way forward and none back. Recently, said Pegleg, the ice must have split open, in an icequake. We were trapped.

Morale hit an all-time low. The veterans, who now seemed very worried indeed, sat down and shook their heads slowly from side to side. My horsehair sweater was as stiff as card, my face was paralysed with cold, and my feet had lost all sensation.

The numbness was moving up my legs. We were trapped on a glacier in the company of two now useless guides, with no way out. It seemed as if the circumstances could not deteriorate any further. But, at that moment, they did.

Oswaldo, who had collapsed on the ice and was huddled in the foetal position, suddenly thrust his right arm toward the sky.

'Loook, dere's beeeg storrm comeng!' he cried.

He was right. A vast snowstorm was approaching fast. I tried to rally enthusiasm to come up with a solution. But the group had resigned themselves to the fact that this time they had been beaten. Bizarre associations began to form in my brain, instead of rational thought. Why were there legless people in all three sections of Gondwanaland? Were the waiter in India, the dancing men on crutches in Africa, now Pegleg, part of some conspiracy?

Had fate planted in my mind that I should visit all three parts of Gondwanaland — and then, perversely, left me here to die?

The first stray flakes of snow began to fall. Oswaldo lay motionless on the ice along with his fellow Patagonians. Kiato was muttering, no doubt reciting a prayer in Japanese.

In minutes we would all be dead.

Never a great talker, Pegleg now gave voice. '*Muerto*' — death — he said.

The other tracker raised his head in agreement: '*Seguro*' — for sure — was his contribution.

Suddenly furious that my epic journey, and my life, should end so disastrously, I searched for an answer. There was little to work with: no real equipment and a team which had lost all hope. But the rush of adrenalin seemed to have done something. The delirium had gone. Now, if I could only think what to do . . . I racked my chilled brains for a solution. The snow was falling faster.

'*Cien mil diabolos*!' A hundred thousand devils? It was Oswaldo shouting. Devils? Magic? Then I remembered the ring, the magic ring.

'Kiato, quickly, give me the ring, I have a wish to make!'

When I had made my wish, I lay back, exhausted. It was then that the faint whisper of sound in the distance became the thudding of rotor-blades. Thc ice patrol . . .

THE END

Glossary

Abyssinia: former name for Ethiopia.
Achhoot: The lowest Hindu caste. Often called 'Untouchables'. Mahatma Gandhi renamed them Harijans, 'people of God.'
Afzelia: Tree — bearing giant beans — common in the savannah of East Africa.
Aga: Sir; term of respect; loan-word from Persian and Turkish.
Alé: South American cult, related to Santeria and Macumba, but devoted to evil.
Agua!: (Water!) Exclamation of delight.
AK47: see Kalashnikov.
Ameranthropoides loysii: A great ape, thought by some to roam the forests of Venezuela.
Amigo: Friend.
Baba: Father or old man. Loan-word from Arabic and Persian. In India may also mean 'baby.'
Babu: Clerk, sometimes used as a pejorative.
Babalawo: Medicine man and spiritual guide involved in Macumba, Santeria and also in ju-ju.
Bacalao: Salted dried cod, popular in Africa and South America.
Balata gum: Gum from the bully tree (used in making golf ball covers).
Banda: Small round — often temporary — hut.
Bedu: (Correctly *Badawi*), nomad of the Arab deserts. Plural: *Bedouin*.
Bindi: Dot — usually red — worn on the forehead by many Hindu women.
Biri: Small hand-rolled tobacco cigarette, popular in India and Pakistan.
Baobab: Tree of the bombax family, (*Adansonia digitata*) found in tropical Western regions of Africa, with a vast grey trunk and gourd-like fruit ('Monkey-Bread'), rich in vitamin C.
Bombilla: Metal tube used with a drinking vessel, usually a small gourd, from which maté is drunk.
Borfima: Object used by many West African secret societies; usually a bag filled with entrails, etc., believed to emanate magical power.
Brahmin: The highest caste in Hinduism.
Burqa: Full-length veil worn by some Muslim women in public.
Burrito: ('Little donkey') term of affection.
Butwa: Secret society of West Africa, particularly Angola.
Buz Kashi: An Afghan game played by horsemen who score goals with a stuffed goatskin.

C-5: A plastic explosive with the consistency of marzipan, it was frequently used by the Mujahedin in Afghanistan.
Caballeros: Gentlemen.
Cachapas: Type of maize pancake (often served with cheese) popular in Argentina.
Candomblé: South American cult, related to Santeria and Macumba.
Caramba: (Appoximately) Good Heavens!
C.F.A.: Central Franc of Africa, the currency of Senegal and some other African nations.
Chadar: Shawl worn by women as a veil. Loan-word from Persian, in which it originally means 'tent.'
Chai: Tea.
Changa'a: Strong home-brewed alcoholic beverage drunk in Kenya.
Chapati: Unleavened flour bread common in India.
Chappal: Sandal, common in Pakistan, correctly *chapli*.
Che: Argentine slang word (pronounced chay): 'pal'.
Chor: Thief; Chor Bazaar, The Thieves' Market.
Colt .38: Small American-made handgun.
Coss: A measure of distance; equal to 2.5 miles.
Creole: A pidgin dialect.
Crypto-zoology: Study of 'hidden animals'; i.e. creatures of fable thought to exist in reality.
Dabba: Cylindrical steel lunch-box.
Dabba-wallah: Person who delivers a dabba.
Dalasi: National currency of Gambia.
Damascene: Inlay of one metal on another. Often gold on steel or silver/copper on brass.
Doh: Two.
Dragunov: Russian-made, highly accurate, sniper rifle.
Dravidian: Non-aryan people of southern India and Sri Lanka: the Hindus, later arrivals, call themselves Aryans ('Arya') by ancient tradition; as do the Persians ('Irani').
Duiker: Small African antelope with short, spiky horns; of the genera *Cephalophus* or *Sylvicapra*.
Durbar: Court, correctly *Darbar Khana* — The large reception room in an aristocratic eastern home.
Ek: One.
Filpai: Elephant foot. Central Asian stylised pattern, often used as a carpet design.
Ganesh: Hindu deity — popular in Bombay — usually represented with the head of an elephant and the body of a man.

Gaucho: South American cowboy: particularly one in Argentina.
Glyptodon: Giant, armadillo-like creature, thought by some cryptozoologists to live in the Patagonian highlands.
Gond: Dravidian, pre-Hindu people of Central India.
Gondwana: Region of Central India named after the Gonds.
Gondwanaland: Name given to the super-continent, thought to have comprised of India, Africa, and South America. Name derived from Gondwana.
Guru: Teacher or mentor; *Guruji* where -ji is a suffix denoting respect.
Halal: Food conforming to Islamic dietary requirements.
Haveli: Mansion; the home of a person of standing in India.
Hijra: Eunuch, a castrate in India.
Hindi: One of the most widely spoken languages of India.
Hindustan: India.
Hombre: Fellow.
Hutu: Agriculturalist tribe located mainly in Rwanda and Burundi.
Jaborandi: Aromatic South American herb.
Jan: Affectionate or familiar suffix to a name: *viz.* Saira Jan.
Ji: (as in Guruji, etc.) term of respect, roughly 'Sir'.
Ju-ju: Fetish used in a ritual or rite (from French joujou) but often now used to denote a West African system of magic.
Kalashnikov: Russian-made assault rifle; (also: Kalashnikov AK47; AK47).
Kamikaze: Japanese suicide pilot in World War II.
KHAD: Afghan Secret Police, operating during the Soviet attempted occupation of Afghanistan.
Kishmish: Mixture of dried fruits and nuts, popular in Afghanistan.
Kohl: Antimony; brittle, silvery metal, used powdered as eye make-up.
Lambada: Erotic South American dance.
Lingala: One of the main African languages of Zaire.
Lingo: The prophet of the Gond people of Central India.
Las Madres: 'The Mothers' (of children who disappeared) during Argentina's 'dirty war' in the 1970s.
Lungi: Loincloth, worn in India and some neighbouring countries. Loan-word from Persian, in which it correctly means 'turban cloth'.
Luo: East African tribe, living largely in western Kenya.
Macanudo: Great!
Masai: Cattle-herding tribe found in Kenya and Tanzania.
Macumba: Brazilian cult based on Yoruba lore, involving spirit possession and the invocation of Yoruba deities in the form of Catholic saints.

Masala: Spice (Arabic-Persian loan-word: originally 'stuff, materials') in Arabic.
Matatu: Privately-owned van offering communal taxi rides: common throughout East Africa.
Maté: Herbal infusion, drunk in Argentina and other South American countries, made from the leaves and shoots of the yerba maté tree.
Matoke: Kind of stewed banana porridge, popular in Central and East Africa.
Mayombero: Form of Santeria, based in Cuba, involving black magic and other rites.
Medeso: Central African dish prepared from black beans.
Megatherium: Giant sloth with hooked claws, once believed to have inhabited southern regions of South America.
MiG: Russian-built jet fighter.
Mira: Plant containing a stimulant, chewed in East Africa.
Mizee Juu: Term of endearment, literally 'number one old man.'
Mughal: Dynasty of Mongols, of the line of Genghiz Khan, who conquered India and were its Emperors immediately before the British advent.
Mokele-Mbembe: Fabulous creature the size of an elephant, thought by some to live in central Africa.
Mujahed: One who fights in a holy war (literally: 'struggler'). There are two kinds of Muslim Jihad: The Lesser, armed struggle, and The Greater, with the mind and tongue, according to the Traditions.
Mujahedin: Plural of Mujahed.
Naan: Unleavened bread eaten in Afghanistan, Pakistan and India.
Namaskar: Hindu greeting, of bowing the head and placing the palms together.
Namaste: Common Hindi greeting (literally: 'I salute all divine qualities in you'); often accompanied by Namaskar.
Nodding donkey: Apparatus used for pumping oil or water from the ground.
Orisha: Deity venerated by the Yoruba tribe of West Africa; as well as by followers of Macumba and Santeria.
Paan: Leaf of the betel palm, combined with an astringent mixture of areca nut, lime, tobacco etc.; the concoction — which is chewed — is very popular in India.
Paisa: One hundredth part of a rupee.
Pakol: Flat woollen hat worn in northern Pakistan (especially in Chitral), and in Afghanistan.
Pampas: Vast grassy plains covering much of southern Argentina.

Panch: Five.
Parsee: Persian Zoroastrians, who settled in Bombay in 1670 at the invitation of the British.
Pashtu: Language of the Pashtuns (incorrectly called Pathans) the most common language in eastern Afghanistan.
Pashtun: Mountain people numbering some twelve million, fabled for their bravery, located mainly in eastern Afghanistan and north-west Pakistan.
Pavarti: Hindu deity, sacred also to the Gond tribe and patroness of Bombay.
PIA: Pakistan International Airlines.
Pilau: (Correctly *Palao*) Central Asian spiced rice dish, popular in Afghanistan, Pakistan and India.
Rouss: ('Russian') Afghan term for the Soviet invasion forces.
Rupia: Rupee, the currency of India and Pakistan.
SA-7 Grail Missile: A Russian-made heat-seeking ground-to-air rocket. Fired from the shoulder, its accuracy and small size have made it popular with guerrillas.
Sahib: Honorific title of address meaning 'Sir' or 'Mr.' in India. Arabic loan-word, it signifies both Friend, Owner and Sir in various usages.
Samburu: Pastoral tribe found in central and northern Kenya, thought to be related to the Masai.
Samosa: Fried pastry triangle filled with meat or cooked vegetables.
Santeria: South American cult, based on West African lore: involving invocations made to Yoruba deities depicted as Catholic saints.
Saree: Long piece of cloth worn by women in India as a robe.
Sayed: (Lord, Prince) Title borne by descendants of the Prophet Mohammed.
Seppuku: Japanese ritual suicide.
Serengi: Stringed Indian musical instrument.
Shah: Title (literally 'king') borne by descendants of the Prophet Mohammed, who also trace their ancestry from the Sassanian Emperors. In India, occurs as a surname among Hindus: who are not of this family.
Shalwar kameez: Pyjama suit worn by men and women, popular in Pakistan. Originating in Iran, its correct name is *Shalwar wa qamisa*: 'Trousers and shirt.'
Shashlik: Pieces of meat and vegetable cooked on a skewer over charcoal.
Shilling: Currency used in Kenya, Uganda and Tanzania.
Silverback: Dominant male of a troop of mountain gorillas, the hairs

on whose back may have turned silvery grey with age.
Songo: Central African dish prepared from stewed cassava.
Sitar: Indian stringed instrument, similar to the lute, with a long fretted neck.
Stinger: American-made ground-to-air missile.
Sushi: Japanese dish, usually of bite-sized pieces of rice and raw fish.
Swami: A Hindu religious instructor.
Talwar: Long Indian sabre.
Tanpura: Large Indian stringed instrument made from a giant gourd.
Thali: Metal tray on which several small individual dishes are placed; originally from south India, now found across the country.
Tilapia: Freshwater fish similar to perch, found in Lake Victoria and other African waterways, forming an important part of local diet.
Tonka beans: Fragrant black bean from a tree in America's tropical regions; used in perfume manufacture. Thought in Venezuela to be lucky.
Toxodont: Giant rhinoceros-like creature covered with coarse hair and thought by some to live in the mountains of Patagonia.
Tutsi: Cattle-herding tribe living mainly in Rwanda and Burundi.
UCLA: University of California, at Los Angeles.
Ugali: Starchy maize flour meal, forming an important part of the East African diet.
Umbanda: South American cult, related to Macumba and found particularly in Brazil.
UZI: Compact Israeli-made 9-millimetre machine-gun.
Wolof: African language spoken in Gambia and parts of Senegal. Takes its name from the Wolof tribe.
Yataghan: Turkish sabre — often slightly curved. The hilt, which has no guard, generally ends in two ear-like protrusions. Also used by Afghans.
Yerba maté: The *Ilex paraguayensis* tree, from whose dried leaves and shoots the maté infusion is made.
Yoruba: People of south-west Nigeria, Togo and Benin: whose lore forms the basis of Macumba and Santeria.